Acts

Acts

The Working of the Holy Spirit

Stephen Kaung

CHRISTIAN FELLOWSHIP PUBLISHERS, INC.
NEW YORK

Christian Fellowship Publishers, Inc.
New York

ISBN: 978-1-68062-092-4

Available from the Publishers at:

11515 Allecingie Parkway
Richmond, Virginia 23235
www.c-f-p.com

Printed in the United States of America

PREFACE

On the day of Pentecost following the resurrection of Christ and His ascension back to the Father in heaven, the Holy Spirit fell upon the 120 of Christ's followers who were gathered together in the upper room of a house in Jerusalem, resulting in the formation of the body of Christ and the birth of the church. And these Spirit-filled believers immediately began to glorify God and to testify concerning the Lord Jesus. Furthermore, through their testimony 3,000 more souls were added to the church on that very same day. All this marked the beginning of the church of God on earth.

Within that first Christian century the church spread far and wide and even reached the very center of the Roman Empire: Rome itself. First through the apostle Peter and then through Paul and the other apostles the gospel of Jesus Christ conquered the known world at that time. The Scriptures provide a glorious record of the power of the glorious gospel of Christ. Indeed, the church is the church triumphant. All glory be to God on high!

May this short historical account of the first acts of the Holy Spirit carried out through the early church inspire all of us who bear the name of Christian to press on towards the completion of God's purpose through His church. Moreover, may we be as faithful as the early church was in bearing the testimony of Jesus!

Contents

Publishers' Note

It should be noted that this series of messages was delivered by the author during the period of October 1972 to March 1973 before a group of Christians who gather together for worship in Richmond, Virginia USA. The texts of these messages were recorded and later transcribed for possible future publication. It should be further explained that in preparing these transcribed messages for today's publication, this entire book's text has been extensively edited and that numerous additional Scripture verses—both texts and/or citations thereof—have been inserted here and there where deemed necessary or helpful to the reader.

Unless otherwise indicated,
Scripture quotations are from the
New Translation by J. N. Darby.

Chapter One

The Days of Travailing

Acts 1:1-5—I composed the first discourse, O Theophilus, concerning all things which Jesus began both to do and to teach, until that day in which, having by the Holy Spirit charged the apostles whom he had chosen, he was taken up; to whom also he presented himself living, after he had suffered, with many proofs; being seen by them during forty days, and speaking of the things which concern the kingdom of God; and, being assembled with them, commanded them not to depart from Jerusalem, but to await the promise of the Father, which said he ye have heard of me. For John indeed baptised with water, but ye shall be baptised with the Holy Spirit after now not many days.

Acts 1:13-14—And when they were come into the city, they went up to the upper chamber, where were staying both Peter, and John, and James, and Andrew, Philip and Thomas, Bartholomew and Matthew, James son of Alphaeus, and Simon the zealot, and Jude the brother of James. These gave themselves all with one accord to continual prayer, with several women, and Mary the mother of Jesus, and with his brethren.

Acts 2:1-4—And when the day of Pentecost was now accomplishing, they were all together in one place. And there came suddenly a sound out of heaven as of a violent impetuous blowing, and filled all the house where they were sitting. And there appeared to them parted tongues, as of fire, and it sat upon each one of them. And they were all filled with the Holy Spirit, and began to speak with other tongues as the Spirit gave to them to speak forth.

In times past we have fellowshiped together in a very general way concerning the four New Testament Gospels. It requires the four Evangelists to present to the world a full picture of Jesus Christ. It is the one and the same Jesus, but because He is of such fullness it requires four different individuals to present Him to their readers.

In the Gospel according to Matthew we are shown Jesus as the King who comes to establish His kingdom on earth; and we who have received Him are the people of His kingdom if we obey Him. In the Gospel according to Mark Christ is presented as the Servant of God—the model Servant, for He came not to be ministered to but to minister and to give His life a ransom for man (10:45). He is both the King of kings and the Servant of all servants. In the Gospel according to Luke Jesus is presented as the Son of man. He is the true Man, the Man after God's own heart—even the new Man who is to be the Head of a new mankind, and according to whom His followers are all to be conformed. Then lastly, in the Gospel according to John Christ is presented as the Son of God: He is God, and to those who are His people He is their very life, He being all and in all to them (Colossians 3:11b ASV).

Now after having fellowshiped together on those four Gospels—that is to say, upon our having seen the Lord Jesus, then we can quite naturally proceed to the book of Acts, and then to the Epistles. In considering the New Testament we should never begin with either the book of Acts or the Epistles; rather, we should always begin with the four Gospels because we must first see the Lord. If first we see the Lord Jesus, then everything else will naturally follow and fall into line. But if at the outset we do not consult the four Gospels for the purpose of seeing Him and instead try to understand—from the later New Testament writings—other things or other doctrines first, then we will go off on a tangent somewhere. It is therefore very basic and necessary for us to realize this truism. The order of the books which we find in the New Testament Scriptures is very meaningful: God wants us first to see His Son, and only after seeing Him are we given to see something further.

The book of Acts, written by Luke the Evangelist, is a continuation of his Gospel narrative on the life and work of Jesus. He tells us that in his first discourse, what is today known as the Gospel according to Luke, he related what the Lord Jesus *began* to do and to teach. But that in his second discourse Luke is intending to relate what the Lord Jesus *continued* to do and teach. In other words, the Gospel of Luke is the beginning of Jesus' teaching and doing. Yes, according to Luke's Gospel account Jesus began to do and to speak, but according to Luke's second discourse—the book of Acts—Jesus has not yet finished His doing and His speaking. And thus the *continuation* of the Lord's speaking and doing forms the content of the book of Acts.

It is rather unfortunate that in our various English-language Bible versions this book is called "The Acts of the Apostles"; however, in this book's original manuscripts there is no such title to be found. Traditionally it has been called "The Acts of the Apostles"; but, having in mind that title as background, a person would quite naturally and preeminently take notice of the doings of the apostles. Indeed, if one reads the book of Acts superficially, one easily gets the impression that the acts narrated therein are those of the apostles. For instance, in the book's first twelve chapters, one would think that it is mainly a narration of the acts of the apostle Peter; and in the second part of the book one would think that it is predominately comprised of the acts of the apostle Paul; with an account of the acts of other apostles added into the book's overall narrative. This, however, is a superficial understanding of this second Lukan discourse, because Luke himself tells us that his intent in writing the second discourse was for the purpose of showing the Lord Jesus *continuing* to do and to teach.

Thus, the book of Acts is not, strictly speaking, an account of the doing and the teaching of the apostles; instead, it is an account of the continuation of the doing and the teaching of the Lord Jesus. In Luke's Gospel we are shown how Jesus began to do and to speak, and in the book of Acts we are shown how He continues to do and to speak. The only difference is that in the Gospel of Luke we have an account of how Jesus began to do and to speak in his own person. In that one Person known as Jesus of Nazareth the Word had become flesh, and so He began doing many things and began speaking many words. And though in the book of Acts we are shown Him still doing and still speaking, Jesus is not doing so in His own person but is now doing so through *a company of people*.

Whereas in Luke's Gospel narrative we are given to observe the Lord doing things and speaking words through the single body of the person known as Jesus of Nazareth, in Luke's Acts discourse the Lord is found speaking and doing through a corporate body—even the body of Christ, the church. Let us further notice that whereas in the Gospel of Luke it is "Christ" who we are told is the one who does and teaches, in Acts it is "the Christ" who is presented as doing and speaking. Please be advised that in Scripture we have two different identities: Christ and the Christ. When the name Christ is used, it refers to himself as a person. But when the phrase, the Christ, is used, it always has reference to His people in a collective sense, that is, it has reference to the corporate body of Christ.

As an example of this latter usage, take note of this Scripture: "As the body is one and has many members, though there are many members, yet there is one body; so also is *the Christ*" (I Corinthians 12:12 emphasis added). In both usages, it is still Christ—Christ in His person and Christ in His corporate body. That is the only difference. In other words, outwardly, there may be some difference, but in reality it is the same Lord who is speaking and doing. Hence, strictly speaking, the book of Acts is not an account of the acts of the apostles; it is an account of the acts of the Lord Jesus Christ by His Spirit through the church. He continues to do and to speak, but it is now in and through a corporate vessel.

Jesus was on earth a little over 30 years—33 years, or some say 33 and ½ years. During those years He did many things, He uttered many words, and they were all very precious. Let us notice as well that the time period of the book of Acts covered approximately 30 some years of activity. Its account began with the ascension of the Lord and ended with the imprisonment of Paul in Rome, the account having thus continued on to about 62 or 63 AD. And hence, like Luke's Gospel, Acts covered some 30 years more of events. Accordingly, during the first 30 years under discussion Jesus began to speak and to do as recorded in Luke's Gospel; and during the next 30 years He continued to do and to speak as recorded in Acts.

We are living in the very last of the last days of the Age of Grace. For this reason it is most essential that we look back to its beginning; that is to say, in approaching the end of this Age, that is the time when a person ought to look back to the beginning of things: that is the only way to see whether a person ends up with that glorious beginning or ends up somewhere else. I believe it is time for God's people to return to the book of Acts for seeing how the Age of Grace began when the mystical, corporate body of Christ—the church—was first formed and for seeing as well how through that body Christ has continued to do and to speak just as He had done before His crucifixion.

After some two thousand years have passed, I have been wondering how close to, or how far away from, that glorious beginning we are. In fact, I wonder even now how we are going to end up, whether or not it will be like a circle and we thus shall end up at that wonderful beginning. I do believe this is the state and condition in which God wants us to end up. I therefore believe it is most essential for us to go back to the beginning and allow the Holy Spirit to show us how everything began.

How was the church—the body of Christ—formed? How does she enable Jesus, the risen Lord, to continue to speak and to do? As we are approaching the end it is important that by the grace of God we be in that body and function in such manner that the Lord is able to continue further and to finish what He has been speaking and what He has been doing. For surely we want Him to finish His doing and His speaking, and to do so gloriously. But if we want Him to do so, which is still to be through a corporate body, we must check to see whether that body—of which we are a part—will allow Him to finish up, because that is the only way He can speak and do. Indeed, it is the intent of the risen, ascended Lord to continue to do and to speak but only through a corporate body. It is therefore very important that He still has a useful, effective body so that He can continue to speak and finish His speaking and that He can continue to do and finish His doing, for God's ultimate design towards men has always been corporate in nature. Unfortunately, too often individual Christian man has stood in the way of God achieving His ultimate design.

In this very connection, we must all acknowledge that we by nature are all self-centered individuals. This is because when sin entered the world, it divided and separated people from one another. And hence, in this respect that has made all of us individualists—whether or not we consider ourselves to be so. For let us take note of the fact that, spiritually speaking, Adam and Eve were separated from each other due to their sin. Even in this matter of our coming to the Lord Jesus for salvation or thereafter in our approach to the things of God, we too often remain as self-centered individuals.

Now it is very true, of course, that in our relationship with the Lord there must be that personal, individual aspect, for nobody else can believe or exercise faith in the Lord Jesus for us. Yes, others can help us to believe, but they cannot actually believe for us. Strange to say, however, in looking back over our entire approach to God and the things of God, we discover that it has all been on an individual, self-centered basis—a basis which is quite different from God's approach towards man. Sooner or later, therefore, God will have to shift us from our individual approach to Him and His interests and commence seeing His corporate approach.

In other words, there must come a day when God will need to show you that your relationship with the Lord Jesus and His interests is more than simply a matter of your *individual* relationship with Him. Yes indeed, the individual side is still there; it is very basic; nevertheless, that is not enough if the Lord is going to be able to finish His speaking and doing. You and I must come to see that through individuals alone He cannot continue to do and to speak what He began to do and speak when He was on earth. At that time Jesus could indeed begin to do and speak through one individual alone—that is, through himself.

But ever since His resurrection and ascension back to the Father there has never been, nor can there ever be, any single individual or even a number of individuals who was or were able to continue the Lord's doing and speaking, other than the risen, ascended Lord himself—He later doing so, however, only through a corporate vessel: even through His many-membered body, the church. Only through that vessel, the body of Christ, does the Lord Jesus choose to continue to do and to speak.

In view of this, I sincerely hope and believe that wherever it may be necessary among us, God will gradually shift our attention and approach towards Him and His interests from merely the individual to the corporate side, from our self-centered state to the divinely-ordained many-membered body of Christ. Only after we have begun to experience this attitudinal shift in seeing things from the divine perspective shall we begin to realize how grand and glorious is God's design. And to this end it is therefore very important and necessary that we come to know more deeply the book of Acts.

This New Testament book begins with the resurrection of the Lord Jesus. After He was raised from the dead He appeared alive to His disciples. He continually taught them the things concerning the kingdom of God. He appeared again and again to them for a period of 40 days and told them that they should not depart from Jerusalem. There they should wait until they received the power from on high (Luke 24:49b), that is, they would be baptized with the Holy Spirit (Acts 1:5b, 8a). Then they would be witnesses of His in Jerusalem, then to all Judea, next in Samaria and then to the ends of the earth (Acts 1:8b). At the end of these 40 days of appearances to His disciples following His resurrection the Lord was taken up to heaven from atop the Mount of Olives just outside Jerusalem (Acts 1:9, 12). Immediately thereafter, the disciples returned to Jerusalem and there they waited for ten days until the stirring events on the day of Pentecost should arrive.

Let us here employ some Old Testament typology first as a way of helping us understand what was about to take place in the lives of these disciples on that particular Pentecost day. In Leviticus 23 are presented all the set feasts or holy convocations of God for the Israelites (all those besides the Sabbath which reoccurs once every week in the year). The first feast, of course, was that of Passover (v.5, but see also Exodus 12). It was to be held in memory of how God delivered the Israelites out of death. On that inaugural Passover night the angel of destruction passed through the whole land of Egypt visiting every house for the purpose of destroying all the firstborn in the land; but God had commanded the children of Israel beforehand to prepare a lamb for each of their households. They were to sprinkle the blood of that slain lamb on the doorposts and the lintel of each house. Then the Israelites in each house were to gather together and roast the lamb and eat its meat as the way of preparing themselves to leave Egypt. Consequently, on that night when the angel of destruction came by each Israelite house and saw the blood, he passed over those houses because blood had been shed and sprinkled. That was the way the children of Israel were delivered out of death and also out of Egypt.

I believe we all understand the spiritual meaning of Passover for us today because Paul tells us in I Corinthians 5 that our Passover is Christ (v. 7b). He is our Pascal Lamb. Like God's people of old, we were all sinners who were condemned to death and destined to be destroyed. But thank God, for us the Lord Jesus is the Lamb of God who takes away the sin of this world (John 1:29). Because we believe in Him and have sprinkled His blood on our hearts (Hebrews 10:19, 22a), destruction has passed over us. For all those who believe in the Lord Jesus, judgment has passed over them and are no longer destined to die but now have eternal life (John 3:14-16). Moreover, we feed upon the Lord Jesus as our food (John 6:35, 51), and by His strength we are enabled to walk out of this world, spiritually speaking. Yes, we are still in this world physically, yet we do not belong to it any longer but we belong to Christ. That is the spiritual meaning for us of the Feast of Passover: it speaks of the death of the Lord Jesus who on the Passover of His day was crucified. The pascal lamb which God as it were had provided the children of Israel was fulfilled in Christ many generations and centuries later.

Now immediately following the set Feast of Passover, and in connection with it, came the Feast of Unleavened Bread, which lasted for seven days. Paul explained to us that our Passover is Christ and that because we have had our Passover, we in this present age are living out the Feast of Unleavened Bread (I Corinthians 5:7). Back then it was held for seven days signifying, in spiritual terms, perfection. Since we have believed in and received the Lord Jesus as our Pascal Lamb, therefore, we today continually experience the reality of the Feast of Unleavened Bread: by this is meant that we should continually remember the Lord, worship Him, and serve Him;

yet, not with leavened bread that betokens malice or wickedness, but with the unleavened bread of sincerity and of truth (I Corinthians 5:8). In other words, after we believe in the Lord Jesus, our whole life is to be one continuous feast of unleavened bread. There should be no leaven in our houses—nothing of evil whether in teaching or doctrine or in conduct or behavior (I Corinthians 5:6-7). We should serve and worship the Lord in the spirit of sincerity and truthfulness.

On the third day after Passover, which was the second day after Sabbath, was the Feast of Firstfruits. The Israelites would collect a sheaf of the firstfruits of barley because barley was harvested in Israel before wheat was. But even before the complete harvest of barley had occurred there would be those first ripe fruits of the barley grain. And the first ripe grains were always the best and served as a guarantee of the more general and complete harvest to come. So the Israelites would cut a sheaf of the firstfruits and wave it before God as an offering to Him. Now according to I Corinthians 15 this speaks of the resurrection of the Lord Jesus, for in speaking on the subject of resurrection Paul wrote there that Christ is the firstfruits and after Him comes the harvest—which symbolically is what we are (vv. 20, 23). Jesus died, but on the third day following His crucifixion He was raised from the dead; and thus the firstfruits betoken the resurrection of the Lord Jesus.

Now following the Feast of Firstfruits, there would occur the Feast of Weeks consisting of seven weeks or 49 days. And on the 50th day, which served to conclude the seven weeks, there was celebrated the Feast of Pentecost. So that by the time of Pentecost all the grain harvests would have been completed. Accordingly, the priests would prepare two loaves of fine flour and bake them with leaven and present them before Jehovah God. Here it was no longer a sheaf of barley grain but ground-up in fine flour that was then made into dough and then baked into two loaves of bread. In Scripture two is the number signifying witness and testimony. Thus, these two loaves here serve as a symbol of the church, for as Jesus himself once observed, "Except a grain of wheat fall into the ground and die, it abides alone, but if it dies it bears the grains of much fruit" (see John 12:24). These many grains are thus being ground into flour, then made into dough, and baked into loaves of bread so that we—as those loaves—may be presented as a satisfying offering to God.

Of all the offerings offered up to Jehovah God back then, those two loaves were the only ones with leaven because all the other loaves spoke of Christ. He was tempted in all things as we are, but without sin (Hebrews 4:15). However perfect we may be, though, there is always the presence of sin in our nature; that is to say, there is leaven. But thank God, even if there be leaven present in us, it is counteracted, spiritually speaking, by the burnt offering, the sin offering, and all the other offerings.

Hence, if the Passover feast speaks of the death of the Lord Jesus, the Feast of Firstfruits speaks of His resurrection; and then the Feast of Pentecost speaks of the birth of the church, which is that mystical, corporate body of Christ through which the risen, ascended Lord is able to continue to do and to speak.

Let us remind ourselves that in between the Feast of Firstfruits and that of the Day of Pentecost there were 50 days. At the time of Jesus' resurrection and subsequent ascension these 50 days were very, very meaningful, although not very much has been described in the Bible concerning them. We know, of course, that these 50 days were divided into two parts—40 days and ten days (Acts 1:3, 2:1a). After the resurrection of the Lord He appeared to His disciples for 40 days. And after He was ascended up to heaven His disciples gathered themselves together with one accord in Jerusalem for ten days. What happened during those 40 days and what happened during the ten days thereafter? Well, though we do not find much in the Bible concerning these 50 days, the little which is there is more than enough for our understanding of what occurred. If we read the relevant Scriptures very carefully, we will learn that the 40-day period was most important.

At the outset we might ask ourselves why it was that after the Lord Jesus was resurrected from the dead He did not simply appear to all the brethren and then ascend up to heaven? We would probably think that that would be the best action to take, for why should He need to remain on earth for 40 more days? Had He not spent some 33 years on earth already? Had He not finished His work of salvation? Since everything was now all right, since everything was altogether finished, why, then, not simply summon all His disciples to the Mount of Olives summit, show himself to them openly, and conclude by saying to them, "Goodbye, dear friends, until I come again"? Would that not have been enough? Indeed, was there any particular reason for Him spending 40 more days on earth? Or was there something further He had yet to accomplish during those 40 days? With respect to the Lord's work of redemption on the cross, that was finished, thank God. As it turned out, however, there was some unfinished business He had to fulfill with His disciples which was most necessary.

Now during those 40 days He appeared to them in a "living state." Let us underline that word living as is found in one of the opening verses of Luke's second discourse concerning all of Jesus' doings and teachings. Though this word in its Greek original has been translated into English as "alive" in most English-language Bible versions, it has been translated by Darby as "living": after Jesus "had suffered" on the cross, He had "presented himself living" to His "chosen apostles" by means of "many proofs," He having been "seen by them during forty days" (Acts 1:2-3). These disciples had previously only known the Lord while He was in His physical body prior to His crucifixion. They had been with Him and had come to know Him for three years or more. They had known that He had been crucified, had died, and had been buried. But now the Lord appeared to them living.

What was the difference between when the Lord was alive before He had died and when the Lord appeared in a living way after He had died and been resurrected? Before He had died on Calvary, the Lord was life ("I am … the life," He had declared, John 11:25; 14:6), but that life was only to be found in that one grain of wheat; it had thus abided alone. But when Jesus appeared to His disciples alive after His resurrection, that resurrection life was now able to be imparted to His disciples and to us. That was the difference. For three years these disciples of His had followed the Lord. They had seen Him, watched Him, observed Him, heard Him, and had even touched and handled Him (I John 1:1). How wonderful and glorious! Such life had never been on earth before; it was a heavenly life that had walked on earth; and as far as Jesus' disciples were concerned there was nothing higher nor more glorious than that. How they must have admired Him extremely much! "Oh!" they must have said to themselves, "if only we could live as You live!" Nevertheless, the more they were with and lived with the Lord Jesus the more they morally and spiritually felt far away from Him, and ultimately hopelessness filled their hearts. Finally, when the Shepherd was smitten, these discipled sheep of His scattered in fear and despair (Matthew 26:31, 56; Mark 14:27; John 16:32). They were altogether finished.

The picture which this situation inspired me to contemplate is that of the potter and his clay as described in Jeremiah 18. There we are told that the potter took up the clay, put it on the wheel, and began to turn the wheel. He placed his loving hands upon the clay and tried to shape it into a vessel. The clay, however, became marred in his hands—and the would-be vessel probably fell to the ground broken. Was it because the potter was not skillful enough? No, it was because there was something in the clay which resisted the hand of the potter. Does the potter throw the clay away? No, he works to reshape this clay again into a new vessel (vv. 1-6).

Let me now apply this scene from Jeremiah to Jesus and His disciples. They had followed Jesus for three years, and as they were in the hands of the Lord He attempted to form them into a vessel, but it broke down; for when the Lord was crucified, the disciples were all scattered and were finished. In spite of all that they had heard, seen and touched, it did not seem to bring them into any useful form. But did the Lord cast them aside? Not at all. Instead, after He was resurrected, He as the master Potter regathered them to himself and made them into a new vessel; but in the process there was a difference. (Of course, with spiritual matters one cannot be too literal.) The difference was that what became marred, cracked and broken in the master Potter's hands was the disciples' old life. Please be advised that He can never make a new vessel out of man's—even Christian man's—old life. Rather, He raises the believers up in resurrection giving them His new life which is most living. Those disciples of the Lord did not live by the old life anymore but they henceforth lived by His risen life that would now be resident within them, and He was therefore able to make them into a new and useful vessel.

It needs to be observed, however, that those 40 days were difficult ones for the risen Lord's disciples. To understand this, let me illustrate what I have in mind by describing what happened with those two disciples of the Lord who were walking from Jerusalem to their home seven miles distant in the village of Emmaus. This had occurred on the very day of Jesus' resurrection. As they walked they talked together and were very sad. They had truly loved the Lord, but He had been crucified three days earlier and was now dead, they said to themselves. However, some women had reported to them and others that the Lord's tomb was empty, that He was risen, and that they had seen Him; but these two disciples had not seen the Lord. Disbelieving those women they were still so downhearted that they decided to leave Jerusalem and head home towards Emmaus. Suddenly, a Man appeared as a fellow traveler and began walking with them; and He asked them what they were talking about, they being so sad of face.

"Oh," they said, "you do not know?!? There is news all over Jerusalem to the effect that this Man Jesus, whom we had considered to be God's mighty prophet, is dead. But the strangest thing is that some women among us His followers say He is alive, but we have not seen Him." Hearing all this, the Lord began to expound the Scriptures to them. And as He opened God's word to them, they felt warm in their hearts and were amazed, for they did not know where this Man had gotten such knowledge.

Now when these three arrived at Emmaus, this Man acted as though He would walk farther; so they urged Him to stay with them, since it was nearly evening. They successfully entreated the Man to stay with them, and soon they all reclined at table for the purpose of dining together on an evening meal. This Man, though, took the bread which was on the table, blessed it, and gave it to them. Upon seeing this, the two disciples' eyes were instantly opened and recognized Jesus: "Ah, the Lord!" But as soon as they recognized Him, the Lord disappeared (Luke 24:13-32).

To me that is one of the strangest things to have ever occurred. It at one time had seemed very strange to me because we all would naturally think that if the Lord wants to appear to someone, then of course He wants that person to know Him; but if, as happened with these two disciples, that person begins to know and recognize the Lord, it became inexplicable to me, as occurred with these two, why He would immediately vanish! Why did He do this to these two disciples? Moreover, during these 40 days this happened not only on this one occasion but it seemed to have occurred many times more, if not every time He had appeared! (This has been repeatedly documented in the following additional Scripture passages: Matthew 28:9-10, 16-18a; Mark 16:7, 12, 14; Luke 24:36ff.; John 20:11ff., 19-25a, 26-29, 30a; 21:1ff.; Acts 1:3, 13:31; I Corinthians 15:5-7.)

As a matter of fact, during this 40-day period the risen Lord would suddenly appear and then disappear. He appeared when His disciples were not expecting His appearance and He disappeared when they recognized Him. Indeed, this happened even to Mary of Magdala, the very first person to see the Lord Jesus in His resurrected living state. She was weeping outside Jesus' tomb whereas Peter and John, after having entered the tomb and found it empty, had immediately thereafter gone to their home. But without her precious Lord, Mary of Magdala had no more home to go to, for He had been her home prior to His crucifixion.

Now while Mary was at the tomb, she heard someone calling her and saying, "Why do you weep? Whom do you seek?" Thinking this to be the gardener, she said: "Sir, if you have taken Him away, just tell me where He is and I will go there and take Him away." And that man simply replied, "Mary." Instantly she recognized that it was the Lord and said: "Rabboni!"—meaning Teacher in Hebrew.

She went forward to take hold of His feet as she had often done before, but the Lord said, "Do not take hold of Me." This must have been quite puzzling to Mary, for had she not taken hold of Jesus' feet frequently in the past? For she had probably washed the Lord's feet many times, but in this instance here the Lord is heard saying: "Take not hold of Me." And after saying a few words of explanation, He left her (see John 20:1-17 ASV mgn.).

Now suppose you love a person very much and you have always done something special for that person. In fact, when the Jews of that day loved a person quite much they would wash that person's feet. Suppose, however, that one day that person refused to let you do it. What would this mean to you? Most likely you would begin to wonder, even as Mary most likely wondered. Yet this kind of thing happened quite often during these 40 days.

As a further instance, on the evening of that same day of Jesus' resurrection, all eleven disciples except Thomas were gathered together in a house with all the doors tightly shut out of great fear of the Jewish authorities. Suddenly, the risen Lord appeared to them and stood in their midst and said to them, "Peace be with you." He then showed them His hands and side, it causing the disciples to rejoice greatly, they having now seen the risen living Jesus. He having next said a few more words of importance, the Lord vanished from their presence.

Then, eight days later, with the disciples once more gathered together, including Thomas, in the same place and all the doors once more being tightly shut, the living Lord appeared again to the Eleven and stood in their midst and said as before, "Peace be with you." Next, He addressed Thomas personally, declaring to him to no longer "be unbelieving but believing." And uttering a few more words, the resurrected Lord Jesus thereafter vanished from their sight as He had done before (John 20:19-29).

Do you understand why He appeared and disappeared over and over again during those 40 days? As I mentioned before, this conduct by the Lord had seemed to me to have been quite strange. Yet, after pondering this matter for some time I came to the conclusion that there was a most important reason, which I will now try to explain.

All the disciples' former relationship with Jesus had been physical in nature. They had seen the Lord, heard Him, and had even touched and handled Him on occasion. In fact, their relationship with the Lord had been very close and intimate—physically. He had been with them and they had been with the Lord, they nearly always having been together in close fellowship. That had previously been their relationship with Jesus, and they had found it most satisfying. But in His various 40-day appearances with them He as it were was now declaring: "You must understand that henceforth your relationship with Me is no longer going to be a physical one; it is going to be totally in the spirit. You shall no longer know Me by the flesh as you once did; instead, you are hereafter to know Me in the spirit. I have appeared to you these several times as a means of drawing you away from the flesh and as soon as you had recognized Me in the spirit, I had disappeared in order that you could begin to understand that from now on this shall be My relationship with you."

Oh, how important that lesson is! How often I have heard believers say, and I myself have said, "Oh, if only I had lived two thousand years ago. If only I had been born a Jew or a Galilean back then. If only I had been born at the same time and place as Jesus had been. If only I could have followed Him and touched Him. Had this been the case with me I would not be lacking in spiritual depth as I am today—indeed, I would be far more spiritual than I am today."

But let us carefully notice what Jesus had said to His disciples when He had announced prophetically to them—even before His death and resurrection—that He would be going back to the Father who had sent Him to the earth: "It is advantageous to you for Me to go away" (see John 16:7a). In response, sorrow had filled the hearts of the disciples (John 16:6, 20a, 22a), for their thought was: "Lord, do not go away from us; stay here, for there is nothing better for us than Your presence with us."

Jesus, however, and knowing their thoughts, proceeded to explain further to His disciples what lay behind this remark to them; for He next said to them: "I say to you the truth that it is much more profitable for you—yea, it is to your best advantage—that I depart; for if I do not go away, the Comforter, who is the Holy Spirit, will not come to you; however, if I return to the Father, I will send the Spirit to you, whom you know objectively already because He has been abiding *with* you, but when He comes, He shall be *in* you" (see John 16:7, 14:16-17 emphasis added).

In other words, the Lord Jesus was saying to His disciples this: "Heretofore I could be *with* you physically, but I could not be *in* you. You must come to realize that there is a relationship which is far better and more advantageous for you than what "with" can provide; there is going to be an "in" relationship with Me which shall be the very best for you. Why, then, would you wish to maintain a relationship with Me on an earthly, physical basis, however satisfying that may have been? No, My dear disciples, there shall henceforth be for you a far better way of relating to Me: it is to be a relationship in the newness of the spirit" (see John 16:7b, 14:16-18).

Is it not true that when we humans see and experience the better, we do not want to change and embrace the best? For that reason the risen Lord had to take away the better relationship His disciples had formerly enjoyed with Him in order that they might want and experience the best relationship with the Lord. And so it is the same with all of us as well.

During those 40 days of appearances and disappearances the Lord Jesus was trying to draw His disciples out from themselves into His resurrection life, to draw them out from the physical into the spiritual. The risen Lord was teaching them a lesson they had never been taught before. Or to put it another way, the Lord was bringing them onto resurrection ground in the realm of the spiritual. Only when these disciples would be able to enter upon resurrection ground by entering into the realm of the spirit would the Lord Jesus be able to fulfill God's purpose of forming them into the body of Christ.

During the same 40 days the risen Lord had talked to His disciples continually about the things concerning the kingdom of God (Acts 1:3b). Whenever I read this Bible passage, I say to myself: "Lord, why haven't You told me specifically what You said concerning the kingdom of God? For that is certainly most important. So, Lord, I would very much like to know what You said about the kingdom in specific terms." I believe we can correctly assume from this Acts passage that the Lord must have revealed many wonderful things to His disciples about the kingdom of God. As a matter of fact, we know that during His ministry of three years on earth He had said a lot about the kingdom of God; but during this post-resurrection period of 40 days it would appear as though He spoke nothing else but that which concerned the kingdom of God; yet, there is no record in Scripture of those things; the record simply states that He spoke of the things concerning the kingdom of God, and nothing more was stated.

Now I think Jesus is the best teacher the world has ever known. I very much admire people who, whenever they teach, can use a blackboard and draw. I lack that ability because if I try to draw a dog it becomes a cat! I realize that visual aid can be very helpful in demonstrating what is being taught. Nevertheless, though the Bible does not inform us exactly what the risen Lord had said when speaking about the kingdom of God, I one day realized that He had continually demonstrated what God's kingdom is! Do you understand what I mean?

We have been told in Scripture that during these 40 days the Lord Jesus would frequently and suddenly appear and just as suddenly disappear before this or that individual disciple or before this or that group of disciples. What is the meaning of this? What, if anything, was being demonstrated by this kind of activity on the part of the risen Lord? I have come to believe that by these actions He was demonstrating what the kingdom of God is: that as Scripture has elsewhere noted, God's kingdom is not eating and drinking—that which is physical in character—but is righteousness and peace and joy in the Holy Spirit—that which is spiritual in nature (Romans 14:17).

So what is the kingdom of God? It is that which is founded on the Lord's risen life, it is that which is solely on resurrection ground. This is therefore to say that the reality of God's kingdom is in the spirit. And the Lord Jesus was using a visual aid, as it were, to demonstrate, by His frequent appearances and disappearances, what the kingdom of God is in its most basic character.

If you want children to better understand what you are saying to them, demonstration is the best way to accomplish this. And do let us realize that these disciples of the risen Lord were still children in terms of growth, spiritually speaking, the Lord even having addressed them as such affectionately (John 21:5a). During these forty days the Lord Jesus was actually attempting to lift them up to a higher level with Him. On the basis of His death, He was ever so slowly but surely raising them up to live on resurrection ground, which would hereafter be a relationship with Him in the spirit. And it required 40 days for the Lord Jesus, by His intermittent appearances and disappearances, to prepare the way for accomplishing this.

On the occasion of Jesus' first of several appearances/ disappearances before His closest disciples, as was briefly described earlier, it had occurred on the evening of the day of His resurrection. And thus having appeared to His disciples, the risen Lord breathed into them and said, "Receive the Holy Spirit" (John 20:22). Having thus received the Holy Spirit they therefore were able to enter into the realm of the Spirit and to be sustained in a spiritual relationship with the Lord. Yet, as was said a moment ago, it took the Lord 40 days to prepare the way for this moment. In the Bible 40 is the number signifying trials and testings of various kinds. It must have been a period of great testing for the disciples, but I think it must have been a great trial for the Lord as well. As a matter of fact, all of Jesus' time with the disciples during the three years or so before His death was a great trial for the Lord, since they had constantly misunderstood Him.

Here I would like to borrow a word from the Scriptures to describe what I believe must have been the reactive experience of the Lord during not only His pre-Calvary three years with the disciples but also these post-resurrection 40 days with them. The word in the Bible I have in mind is the word travail: "Out of the travail of His soul He shall see His seed" (cf. Isaiah 53:10-11a ASV). That refers to His death on behalf of His seed—even all those who believe on Him. Because of His death, He has given birth to all—including first the disciples of His day—who have believed in Him; but those 40 days after Jesus' death and resurrection were a continuation of this travailing. He travailed for His disciples in order that they would be lifted out of themselves into His risen life, out of their flesh into the spirit, even out of the old creation into the new—all such so that God would be able by His one Spirit to form them into Christ's mystical, corporate body. Those 40 days, like the previous three years prior to Calvary, constituted days and days of travail for the Lord Jesus.

The Lord thereafter ascended up to heaven from the Mount of Olives; and in obedience to His command the disciples returned to Jerusalem for ten days of waiting. (Ten in God's word is the number signifying the taking up of responsibility—for example, ten fingers comprise a person's two hands.) When the Lord ascended from the Olivet Mount, there were probably more than 500 brethren present—in the opinion of most Bible commentators—because in I Corinthians 15 we are told that on one occasion the Lord had appeared to more than 500 brethren all at once (v. 6a). This has led to the belief that this occasion most likely refers to the time of His ascension. But oddly enough only 120 gathered back in Jerusalem and remained together in what Scripture has termed "the upper chamber" (Acts 1:13a). Though most likely the greater part of these 500 did return to Jerusalem from Olivet, after a day or two, or perhaps even a few days, these brethren apparently could not bring themselves to remain faithful to the Lord and instead began to scatter. It would seem, in fact, that they had ultimately returned to their homes in Judea, Galilee, and elsewhere, or else entirely disappeared; but the 120 brethren faithfully assembled together in the so-called upper room and gave themselves to continual prayer with one accord (Acts 1:14a).

There is nothing which tests one's flesh more than engaging in corporate prayer. There is nothing which will try one's flesh more than praying together. There is nothing more challenging than giving oneself to continual prayer together with one accord. It is much easier for a person to go out and do something together with others, but to give oneself to prayer with others in one accord is very difficult.

Why did these 120 believers come together in the upper room to pray? Well, the Lord had said to them: "Remain in the city and wait until you be clothed with power from on high" (see Luke 24:49b). How did they wait? Did they sit there and simply wait passively? No! They knew that if the Lord said for them to wait until they received power from on high, He expected them to wait actively, not passively. So they gave themselves to prayer together. They realized that there was only one thing they could do and that was to pray.

What kind of prayer was it that they prayed? It needs to be understood that God has a particular principle related to all of His work concerning the new creation. With respect to the old creation, when God created the heavens and the earth, He did so all by himself. He did not ask for man's help. In the work of the new creation, however, God has set forth a principle which binds Him not to do anything unless He has acquired the cooperation from man.

I remember what brother Watchman Nee once said: "God is almighty in heaven, but His power on earth is restricted by man." This is not because man has such power by which to limit God; rather, it is because He has set down a principle which it is His good pleasure to follow and observe. So far as the new creation is concerned, God will not do anything until He secures a response from His people on earth who shall ask Him to do what He very much wants to do. That is why we find in Matthew 18 these words of Jesus to His disciples: "If you bind something on earth, God will also bind it in heaven; and if you loose something on earth, He will also loose it in heaven" (see v.18). What does this passage mean? It means that the earth governs the heavens; yet, in the matter of binding, for example, it is the heavens that want to bind but the heavens will first share its burden with us on the earth so that we will take up that burden and pray: "Lord, we want this thing bound." And in response the God of the heavens will say: "All right, I will bind it."*

After giving up His body in the flesh on the cross, the risen Lord takes upon himself a corporate body by which and through which to continue His speaking and His doing. That is what He wants, for He earnestly travailed for that during all three years and during all those 40 days; but the risen Lord cannot and will not continue speaking and doing all alone, for He is bound. He therefore told the brethren to return to Jerusalem and wait. They understood, and so they went back to the city where, in the upper room, they did not just sit there or rest there and wait as though believing that the power from above would come down automatically. No, such things of the spirit never will. That is not God's way with the new creation. This the disciples now fully understood. These 120 brethren had entered into fellowship with the afflictions of Christ concerning His body, which is the church (cf. Colossians 1:24 ASV). In their coming together, it was a most difficult, trying challenge to their flesh to let go of self-interest. But in view of what the Lord wanted, which is a body, they wanted it too. They were willing to come together to give themselves to continual prayer with one accord.

What one word can describe what these brethren were doing? Is it not this same word of travailing? They were travailing for the birth of the church. They, as it were, were now fellowshiping with the risen Lord in His travailing. Indeed, it was on the basis of the travail of the Lord Jesus that they were able to fellowship. It was by His resurrection life within them

---

* A presentation of this Biblical understanding can be found in Watchman Nee, *The Prayer Ministry of the Church* (New York: Christian Fellowship Publishers, 1973), the opening chapter, pp. 8-35.—*The Publishers*

that enabled them to travail together with the Lord. Do bear in mind that this has nothing to do with atonement. Jesus was all alone bearing our sins all by himself. Yes, we receive the good of His atonement for mankind, but we do not share in it. So far as the new creation is concerned, however, these 120 brethren gave themselves to continual travailing prayer. It was praying with a purpose: they wanted what their Lord wanted.

What if all 500 brethren had gone home? What would have happened? Its result cannot easily be imagined. But let us try. What if the risen Lord had ascended back to heaven without God having been able to form a body for His Son on earth? The Lord Jesus would have been shut up, He being able neither to continue speaking nor to doing; in other words, He could not finish what He wanted to say and what He wanted to do. But thank God, though the majority of those more than 500 brethren seemed to have scattered hither and yon, there were 120 of them who were willing to give themselves to continual travailing prayer for the birth of the body of Christ. Not only was the Lord Jesus travailing but now His brethren on earth—the 120—were travailing with Him for the bringing forth of that which would be most essential to His continued speaking and doing: the body of Christ, the church.

Moreover, during those ten momentous days of waiting and travailing, they were not only praying, they were also making personal adjustments with the Lord and with one another. People cannot pray together over a period of time without their having to make many adjustments. The Bible only cites one adjustment that was made: they filled in the vacancy of Judas Iscariot with brother Matthias, who was now numbered with the Eleven (Acts 1:21-26). But from our own experience we can understand that among these 120 brethren there must have been many personal adjustments which had to be made with the Lord and with one another during these ten critical days.

Now after ten days of these 120 travailing together, the day of Pentecost was to be accomplished. For suddenly a sound out of heaven like unto a hard breathing filled all the house where they were sitting and there appeared parted tongues, as of fire, coming upon each one of them. At this moment they were all filled with the Holy Spirit and began to speak in other languages as the Spirit gave them utterance concerning the great things of God (Acts 2:2-4, 11b). What had happened? It was nothing less than the birth of the church. This was as great a miracle as was Christ being born through Mary. This latter was personal, but the former was corporate in nature. The latter became the foundation, the former became the superstructure. One was the beginning, the other became the continuation. Yet let us never forget that Christ and His church are one, not two. It is the same Christ who is speaking and doing through the law and principle of travail.

What we need in our day is to know what God wants and to travail together for that. And such will be a working together with God and not for God. Out of this kind of situation that which God wants will come into being. Here it was the birth of the church, the beginning of the body of Christ. And we clearly see how the risen and ascended Lord Jesus could speak and do things through that now mystical, corporate body of His just as He had been able to do formerly when He was in that physical body of His as Jesus of Nazareth. And this, to put it most succinctly, is actually the content of the book of Acts.

What in these days I pray to the Lord about is this: the Lord needs a body, and the church is that body, even the body of Christ; in fact, it is the extension of Christ. Furthermore, it is through that body that He is to speak and to do as He used to speak and do; nevertheless, it must be stated most earnestly that such speaking and doing by the Head of the church cannot be realized if there is a lack in travailing on our part. The Head of the body has travailed, and the early church had travailed; but have we? That is the key issue in our day.

Our heavenly Father, how we praise and thank Thee for sending Thy Son, the Lord Jesus, to this world to take upon himself human flesh, and in that fleshly body of His He began to speak and to do. Oh, our heavenly Father, how we praise and thank Thee that after the Lord Jesus has accomplished the work of redemption He has risen from the dead and is now seated at Thy right hand, waiting for Thy enemy to become Thy footstool! But Thou hast sent the Holy Spirit. Oh, that we, having been baptized into one body, shall enable the Lord to continue to do and to speak. Oh Father, what a privilege but what a responsibility! We humble ourselves before Thee. We ask Thee to show us Thy mind. We pray that Thou wilt enable us to travail with Thy Son for His body's sake. Oh, we worship Thee together. In the name of our Lord Jesus. Amen.

Chapter Two

The Birth of the Church

Acts 2:1-21, 33, 36—And when the day of Pentecost was now accomplishing, they were all together in one place. And there came suddenly a sound out of heaven as of a violent impetuous blowing, and filled all the house where they were sitting. And there appeared to them parted tongues, as of fire, and it sat upon each one of them. And they were all filled with the Holy Spirit, and began to speak with other tongues as the Spirit gave to them to speak forth.

Now there were dwelling at Jerusalem Jews, pious men, from every nation of those under heaven. But the rumour of this having spread, the multitude came together and were confounded, because each one heard them speaking in his own dialect. And all were amazed and wondered, saying, Behold, are not all these who are speaking Galilaeans? and how do we hear them each in our own dialect in which we have been born, Parthians, and Medes, and Elamites, and those who inhabit Mesopotamia, and Judaea, and Cappadocia, Pontus and Asia, both Phrygia and Pamphylia, Egypt, and the parts of Libya which adjoin Cyrene, and the Romans sojourning here, both Jews and proselytes, Cretans and Arabians, we hear them speaking in our own tongues the great things of God? And they were all amazed and in perplexity, saying one to another, What would this mean? But others mocking said, They are full of new wine.

But Peter, standing up with the eleven, lifted up his voice and spoke forth to them, Men of Judaea, and all ye inhabitants of Jerusalem, let this be known to you, and give heed to my words: for these are not full of wine, as ye suppose, for it is the third hour of the day; but this is that which was spoken through the prophet Joel, And it shall be in the last days, saith God, that I will pour out of my Spirit upon all flesh; and your sons and your daughters shall prophesy, and your young men shall see visions, and your elders shall dream with dreams; yea, even upon my bondmen and upon my bondwomen in those days will I pour out of my Spirit, and they shall prophesy. And I will give wonders in the heaven above and signs on the earth below, blood, and fire, and vapour of smoke: the sun shall be changed to darkness and the moon to blood, before the great and gloriously appearing day of the Lord come.

Having therefore been exalted by the right hand of God, and having received of the Father the promise of the Holy Spirit, he has poured out this which ye behold and hear.

Let the whole house of Israel therefore know assuredly that God has made him, this Jesus whom ye have crucified, both Lord and Christ.

I Corinthians 12:12-13—For even as the body is one and has many members, but all the members of the body, being many, are one body, so also is the Christ. For also in the power of one Spirit we have all been baptised into one body, whether Jews or Greeks, whether bondmen or free, and have all been given to drink of one Spirit.

Today I would like to speak in greater detail, than was shared last time, on the birth of the church—the body of Christ. It all began with the 120 brethren who had obeyed the command of the risen Lord Jesus to remain in Jerusalem to await the fulfillment of the promise of the Father to receive power from on high (Luke 24:49). And these 120 disciples of the risen and now ascended Lord gave themselves for ten days to continual travailing prayer with one accord (Acts 1:14a).

And numbered among these 120 were the twelve apostles, if we consider brother Mathias as hereafter one of the Twelve in place of Jesus' betrayer, Judas Iscariot. From the days of John the Baptizer these twelve disciples/apostles had been with Jesus all the way through until the day on which the risen Lord was taken up into heaven (Acts 1:16-26). Indeed, during those three years in company with Jesus they had known Him, heard the call of discipleship, and had left everything to follow the Lord. They were with the Lord when He was speaking, and they were with the Lord when He was doing many things. They were, as it were, with the Lord through His death, through His resurrection, and during those 40 days of His appearing. And they were together, travailing in prayer, for ten whole days. What wonderful people! These twelve apostles had thus had a very good background and history with Jesus. Is it possible that anyone at any time could have found any twelve people who possessed a better background or more solid history with the Lord Jesus than these men? Such would not have been easy to find, in my estimation.

Along with the twelve apostles were some women also (Acts 1:14a). These were the same women whom we find mentioned in Luke 8. As Jesus had traveled about Israel preaching the gospel of the kingdom with His disciples, these women had ministered to both the Master and His disciples "of their substance" (vv. 2-3). And when Jesus was crucified, the Eleven had been so frightened and fearful for their lives that they had fled and hid themselves behind closed doors (Matthew 26:56b; John 20:19, 26). However, some of these same women—though considered the "weaker vessel" (I Peter 3:7)—were bravely present at Jesus' crucifixion (Matthew 27:55-56, Mark 15:40, Luke 23:49). They had witnessed Jesus' body being taken down from His cross, had seen the place where He was buried, and had even gone early on the resurrection morning to anoint His body with prepared spices (Matthew 27:55-56 again, 28:1; Mark 16:1-2; Luke 23:55-56, 24:1; John 19:25).

These women were the ones as well who were the first followers of Jesus to see Him in His risen state before all the other disciples had done so (Matthew 28:9a, Mark 16:9, John 20:11, 14-16). Moreover, they were also the ones to whom both angels and the risen Lord himself had given various messages which they were to convey to the Eleven following His resurrection (Matthew 28:5-7, 8b-10; Mark 16:5-7; John 20:17b). Indeed, as one very dramatic instance of this, it was to Mary Magdala to whom the risen Lord had said: "Go to my brethren and say to them, I ascend to my Father and your Father, and to my God and your God" (John 20:17b again). Without a doubt these were truly wonderful women.

Not only were these women among those who were present in the upper room; the Scripture indicates that the mother of Jesus, as well as His brethren in the flesh, were also there (Acts 1:14b). Jesus' mother was the most blessed among all women (Luke 1:42, 48b). Oh, how she gave her body to God that out of her womb the Son of God might be brought forth in flesh and become a man! And though she had been told by the prophet Simeon that a sword would go through her soul (Luke 2:25, 34a, 35a), she was willing to accept what God had willed for her. What a wonderful woman Jesus' mother indeed was!

Concerning Jesus' brethren in the flesh, however, they had not at first believed in the Lord while He was living (Matthew 13:57a, John 7:5). They had even been sarcastic, as it were; for at one point these flesh-and-blood brethren of the Lord had advised Him in the following manner: "If you want to be famous, do not hide yourself in our hilly backwoods country here in Galilee; rather, you should go up to the soon-coming Feast of Tabernacles at Jerusalem and show yourself; then you will become famous" (John 7:2-4). Though they had not believed in Jesus back then, oddly enough here they now were, present in the upper room. Evidently, after Jesus' resurrection, something must have happened. For we know that the risen Lord had himself appeared to His brother James (I Corinthians 15:7a). Furthermore, this same brother, together with another of Jesus' brothers—Judas or Jude (Matthew 13:55, Mark 6:3a)—later wrote two of the Epistles we have in the New Testament canon: those of James and Jude. Thus, these two, along with Jesus' other brethren in the flesh (see again the Matthew and Mark verses) had at some subsequent point turned to the Lord and were now giving themselves totally to Him in belief and trust as those who were numbered among the 120.

I believe it can be said with confidence that all the rest of the 120 people present in the Jerusalem upper chamber were the elite—the "cream of the crop" of the Lord's many followers. And these 120 disciples were together for ten whole days giving themselves "with one accord to continual prayer" (Acts 1:14a). Think of that! What potential power! In the whole world one cannot find a better and more spiritual congregation than these 120 assembled people. In fact, any observer would be extremely satisfied with such a congregation. Moreover, if I were privileged to be in that congregation myself, what more would I wish or want? It was such a wonderful congregation of people who were gathered together with one accord there in that upper room. Indeed, in observing such a congregation anyone would conclude that that was sufficient for God's will and purpose in the earth to be accomplished: there would be no need of the Pentecost experience; for surely He could use this congregation of 120 believers in Christ to serve as His witness to the whole world. Nevertheless, the risen Lord had commanded, "Wait" (Acts 1:4-5).

Here was a congregation of 120 members, the best one could ever hope to have on this earth, and yet the Lord said, "Not sufficient." What the risen and now ascended Lord had wanted was not a congregation, for such an assemblage of people cannot be that vessel through which He would be able to continue to speak and to do. What He needed then, and what He needs yet today, was and still is a body. We would be satisfied with a congregation if such were composed of the best members possible. However, the Lord Jesus would not have been satisfied back then with the best possible congregation of good members in this world; instead, He would have wanted—and still wants—a body, because only a many-membered body could and can be that vessel through which to express himself fully.

We must see the difference between a congregation and a body. If I may say so, it is the difference between heaven and earth. A congregation can be organized by man, but a body must be born by the Spirit. A congregation may be a gathering of many members—even a gathering of superior members, as in the case of these 120 brethren. And in that case every individual is superior and they can all come together and pray. But, they are simply 120 individual Christians. Though they may come together to pray, they are not one body; they are still 120 individuals. But a body consisting of 120 members is a radically different entity. Indeed, the reality for these 120 is not a matter of their congregating together but a matter of their being constituted one body. Even when they are not together, these 120 are nonetheless one because their oneness is organic in nature and not organizational as such. There is a kind of unity in a body which you do not find in a congregation.

What the risen and ascended Lord is therefore seeking after as a continuation of himself on earth is not a congregation or even many congregations but is a body. Only the latter can continue His speaking and His doing; accordingly, there had to occur what happened on the day of Pentecost ten days following the Lord Jesus' ascension. That was the day when that body of Christ—the church—was formed and born of the Spirit. The church, if she is truly the church, cannot be organized but only born. If many believers are *organized* together, they have become a congregation; but if they are united into oneness *organically*, they have become a body.

How was the church born? We find here a congregation of 120 excellent people. They prayed together with one accord, they all possessing a good spirit. But the risen Lord had indicated that that was only to serve as a preparation for the actual event of Pentecost; and hence, the period of preparation did not constitute what He ultimately had in mind when He told His followers to wait for the Father's promise to appear. To the contrary, it was only when the 50th day since Passover had arrived and the 120 were still praying together that the Lord's ultimate desire and purpose for that day was fulfilled.

I do not know exactly how early, but these 120 must have met very early in the morning. And when they were once again together in one place, there suddenly came forth a sound out of heaven as of a violent, impetuous blowing. In different Bible versions there are different descriptions given of this phenomenon: "a sound as of the rushing of a mighty wind," "a sound as of a rushing mighty wind," "a noise like a violent, rushing wind," and so forth. As a matter of fact, the New Testament's Greek original conveys the idea of a sound as of a continuous, hard breathing. And it filled the whole house where they were sitting. Then there appeared to them parted tongues as of fire—not actual fire but, "as of fire." And these tongues came upon each one of them. Then they were all filled with the

Holy Spirit and began to speak with different tongues as the Spirit was giving to each of them utterance. Now that was the accomplishing of the day's event of Pentecost.

What do we notice here? Well, there was the sound as of continuous hard breathing; there was the sight of parted tongues like fire; and the sound filled the whole house. Each of those fire-like tongues came upon every one of the 120 disciples and they began to speak in different languages as they were given utterance by the Spirit. Thus, we take special notice here, do we not, of the sounds of hard breathing like a mighty rushing wind and those different language utterances, and we also take special notice of those fire-like tongues which rested on each and all of the disciples. Yet, I would inquire, Is that all which is to be noticed—sounds and sight? What is the real meaning which lay behind these spectacular phenomena?

Is it not true that we are very often attracted by both sound and sight but we overlook or forget their actual meaning? G. Campbell Morgan, considered the prince of Bible expositors, once observed, "How often we remember the incidentals and forget the essentials." Yes, there was the sound, as of hard breathing. And there was the sight of tongues like fire. Yet, if I may state it as such, those phenomena were, in this event, the "incidentals," though it must be acknowledged that they were spectacular in nature. However, what were the "essentials" which are necessary for us to understand? First, the sound was that of God breathing upon all the 120 believers present, which was really the baptism with the Holy Spirit. And second, the sight here of fire-like tongues was actually the manifested gift of the Holy Spirit enabling all the 120 to speak in languages not their own. Consequently, what occurred in that upper room on Pentecost day was far more than the presence of sound and sight. These 120 brethren of the risen and ascended Lord Jesus were baptized with the Holy Spirit, and a body—even the body of Christ—was formed on that momentous day.

We are frequently attracted by outward things, and very often we begin to lose sight of what God has really done to us and for us. It is quite true that very often the seen is that which accompanies the unseen, but it is the unseen that is the reality. On the day of Pentecost something tremendous and most essential happened; it was not simply a spectacular sight. These 120 people were baptized into one body in the power of one Spirit. In one Spirit they were baptized into one body (I Corinthians 12:13a). And hence, they were no longer a congregation of 120 members; they instead had become a body of 120 members. That essentially is what happened on the day of Pentecost.

Did other people in the city hear the sound? In most English Bible translations the relevant passage (Acts 2:6a) reads that "the sound was heard" by others elsewhere in Jerusalem. Strictly speaking, however, most likely only the 120 in the upper room heard the sound and beheld the fire-like tongues coming upon themselves. The Authorized Version Bible more accurately translates the passage as follows: "Now when this [which had occurred] was noised abroad, the [city's] multitude came together…"; and the Darby Bible accurately translates the passage from the Greek this way: "But the rumour of this [which had occurred] having spread, the [city's] multitude came together …" Hence, it was not the event's sound which had spread but a rumor had begun to spread throughout the city that something out of the ordinary had apparently occurred in the upper room of this particular house. And this rumor had caused people from all over Jerusalem to commence gathering at this place.

Now it is obvious that all these people from elsewhere in Jerusalem could not possibly gather in or around the upper room itself. Evidently, therefore, as a result of the rumor having spread far and wide concerning what had happened in the upper room which thus drew a multitude of people to commence gathering at the house, the 120 disciples decided to move themselves from the upper room to another location. They decided to relocate to either a place near the temple—perhaps in Solomon's Porch—or else perhaps inside the temple area itself, at either place of which thousands of people could be accommodated. Some observers have even noted, in fact, that probably the upper-room house was not that far from the temple, which factor would make this relocation quite feasible. In any event, all this must have occurred early in the morning; and thus, by the time the multitude of people had assembled themselves at some location in or near the temple, it was already nine o'clock—the time of the morning sacrifice and prayer in the temple.

Hence, we come to know that the inhabitants of Jerusalem and those Jews visiting the city from Judea and Galilee and from elsewhere in the known world of that day had not heard the sound or witnessed the sight of this extraordinary event because they were not in the house nor in its upper room. As a matter of fact, by the time the first of these inhabitants and those from outside Jerusalem had arrived at the house, both sound and sight had ceased. Nevertheless, what they did hear and see were these 120 disciples of Jesus who were now on fire for the Lord, were uttering foreign languages, and speaking of the mighty things of God. Thus, though the appearance of things surrounding this miraculous occurrence was different to these two groups of people, nevertheless, the essential result remained the same: these 120 believers in the Lord Jesus had become united by baptism into the one body of Christ. At its essence, therefore, that was what had really happened in that upper room on the day of Pentecost.

What, then, is the spiritual significance of Pentecost? And what was the manifestation of this baptism with the Holy Spirit? Well, as people continued gathering in the temple area they heard these 120 believers in Christ speaking in their own dialects. Think of that! Here were those 120 people all speaking at once, with thousands of bewildered onlookers gathered around them and hearing the great things of God being spoken about in these onlookers' own languages.

How did the interaction between the speaking on the part of the 120 and the hearing on the part of the thousands of onlookers play itself out in some sort of orderly fashion? I am not certain of the answer. But let us suppose we are 120 people present in one place and we are all speaking simultaneously but in different languages in the presence of many other people who are gathered around us. Yet, they cannot understand what is being said because of the confusion caused by many languages being spoken all at once! That which I have just described is what must have initially confronted this multitude of onlookers.

So I have asked myself how, on the day of Pentecost, did order emerge out of an obviously confusing situation? I do not know for sure, but perhaps the way order was soon established was as follows. Here were 120 people each speaking in a different tongue; and so, a number of the onlookers ended up gathering themselves to that person of the 120 who was speaking in their language; and conceivably, therefore, that person would be uttering the great things of God to perhaps 30 or 50 onlookers. If so, then this would mean that each of the 120 believers would be speaking to a small group—here a group, there a group, and elsewhere another small group. And hence, everybody among the gathered multitude could hear without any further confusion. There would be order.

Why, though, we might ask ourselves, did God apparently think it necessary for there to appear the speaking in various tongues on the day of Pentecost? In order to give answer to this question one cannot avoid looking afresh into chapter 11 of the Old Testament book of Genesis. For there we learn that all the world's people in that ancient period had possessed but "one language and the same words." And at a certain point in their history they had traveled from the East and ended up settling down on a plain in the land of Shinar (most likely it being the area of Babylon) where subsequently they had come up with the proudful intention of building a city with a tower which they thought could reach up to heaven itself. Indeed, concerning this tower they boastfully said among themselves that by this endeavor "we will make a name for ourselves and not be scattered over the face of the earth." In response, however, God did two things: He first confounded these people's one language so that they could not understand one another's speech, and then He scattered them abroad over the whole earth (vv. 1-8).

Let us understand that when God first created mankind all people spoke the same language and thus they could understand each other. Moreover, by their being able to speak in one language they were able to draw themselves together, journey together and ultimately begin constructing a tower for themselves against God. This rebellion against Him caused Jehovah to disturb and confound these people's speech by imposing upon them different languages which thus hindered them from understanding each other and ultimately they scattered abroad throughout the earth. Hence, the variety of tongues or languages which came into existence was actually a sign of a divine curse upon the earth's people back then and caused them to be scattered.

However, on the day of Pentecost God reversed the entire situation with respect to the multitude of onlookers gathered around the 120 disciples of the risen and ascended Lord Jesus. Whereas heretofore the earth's people had been divided and scattered because of being cursed with a variety of languages due to their rebellion against their Creator, God now grants, on this day of Pentecost, the gift of tongues in order to draw people together into one. So that instead of a sign of curse, this Pentecost experience became a sign of blessing. Instead of people continuing to be scattered, Pentecost commenced drawing people together: out of every tribe, tongue, people and nation of that day God by His Spirit had gathered believers together—both the 120 and a multitude of others—to His name (cf. Revelation 5:9b), and the result was the birth of the church, the body of Christ, and her immediate enlargement from those in the multitude who turned to Christ. Hence, the reason God bestowed the gift of tongues on that momentous Pentecost day was for the purpose of reversing the curse by His regathering in Christ a people to and for himself.

Let us next consider in some detail what then occurred on this Pentecost day with regard to the interaction between the apostle Peter and the Eleven on the one hand and the multitude of people on the other—but constantly seeking throughout to relate these various details to the meaning of the baptism with the Holy Spirit and thus come to a full realization what this baptism gives to us. First of all, the people were amazed, perplexed, they asking one another what might be the meaning of their being able to hear spoken in each person's language the great things of God. But some of them began to mock those speaking in various tongues by saying: "Oh, these people are just full of new wine, that is all."

Hearing this, the apostle Peter and the Eleven stand up together, for now that they were a part of the corporate body of Christ, it was no longer a matter of one member alone—in this instance, Peter—standing up and speaking. And so Peter began to say, "You men, these people are not drunk, as you suppose, for it is only the third hour of the day." Back then, the third hour of the day would be nine o'clock in the morning: the time of morning prayer. According to Jewish custom of that day, before offering up their morning prayer, the Jews would neither eat nor drink anything. In fact, if they were going to drink anything, the time for doing so would only be after and not before having their morning prayer. And hence, stated Peter, these 120 people were not drunk.

On the contrary, far from these people being drunk, explained Peter, "*this* that you are hearing is *that* ..." This is what? This is that which was prophesied by the prophet Joel of old:

> And it shall be in the last days, saith God, that I will pour out of my Spirit upon all flesh; and your sons and your daughters shall prophesy, and your young men shall see visions, and your elders shall dream with dreams; yea, even upon my bondmen and upon my bondwomen in those days will I pour out of my Spirit, and they shall prophesy. And I will give wonders in the heaven above and signs on the earth below, blood and fire, and vapour of smoke: the sun shall be changed to darkness and the moon to blood, before the great and gloriously appearing day of the Lord come. And it shall be that whosoever shall call upon the name of the Lord shall be saved (Acts 2:17-21 quoting Joel 2:28-32a).

Hence, in reply to the multitude of people asking one another, What does this that we hear from the mouths of these 120 people mean, Peter, quoting the prophet Joel, declared to the multitude that this which they were hearing is that which the prophet of old had prophesied. And when Peter had finished speaking forth the gospel to the multitude of people that morning, 3,000 of them received what God had prophesied through Joel, namely, the outpouring of the Holy Spirit upon them.

However, in our carefully reading what Peter had quoted from Joel, can it be said that *this* which was manifested through these 120 believers is the *that* of Joel in *every* respect? For among the many and varied signs in Joel's prophecy of what would happen when the Holy Spirit would be poured out upon flesh in the latter days, we read of such signs mentioned as that young men shall see visions and old men shall dream dreams, to cite but two of the many signs Joel described. On the day of Pentecost, though, there were neither visions nor dreams coming forth; instead, there was manifested only the gift of tongues. One can rightly conclude, therefore, that the outward appearance of things related to the Holy Spirit's outpouring may differ from instance to instance; in other words, God may give different signs at different times; nevertheless, the essential element is the same in all instances: this is that.

Now towards the end of Peter's gospel sermon, the apostle began his conclusion with these meaningful words: "This Jesus God raised up [from the dead], whereof all we are witnesses. Having therefore been exalted by the right hand of God, and having received of the Father the promise of the Holy Spirit, he has poured out this which ye behold and hear" (Acts 2:32-33). Jesus, declared Peter to the multitude, has not only been raised from the dead, but by His ascension into heaven (cf. v.34) He has also been exalted to the right hand of God the Father. And in turn, this same Jesus, added the apostle, having received from the Father the promise of the Holy Spirit, has poured out upon me and the others here this which you all now see and hear.

Before proceeding further let us recall that as the risen Jesus was being taken up into heaven from the Mount of Olives, these 120 brethren and others who were gathered at the Mount beheld Him ascending upward. But at a certain moment a cloud received Him out of their sight and hence they could no longer witness Him ascending, though they assumed He was still going up and up and up. Yet how could they know for certain that this Jesus had in fact arrived at the Father's right hand? They had for sure seen Him ascend perhaps halfway up, or perhaps at least a little distance, only to disappear totally from their sight (see Mark 16:19; Luke 24:49-51; Acts 1:4, 8-12). How, then, could they be absolutely certain—as Peter had confidently declared—that this Jesus, raised from the dead, had also now been exalted to the right hand of the Father? Where, indeed, was the proof? The proof was the outpouring of the Holy Spirit. If the ascending Lord Jesus had not arrived and been exalted to the Father's right hand, then He could not have received from the Father the promise of the Holy Spirit; and thus the Spirit could not and would not have been outpoured. The very descent of the Holy Spirit upon these 120 believers in Jesus was demonstrable proof of His exaltation.

Returning now to Peter's sermon to the multitude, after giving a parenthetical explanation quoting the first verse of Psalm 110, the apostle concluded the main portion of his sermon with these forthright words: "Let the whole house of Israel therefore know assuredly that God has made him, this Jesus whom ye have crucified, both Lord and Christ" (Acts 2:36).

A principle in English grammar states that whenever the conjunctive adverb, therefore, appears in a given text, it signifies that what follows it has a connective consequence to what has been said prior to the adverb. In other words, there is stated a cause that is followed by a result. Hence, what we find being asserted here in this verse 36 is connected to its cause which is to be found in verse 33, with the in-between verses 34 and 35 constituting the parenthesis alluded to a moment ago, which reads: "For David has not ascended into the heavens, but he says himself, The Lord said unto my Lord, Sit at my right hand until I have put thine enemies to be the footstool of thy feet." It is the Lord, of course, who has been exalted to the right hand of God, not David.

What, then, is the consequence or result of Jesus having ascended and been exalted to the Father's right hand and the outpouring of the Holy Spirit which flowed from that exaltation? The apostle Peter convincingly stated the matter this way, employing as he did the conjunctive adverb: Therefore, let all the house of Israel know with certainty that God has made Him—this Jesus whom you did crucify—both Messiah and Lord overall. His Messiahship signifies Lordship, and thus this Jesus now reigns at the right hand of God as both Messianic King and Lord of all. In this connection, let us notice what Psalm 2 has to say: "I have anointed my king upon Zion, the hill of my holiness. I will declare the decree: Jehovah hath said unto me, Thou art my Son; I this day have begotten thee. Ask of me, and I will give thee nations for an inheritance, and for thy possession the ends of the earth" (vv. 6-8).

Of course, the reference to Zion here does not point to the earthly Zion but to the heavenly one. At the ascension of the resurrected Son of God, the Father anointed Him as King. There is a spiritual connection between this passage from Psalm 2 and Psalm 133—both psalms composed by King David of old. In the latter psalm David described how the anointing oil was poured out upon the head of Aaron the Jewish high priest of his day, how then the oil flowed down upon his beard, and ran down to the skirt or very bottom hem of his garment. Such is an earthly picture of what happened at the Father's throne in the highest heaven. For when Jesus—who is the High Priest of our confession (Hebrews 3:1b)—had ascended to heaven, His Father anointed Him as Lord over all. Moreover, that same anointing oil—a type of the Holy Spirit—flowed down over the rest of His body. Thus, it is a picture of the Holy Spirit being outpoured as the result of Jesus having been exalted to the right hand of His Father.

Here, therefore, we have provided to us the first essential meaning of the baptism with the Holy Spirit: it is that we may see Jesus Christ as the Lord over all. In fact, I Corinthians 12 informs us that unless a person is in the Holy Spirit, that one cannot say, "Jesus is Lord" (v. 3 ASV). In other words, it is not a matter of outward speech but that of an inward spiritual reality. How, then, can we utter with all realness that Jesus is Lord? It can only be in, by or in the power of the Spirit: it is the Holy Spirit who enables us to see, announce or declare that Jesus is Lord. Hence, this is the first true meaning of the baptism with the Holy Spirit: that Jesus is Lord.

If a person is filled with the Holy Spirit, that person should be able to see and declare Jesus as the Lord. If a person does not see Jesus as Lord, if he does not honor Him as Lord and Head that one is not filled with the Holy Spirit. How, though, can we be filled with the Holy Spirit? If we can see that Jesus is Lord, we will be filled. Instead of seeking for an experience, let us seek to see Jesus as Lord. Then we will experience the filling of the Holy Spirit. That, then, is the first meaning of the baptism with the Holy Spirit—that Christ Jesus must be Lord; in other words, the Head must be in His place, and then the body can and will be formed. Consequently, on the day of Pentecost the outpouring of the Holy Spirit was the proof of the exaltation of Christ, and the outpouring of the Holy Spirit was to bring those who believe under the headship of Christ.

The second meaning of the baptism with the Holy Spirit is explained in I Corinthians 12: "In one Spirit were we baptized into one body, whether Jews or Gentiles, and we were given to drink of one Spirit" (see v. 13). All the people who were present on the day of Pentecost were Jews. The 120 believers were all Jews, all of the 3,000 who responded to Peter's preaching were either Jews or proselytes, but mainly they were Jews. Somewhat later, in the house of the Roman centurion, Cornelius, those gathered there were all Gentiles (see Acts 10). In all of Scripture there are only two instances wherein reference is made to the phrase, "baptized with the Holy Spirit." And in both instances the phrase is related exclusively to what happened with respect to the 120 disciples in the upper room on the day of Pentecost and exclusively to what occurred later in the home of Cornelius (see Acts 1:5 which is in relation to the upper-room event, and Acts 11:15-17 that is in relation to the Cornelius-household event). Aside from these two passages this term "baptized with the Holy Spirit" is never used in Scripture.

Why is this the case? Let us recognize that at Pentecost this baptism only involved the Jews, which was only part of what was needed to occur in forming the body of Christ—the church. There had to be another part to make the baptism complete; and that occurred in the Gentile house of Cornelius. Consequently, when *both* Jews *and* Gentiles were baptized with the Spirit into the one body of Christ, that completed the birth of the church. Strictly speaking, what happened at Pentecost and in the home of Cornelius can never be repeated. For let us be very clear that the baptism with the Holy Spirit is a *corporate*, and not an individual, experience; for as I Corinthians 12 makes most clear, it is by the "one Spirit [that] we have all been baptized into one body [—the body of Christ], whether Jews or [Gentiles] …, and have all been given to drink of one Spirit" (v. 13). Hence, we are all one body in Christ, and that, at its core, is what "the baptism with the Holy Spirit" is. It is necessary for us to see clearly what the word of God says. I would say again that the baptism with the Holy Spirit is a corporate experience and not an individual one: it is for the entire body of Christ, the whole church.

Nevertheless, though the being "baptised with the Holy Spirit" (Jesus' words of anticipation quoted in Acts 1:5b) happened only once never to be repeated and was exclusively corporate in nature, that does not mean we as individual Christians cannot and should not have a personal experience of being "filled with the Holy Spirit," which all the 120 believers on Pentecost day had experienced personally (Acts 2:4a) in addition to their experiencing being baptized with the Holy Spirit into one body. For we read in Acts 4 that many, if not all, of those 120 believers who had experienced that unique baptism were the same believers who shortly afterwards once again "were all filled with the Holy Spirit" (v.31), since this personal individual experience of theirs was based on the reality of what had happened earlier in the upper room. Just as our experience of resurrection life today is based on the historical fact of the resurrection of Christ which happened long ago, so also our experience by faith today of the infilling of the Holy Spirit is based on the historical fact of the baptism with the Holy Spirit that had occurred on the day of Pentecost long ago.

Now the experience of the 120 believers with the Lord Jesus concerning the place and operation of the Holy Spirit in their spiritual lives actually came to them in bits and pieces, if I may phrase it that way. First, I need to make the following observation, that during Jesus' earthly days—and in view of His death—these disciples of His must have been regenerated by the Holy Spirit before the Son of man's death had taken place. In support of this view let us notice what Jesus had declared to Nicodemus prior to His death and in view of His coming death on the cross: "That which is born of the Spirit is spirit. … [Therefore,] … you must be born again" (John 3:6b, 7b NASB). Moreover, in that same conversation with Nicodemus this Son of man also declared this: "As Moses lifted up the [bronze] serpent in the wilderness, even so must the Son of man be lifted up: that whoever believes may in Him have eternal life" (vv. 14-15 NASB). These words of the Son of man obviously point to the cross. It is on the basis of Jesus' death on Calvary's cross that the Holy Spirit regenerates believers in the Lord Jesus. Surely, though, these early disciples of His had experienced the Spirit's regeneration even though the Son of man's crucifixion had not yet occurred. Please do not ask me to explain more; for I cannot. Nevertheless, we have to believe that this was the way it was with these early believers in the Son of man. I have to believe that disciples of His like Peter and John certainly must have been regenerated by the Holy Spirit prior to Jesus' death. We cannot push their experience of regeneration to a time following the Calvary event; we have to believe that these earliest disciples of the Lord were born anew of the Spirit during the earthly days of Jesus and in view of His coming death. And that, of course, was the first step in the experience of these 120 with the Lord Jesus in regard to the place and operation of the Holy Spirit in their spiritual lives.

What was the next step? Let us recall that on the day of Jesus' resurrection, He had appeared to the Eleven, breathed into them, and said to them, "Receive the Holy Spirit" (John 20:22). Was this merely a symbolic act on the part of the risen Lord? Not at all; this was real, it being the fulfillment of Jesus' promise to His disciples that "in that day"—the day of His resurrection—the Holy Spirit as the Comforter, Guide and

Counselor would come and dwell in them (John 14:20a—here, the phrase "in that day" is uttered by Jesus within the context of His promising His disciples that He would be coming back to them in the Person of the Holy Spirit to indwell them: John 14:16-20). Hence, for these early disciples the beginning of their experience of the *indwelling* of the Holy Spirit occurred on the day of Jesus' resurrection. And that constituted for them the second step.

Let me review briefly what has thus far been explained concerning the steps these early believers in Jesus were experiencing in their relationship with the Holy Spirit. First, their regeneration or second birth by the Holy Spirit connected them with the Lord's sacrificial death in their receiving eternal life by having believed in Him. And second, their receiving the indwelling Holy Spirit as the Comforter and Guide in them connects these early disciples with the day of Jesus' resurrection: without the Holy Spirit indwelling them, how could 120 people continue together for ten whole days? Indeed, without the indwelling Spirit of God, they would not be able to do so for a mere ten hours! For recall how often the Twelve—even when Jesus was present—quarreled among themselves! But there in that upper room there was no more quarreling: they were under the control and leadership of the Holy Spirit in them, and thus they could pray together with one accord for ten days without any negative disruption whatever! Can people accomplish that without the Holy Spirit? Impossible! Hence, these disciples had not only experienced the Spirit's regeneration, they also now possessed the Spirit indwelling them. On the day of Pentecost, however, there came the third step in their experience of the Second Person of the Trinity: there descended upon them the outpouring of the Holy Spirit and thus they were filled with the Holy Spirit.

Let me use an illustration. Here is a cup into which you pour some water. There is now water in the cup, but the water has not risen to the brim, nor is it overflowing. Like these cups this was the condition of the disciples in relation to the Holy Spirit in them *before* the day of Pentecost. These disciples all had the Spirit in them, but the Spirit was not overflowing. On the day of Pentecost, however, it was as though an overwhelming shower of the Spirit had come upon these disciples; and hence, there was such an outpouring of the Holy Spirit that one could describe these disciples' experience as that of their being filled to overflowing. Now that was Pentecost. In other words, the work of the Holy Spirit was consummated in the lives of these 120 believers on the day of Pentecost. That was the third step in their experience of the Holy Spirit.

What, though, was the experience of the 3,000 who heard and believed the gospel on that Pentecost day? Did they have to go through those same steps—one, two and three? For them the Lord had already died; He had already been resurrected; He had already ascended and been exalted. All was now done, and even the Holy Spirit had been outpoured. Would it be necessary for these 3,000 believers to first be regenerated by the Holy Spirit, then wait for a certain period to experience the indwelling Holy Spirit, and then wait for another period to receive the outpouring of the Spirit? The Bible does not say that. On the contrary, what Peter preached to these people was very, very simple. Do we remember what he said? He said, "Repent." They had not repented yet. The apostle therefore proceeded to instruct them as follows: "Repent, and be baptised, each one of you, in the name of Jesus Christ, for remission of sins, and ye will receive the gift of the Holy Spirit. For to you is the promise and to your children, and to all who are afar off, as many as the Lord our God may call" (Acts 2:38-39).

Repent, be baptized, and receive the gift of the Holy Spirit. That phrase here, the gift of the Holy Spirit, does not have reference to the diverse gifts of the Spirit; rather, it points to the Holy Spirit as a gift—the Promised Gift of God the Father and His Son the Lord Jesus Christ (Luke 24:49; John 14:16, 14:26, 15:26a; Acts 1:4b, 2:32-33). And this promise, added Peter to the multitude, was for them, for their children, for those who were near, and for those who were far away—even for as many of them as God might call and might believe. From this it can be rightly concluded that the entire so-called three-step experience of the Holy Spirit for those 3,000 people who believed on that Pentecost day could be and should be experienced all together all at once. And in fact, that was truly the experience of the 3,000 from among the multitude who did believe.

In other words, the experience of the Holy Spirit by these 3,000 believers did not come to them in piece-meal fashion as had been the case with the 120 believers. To the contrary, they received the Holy Spirit in His totality all at once. They were regenerated on that day, they received the indwelling Holy Spirit on that day, they were filled with the Holy Spirit on that day, and they also became part of the body of Christ—the church—on that same day. Accordingly, the body grew from 120 members to 3,120 members within that one selfsame day. Beyond any dispute, that is precisely what happened on the day of Pentecost.

Do please understand that the baptism with the Holy Spirit brings us into a realization of Jesus as Lord, even our Head; furthermore, it brings us into the church, the body of Christ, as members one of another; and consequently, the risen, ascended and exalted Lord Jesus can continue to do and to speak because this body of His is none other than the extension of himself on earth. That fact does not mean, though, that there is no manifestation of spiritual gifts. Surely there is such a manifestation. On the day of Pentecost the gift of tongues was given for a distinct purpose: for gathering together those scattered people of His into the one body of Christ. But then we learn from I Corinthians 12 that the Holy Spirit, according as it pleases Him, bestows gifts to different members for the edifying and building up of the body (vv. 4-12 ASV).

Let me illustrate the matter this way. In the tabernacle of old, and later in the Jerusalem temple, after all the furnishings had been made and set up according to divine order, there remained one very important task to be done before God's house could come alive. What was that task? All had to be anointed with holy oil—both furnishings and priests. Such anointing had somehow quickened all into life (Exodus 40:9, 13-15a, 34-35; I Kings 8:10-11).

Likewise, when we believers receive the Holy Spirit, He quickens us into life and we become members of Christ's body with each of us having a function. The Holy Spirit fills us and activates that function by giving each of us a gift as a manifestation of the Spirit (I Corinthians 12:1, 7 Darby). It is not your or my manifestation but that of the Holy Spirit: He manifests himself through all these gifts. And as these spiritual gifts are activated and begin to function, they are not to be put into operation for personal display but are for the building up of the body in love (Ephesians 4:15b-16).

So, yes, there will indeed be manifestation of the Spirit's gifts. Let us bear in mind, however, that there is the gift of the Holy Spirit in and of himself, and there are the gifts of the Holy Spirit which are bestowed by Him: yet, the one is primary, the other is secondary. Or to put it another way, the Holy Spirit is himself a gift—even the gift of God; and because we have received the Spirit as God's gift, He, the Spirit, will gift us with gifts according as it is His will and pleasure. And all these manifestations of the Spirit in His granting spiritual gifts are for the edification or building up of the body of Christ. Let us thank God that we are in the body, but how we need to be filled with the Holy Spirit in order that we may be living, functioning members of that body!

What does it mean to be filled with the Holy Spirit? It means that you are under His control. If you really give yourself to the Lord and are under the control of the Holy Spirit, the Latter will activate you as a living, functioning member of the body of Christ. On the other hand, if you are not filled with the Holy Spirit and are therefore not under His control, then, yes, you are still a member but you are a non-functioning, almost a dying, member. That is the difference between being filled with the Spirit and not being filled.

I do hope we can see what God is really after—that the baptism with the Holy Spirit is much more than a personal experience and much more than a manifestation of one kind or another by the Spirit. What God is truly after is a body that functions under the control of the Head (Ephesians 1:22b, 5:23b; Colossians 1:18a, 2:19a) so that the Head—even the risen, ascended and exalted Lord Jesus—is able to continue His speaking and His doing on earth through that body of His. If we fail to see God's primary concern and merely attempt to lay hold of the secondary or the incidental, then I am afraid we miss what God is really after.

May the Holy Spirit therefore help us to enter into God's full thought concerning how the body of Christ—the church—was formed and how its members are activated into functioning together under the headship of Christ so that His body may be built up in love (see again Ephesians 4:15b-16). If we truly come to see this, we will have understood the beginning of church history.

Dear Lord, our one desire is to see what Thou art really after. Lord, we pray that we may see that Thou art after a body, a living body under Thee, the living Head, and that Thou dost desire to continue to speak through this body. Oh, that we may be filled with Thy Spirit as functioning members of the body through which Thou art able to express thyself. And Lord, it is all for Thy sake and for Thy glory. We pray that we may be delivered from confusion and really know Thy mind. Oh Lord, do help us. We ask in Thy name. Amen.

Chapter Three

The Life of the Church

Acts 2:37-47—And having heard it they were pricked in heart, and said to Peter and the other apostles, What shall we do, brethren? And Peter said to them, Repent, and be baptised, each one of you, in the name of Jesus Christ, for remission of sins, and ye will receive the gift of the Holy Spirit. For to you is the promise and to your children, and to all who are afar off, as many as the Lord our God may call. And with many other words he testified and exhorted them, saying, Be saved from this perverse generation. Those then who had accepted his word were baptised; and there were added in that day about three thousand souls.

And they persevered in the teaching and fellowship of the apostles, in breaking of bread and prayers. And fear was upon every soul, and many wonders and signs took place through the apostles' means. And all that believed were together, and had all things common, and sold their possessions and substance, and distributed them to all, according as any one might have need. And every day, being constantly in the temple with one accord, and breaking bread in the house, they received their food with gladness and simplicity of heart, praising God, and having favour with all the people; and the Lord added to the [church] daily those that were to be saved.

Acts 4:32-35—And the heart and soul of the multitude of those that had believed were one, and not one said that anything of what he possessed was his own, but all things were common to them; and with great power did the apostles give witness of the resurrection of the Lord Jesus, and great grace was upon them all. For neither was there any one in want among them; for as many as were owners of lands or houses, selling them, brought the price of what was sold and laid it at the feet of the apostles; and distribution was made to each according as any one might have need.

We have been considering together Luke the Evangelist's second New Testament writing, the book of Acts. And in the course of our first two discussion times previously we came to see that during the last ten days of the 50-day period between Jesus' resurrection and the events of Pentecost there occurred the days of travail which brought in the birth of the body of Christ, the church of the living God. Today I would like for us to go a step further and consider what I believe should quite naturally be the next aspect to be discussed: the practical life of the body or church of Christ.

We have to thank God that in reading the Bible we find that He often shows us life before we are given teaching. God often demonstrates first before He instructs. I think that is a definite advantage because if we are taught first we will try to implement it apart from the agency of the Holy Spirit. Our approach may be that if we are given a teaching on some aspect of the spiritual life first before it has been demonstrated in actuality, then our mentality may too likely be: "All right, now that we have the teaching, let us go forth and implement that teaching on our own." Hence, too well aware of this tendency in mankind, God often does not teach us in His word first but initially demonstrates the teaching according to His Spirit. In the present case, therefore, what is presented to us in Scripture first is the spiritual life of these believers before the teaching is given regarding how they should conduct themselves.

That is why in the New Testament canon there are the four Gospels before the book of Acts, and why there is the book of

Acts before the Epistles. Whereas in the book of Acts we do not find much teaching but far more the demonstration of life, in the Epistles we have much more of the teaching which explains that life. Hence, in reading the history of the early church, what we see at its beginning is a showing forth or a giving demonstrable evidence that a body has been born—that a church has been born by the agency of the Holy Spirit. In other words, we are shown how that body lives and how the church functions. In fact, we do not see teaching about that life but we do see a great deal of demonstration.

As was noted earlier, the 120 brethren had possessed a very good spiritual background. They had had a lengthy two- or three-year history with the Lord Jesus. And because of this, after they were merged into one body we could certainly expect a wonderful body life to be exhibited. But just as those 120 believers were starting to live as one body, 3,000 more believers were added. This, of course, presented a problem; for those 3,000 newcomers were obviously not nearly as mature as the 120. Though they were indeed pious Jews and knew a lot of the Old Testament and may even have had some contact with Jesus while He was on earth, nevertheless, in comparing these 3,000 with the 120, we realize there was a great disparity between these two groups of believers.

Humanly speaking, the 120 could quite reasonably be sent forth and could live out that body life because they were ready for such. The 3,000, however, were not ready to be fitted into the body or church life; for if they were immediately to come into body life, they would entirely dilute the life of the 120. The human mindset would maintain that the situation would be very difficult for all concerned. In fact, if that situation were left up to us to resolve, we would more than likely wish to assemble all those 120 spiritual believers and have them say something like the following to the 3,000: "You newcomers are just beginners in the faith; we need to wait a while until you all have matured sufficiently enough before having you join in with us; for this is a 'college,' after all, and not a 'kindergarten'." Yet, the wonderful reality about the life in the body of Christ is that there can simultaneously be both mature and immature members—there can be both spiritual giants and babes in Christ and various other levels of spiritual growth in between. Indeed, in the family and household of God—the church—there can be, and are, fathers, young people, and children in the faith who can fit in together with each other (I John 2:12-14, 18, 28a).

Let us clearly understand, therefore, that at the very beginning of the church life back then, there were fathers and mothers, young men and women, and numerous babes in Christ. Yet the wonderful fact is that those babes were very soundly born. For though they had heard the gospel for the very first time, they instantly said, "What shall we do?" They were pricked in heart but they did not know what to do. So Peter and the eleven apostles instructed them, saying: "This is what you should do: Repent and be baptized in the name of the Lord and receive the gift of the Holy Spirit." Moreover, Peter used many other words in exhorting them to be saved from the perverse generation of that day. And those who accepted his word were baptized (Acts 2:41a). The Greek word translated into English as accepted here in this passage means "to receive in full"—that is to say, their accepting the word preached was a complete acceptance: they repented; they accepted the Lord Jesus; they were baptized; they received the gift of the Holy Spirit; and they were saved from this world.

Hence, those 3,000 had become living members of that living body right away. Very often we think those who are mature can function, but those who are newly saved must wait for years before they can open their mouths. But in this instance here in Acts we find that right away the body of Christ had been enlarged to include 3,000 more members. Instantly there was merged together in one body in the Spirit both older and younger, both mature ones and babes. And every member was living and functioning. The functions may have been different among these body members; nevertheless, they all functioned.

The Bible says that they persevered in the teaching and the fellowship of the apostles, in the breaking of bread and in prayers. The word they here refers not just to the 120 but to the 120 plus the 3,000. That word referred to every child of God at that time who was in the church in Jerusalem. They *all* persevered; they *all* continued steadfastly; they *all* lived in accordance with the teaching and the fellowship of the apostles. That is the scriptural description of how these believers lived out the body life together.

Now what exactly was the teaching of the apostles? It was none other than the teaching of Christ. Before Jesus had ascended back to the Father He had said to His disciples: "Go into all the world and make disciples of the nations and baptize them in the name of the Father, the Son, and the Holy Spirit, and whatever I have commanded you, teach them" (see Matthew 28:19-20a). The apostles therefore simply taught the 3,120 believers the teaching which they had received from Christ. Paul echoed this same understanding in writing to the Corinthians this: "What I have delivered to you is what I have received from the Lord" (see I Corinthians 11:23a). This thus signifies that the apostles cannot teach what they like, that what they teach cannot be their own special teaching. Not at all! The apostles taught nothing but the teaching of Christ Jesus. In other words, the risen and ascended Lord is found to be teaching His people through His apostles. It was not the teaching of man; it was the teaching of the Lord Jesus.

Yet that being true, how did the apostles teach these 3,120 members in the body of Christ? Their teaching did not come from man nor from the wisdom of man; their teaching came by way of revelation from God. That was the way these apostles taught. They simply taught what they had received from the Lord Jesus by revelation. They taught what they themselves had seen, what they themselves had experienced. Their teaching was not dead doctrines or theory. Their teachings constituted living words of God. Therefore, those who received their teaching back then did not receive it as being man's word but as being the very word of God. It was not some theory conjured up in their mind but was that which they continually abode in. They experienced the teaching of the Lord Jesus and then they practiced it. Hence, the teaching of the apostles was the teaching of Christ and it is found in the Bible, but it is that which is breathed upon and quickened or made living by the Holy Spirit.

We could therefore say that the ministry of the apostles was a living ministry. It was under the administration of the Spirit, and because of that, their teaching was most powerful. Those who received the apostles' teaching received it in their spirit. And so it worked in their lives. Such Holy Spirit-administered teaching was therefore not something which went from one mind to another mind; it was that which was imparted from one spirit (that is, from the apostles' spirit) to the renewed spirits of others. It was the impartation of Christ through the apostles and was the receiving of Christ in the spirits of those 3,120 believers, and by that means they grew in the grace and knowledge of the Lord Jesus (II Peter 3:18). Such, then, was the teaching of the apostles, and all these people in the body of Christ back then persevered or continued steadfastly in that teaching.

But these saints also persevered in the fellowship of the apostles. What was that fellowship? Had these apostles *formed* an exclusive club of their own known as the apostles' fellowship? Not at all! On the contrary, they had *joined* an exclusive club themselves. They had become members of the exclusive club of the Father and of the Son in the Holy Spirit. The apostle John, in his first epistle, had written: "What we have seen and heard, what we have contemplated and handled, we have reported to you in order that you also may have fellowship with us; and our fellowship is with the Father and with His Son" (see I John 1:1, 3). The apostle Paul made a similar declaration: "We have been called into the fellowship of God's Son Jesus Christ" (see I Corinthians 1:9b).

From all this, then, we can conclude that the fellowship of the apostles is not a man-made one but is the fellowship of God's Son Jesus Christ. And the fellowship of God's Son Jesus Christ is that which is between the Father and the Son in the Spirit. Oh! That is the most exclusive club in the whole universe!—this being composed exclusively of the Father and the Son in the Spirit, that is all. And what fellowship the Father and the Son have had and continue to have in the Spirit! That is real fellowship. These Members of *this* club share everything because They are one. They are one in heart, one in love, one in purpose, one in everything. Indeed, there are no hesitant moments out of fear, doubt or disinclination to share, no drawing back from one another for any reason; on the contrary, They are open and free, committed the One to the Other, and are perfectly harmonious together. How glorious it is! In *this* fellowship there is no shadow, no darkness, no jealousy, no prejudice, and no fear. Oh, the fellowship of the Son with the Father in the Spirit is truly most glorious!

But then the Father and the Son agreed to enlarge their exclusive club's membership: "Let Us include man in our fellowship. Let them participate with Us in what We have." That is why the Lord Jesus came into this world—to bring additional members into that fellowship. He came into this world to open the door to others for them to be included in His fellowship with the Father. And to that end, let us recall that after His death and resurrection He told Mary of Magdala to go and say to His brethren, "I ascend to my Father and your Father, and to my God and your God" (John 20:17b). Thus, all Jesus' disciples were called into Jesus' fellowship with the Father in the Spirit; and here in Acts we learn that the apostles had joined and become a part of that glorious fellowship.

How, though, had they joined that fellowship? It was not by official means and ways. Instead, it had occurred through the

Spirit, for God had put them in Christ; and being in Christ, they had instantly come into that fellowship. That is what was meant in Acts regarding the "fellowship of the apostles." They fellowshiped with Jesus the Son and with the Father in the Spirit. What a fellowship they all now enjoyed!

Furthermore, let us also recall that portion of Jesus' great intercessory prayer in which He prayed to the Father concerning His then current disciples and those they would reach with the gospel: "I pray not only for these My present disciples but also for those who shall believe on Me through their word: that they may all be one, even as You, Father, are in Me and I am in You, so that they also may all be in Us" (see John 17:20-21b). By this, therefore, we come to understand that God, through the gospel word preached by those early apostles of the Lord Jesus, extended to the 3,000 who believed on Jesus that Pentecost day the privilege of being included in that glorious divine fellowship. Moreover, by the preaching of the gospel to usward we too have been drawn into that fellowship of the Father and the Son in the Spirit. And that is what "the fellowship of the apostles" consisted of. Just as "the teaching of the apostles" was not another or man-devised teaching but was the entire body of teaching of Christ in the Spirit, so "the fellowship of the apostles" was not some humanly-devised fellowship, either: it was, and is, the fellowship of God the Son with God the Father in God the Holy Spirit.

Now teaching has reference to truth; whereas fellowship has reference to grace. On the one hand, the Jerusalem church persevered in the teaching of the apostles; those 3,120 members of the body in Jerusalem received all the truth which is in Christ. It is as the apostle Paul has written: "... you have heard Him (i.e., Christ) and have been taught in Him according as the truth is in Jesus" (see Ephesians 4:21). God's truth is to be found in Christ Jesus because only in Him is there the "yea and amen of God" (see II Corinthians 1:18-20). That is the teaching of the apostles which the 3,120 received and persevered in back then, and that is what we too must receive and persevere in. On the other hand, there is also the fellowship of the apostles which they persevered in: it was and still is, a sharing or common participation in a partnership of togetherness in Christ in the Spirit. That is the fellowship of the apostles which the early church in Jerusalem experienced and persevered in. Both the teaching and the fellowship which the body of Christ back then persevered in was not greater or lesser than the teaching and fellowship of the apostles. The Jerusalem church of that early day neither exceeded nor limited the extent of the teaching, nor was the fellowship which she maintained in those early days larger or smaller than the fellowship of the apostles.

That, then, is how the body of Christ lived out its life in the Spirit together at the beginning. The believers of that day received all the truth which is in Christ: they did not receive just one or two or a few truths, nor did they add in various human-devised theories, but they received all the truth which is in Christ as delivered by the apostles. Moreover, all the members of the body had fellowship with one another. Indeed, the scope of their fellowship was that of the body itself. That, therefore, was how these believers truly lived out the church life. And if we today experience and persevere in the teaching and the fellowship of the apostles, we too shall be living out the body or church life.

Now the teaching and fellowship of the apostles are especially demonstrated both in the breaking of bread and in the prayers. What is meant by the breaking of bread? Recall that on the night of His betrayal, the Lord Jesus gathered His own around Him. And towards the end of their celebration together of the Passover Feast, He took a loaf, blessed it, broke it, and gave to His disciples, and said, "Take, eat, all of you. This is My body broken for you. Do this in remembrance of Me." Afterwards, He took the cup, gave thanks, and passed it to His disciples, and said, "This is the cup of the new covenant, sealed with My blood. This do, as often as you shall drink it, in remembrance of Me" (see both Matthew 26:26-28a and I Corinthians 11:23b-25). The apostles well remembered that historic breaking of the bread and the drinking of the cup inaugurated by the Master. We therefore find in the early church that they broke bread every day and not just once a week, because their breaking of the bread was the act of their remembering the Lord. The breaking of bread in the early church became the very symbol of their life together. Their life was centered upon Christ and based completely upon Christ because His blood had cleansed them and His life now sustained them. They lived because of Him, and they expressed their love towards the Lord by breaking the bread. This was part of the teaching and the fellowship of the apostles.

This reminds me of an incident in the life and work of a particular Bible translator. In times past some people have asked me what version of the Scriptures I use, and sometimes I hesitate to mention it because it is not a popular version. I use the version called the *New Translation* by John Nelson Darby. Darby lived in the 19th century in England, and with some helpers he translated the Bible from the Hebrew and Greek into German, into French, and into English. And when he was translating the Bible with his helpers, they would break the bread and drink of the cup every day. This was because in laboring together on these various translations, they were afraid that by being occupied with so much mental work their hearts might be drawn away from the Lord. And hence, they participated together in the Lord's table daily in order that their hearts—in their remembrance of the Lord Jesus in this way—might be kept in the love of Christ. I think that was something most beautiful and precious.

Today we sometimes treat this matter of Communion as nothing more than a formality. Either it is engaged in four times a year or once a month or even only once a week, but too often we consider it to be a ritual, a Christian ceremony, or a sacrament. This was not so, however, with the believers in the early church, for this was the way by which they expressed their perseverance in the teaching and the fellowship of the apostles; in fact, their having daily communion demonstrated that their lives were centered upon Christ. It was the way by which they kept their hearts in love with Christ and was the way by which they kept themselves always in gratitude and worship.

We see, then, that the early church persevered in the teaching and fellowship of the apostles by the breaking of bread. Christ was the center of all the teaching; Christ was the center of all their fellowship. If in our day any teaching or doctrine is not centered upon Christ, it will soon become that which is in opposition to Christ. Whatever the teaching or doctrine and whatever the fellowship may be, and no matter how correct or pleasant it may be, if it is not centered upon Christ, it will eventually degenerate into something foreign to Christ and His kingdom purpose.

Permit me to address this subject of fellowship further. Essentially, fellowship is the sharing of Christ. It is not conversing together about this or that matter of interest and it most certainly is not talking about nonsensical things. Moreover, fellowship is not an activity for criticizing this person or that and certainly not doing so behind that one's back: "Oh, I had good fellowship with brother and sister so-and-so, for we all ended up agreeing that sister so-and-so over there is very bad." That is not the meaning of fellowship, for such is not at all edifying. Rather, fellowship is centered upon, and is a sharing of, Christ. And the breaking of bread together by the saints in the early Jerusalem church was symbolic of the fact that they were Christ-centered people. Each of these saints would have agreed with what Count von Zinzendorf of the Moravian Brethren in Germany once remarked: "I have only one passion in this world and that is Jesus Christ."

Two activities which Christians neglect very much today are the breaking of bread and prayer. Some Christians claim that having the Lord's Table once a week is too much, so they reduce it to once a month; but that too is too much, so it is reduced to once in a season; yet even that is too much, so it is reduced still further to only at Easter and Christmas, as though Communion is a most minor observance for Christians to participate in. But let us also consider the spiritual activity of prayer together engaged in among believers in the church. Whenever a minister of the word is to preach, the church's meeting place is filled, but when the meeting of the church is for prayer, like the sparrows who alight at one's door, there are only a few who attend. And what is even worse, some churches today have no prayer meeting at all. Is any of this an expression of a true church?

"And all that believed were together." They did not come together in order to *be* one; on the contrary, it was because they *were already* one that therefore they came together. This togetherness was more than physical in nature; it in addition was a togetherness in the Spirit. Indeed, these believers knew they were one, that they were related to one another, and that they recognized that they could not live without each other. Hence, they *had* to be together.

Brother Watchman Nee once visited an elderly brother, George Cutting, who wrote the noteworthy booklet, "Safety, Certainty, and Enjoyment"—a wonderful piece of Christian literature which has helped many, many people in their spiritual journey in Christ. So when brother Nee went to England one year, he purposely visited that brother who was then in his nineties. Not being too clear in his mind at that time, brother Cutting would awaken from slumber and be very clear for a few minutes but would then enter into a semi-comatose state. Now when brother Nee returned to China, he told us that during his visit with brother Cutting, he would awaken and speak to brother Nee these few words: "He cannot do without me; I cannot do without Him. I cannot do without Him; He cannot do without me." He was, of course, referring to the Lord Jesus, and he uttered only these few words before going off into the comatose-like state once again.

Brother Nee went on to remark that we Christians often say that we cannot do without the Lord, but do we also know that He cannot do without us? Brother Cutting knew this very well. However, brother Nee was prompted to add the following: "Yes, it is quite true, we cannot do without the Lord and He cannot do without us; yet, there is an additional reality: that neither can you do without me and I cannot do without you." Now *that* is true togetherness in the Spirit.

How much in our day are we conscious of the body life? Do we really know that just as we cannot do without the Head of the body, we cannot do without our brothers and sisters? We have to be together because we are one.

"They had all things [in] common" (Acts 4:32c, 2:44b ASV), for no one "claimed that anything belonging to him was his own" (4:32b NASB). In other words, everything was voluntarily at the disposal of the brothers and sisters. Were they forced to do that? Was there any teaching which required them to do that? Not in the least. They were so delivered from the spirit of selfishness, self-possessiveness, and self-interest, and were so full of the love of Christ that they could no longer claim, "This is mine."

There is a very strong urge in our flesh to self-possessiveness: we want to own things. We are impelled by our flesh to say, "This is mine." We can see that impulse even in a little child: "This toy is mine; you cannot touch it!" Self-possessiveness is a fallen instinct of man. It is there, for whether it is expressed in a big way or a small way, it is present in mankind. It is the expression of individualism. But when the grace of God comes in—when the love of Christ has so filled us—we are completely delivered from individualism, but not, of course, our individuality. Those believers in the early church were still individuals; they had not lost their individuality; but they were delivered from individualism. Such was the expression of true body life. The spirit of self-possessiveness was gone. They were one, and so they shared everything in common.

We need to be clear here that, strictly speaking, this expression of body life in the Spirit is not to be confused with communal life or life in a commune. In America there appears to be a move afoot among some of God's people whose hearts have been touched by the Lord of longing to live in community together. And as a consequence, many communes or communal groups have been or are being established. Quite a few so-called Christian communities are being organized.* Let me explain what is on my heart in order that no one misunderstand me.

On the one hand, if the love of Christ has constrained a particular local expression of the body of Christ, then its members are already a community. In fact, the church, by definition, *is* a community. Her brethren share everything one with another. Selfishness is gone and everything is shared in common; yet this is the action of the whole church and not just a few special people who organize themselves into a community or a commune. We must recognize that the church's community life is not that which people go out and organize. It is not a teaching which someone tries to copy; instead, it comes about as a result of the love of Christ within brethren giving them such a sense of body consciousness that they, as it were, live with the other brothers and sisters as one body. No one among themselves says, "This is mine."

As a matter of fact, because there were so many poor believers among those who had received the Lord on Pentecost day that many more fortunate ones among them sold their property and laid its proceeds at the feet of the apostles for them to distribute to each according to everyone's need. It was not a requirement that every property owner among these believers

* The reader should bear in mind that these observations were being voiced during the early 1970s; but since then, such a movement has diminished considerably.—*The Publishers*

had to sell their property; to the contrary, it was all *voluntary*. Even those who had not sold their property or goods voluntarily opened their houses for the church. Otherwise, if they all had sold their property, the church would have had no places in which to meet from house to house.

This sense of community is not something organized or manufactured. It is a spontaneous expression of the love of Christ in those who comprise the church local; they possess the consciousness of body life. And when anyone becomes aware of this, that one knows that this is the genuine reality of the body of Christ.

In the human psyche there seems always to be present this aspiration for man to try to create this kind of utopian communal life. Several years ago I went to Israel, and I visited a few kibbutzim, the Jewish term for collective farms, settlements, or communes. And I was deeply impressed. Their inhabitants had come together: they lived together, ate together, and worked together. They individually did not possess anything; all their possessions belonged to the kibbutz. These people, having witnessed the division and the selfishness that was in mankind all around them, their good selves naturally aspired to create such a commune. But though I was deeply impressed, I knew that the kibbutz did not answer to the heart of God. What can only please God is not a copy, is not an involuntary entity created by man; it's not even a voluntary humanly-organized entity. Rather, it is that which is the result of the work of the Holy Spirit in our lives. As we go on in the Christian life I believe we shall discover how true that is.

The apostles never taught the following: "Every one of you who has property must sell it and give the proceeds from its sale to the church." Even when, as is learned from Acts chapter 5, Ananias and Sapphira, as a means of making a name for themselves, sold their property, held back some of the price, laid the rest of the price at the apostles feet, and deceptively made it appear as though it was the total price, Peter made it clear that this was a voluntary act on their part; for he said this to Ananias: "While your land remained unsold, did it not remain your own? And even after it was sold, was not the money gained still under your control? Why, then, did you lie to the Holy Spirit?—for you have lied not to men but to God!" (see vv. 1-4) Here we see that this was a matter purely between the brethren and the Spirit of God. He is the One who constrained the brethren in the early church to do good voluntarily and not under any compulsion or force. And such was the way they lived out the Christ-life in those early days. That was the life of the early church. And that is the expression of true body life.

These believers met every day in the temple, observed the breaking of bread in their homes, ate their food with joy and thankfulness, constantly praising the Lord, and thus gained favor with all the people in the city; and so the Lord added to the church daily those that were being saved. Church life is an assembling life and these early church brethren assembled together every day. Now probably our reaction would be to say that that is impossible today with us. Yes, but the principle is still valid to maintain. Let us not forsake the assembling of ourselves together, especially when we know the day of His return is near (Hebrews 10:25a, c). How we need to come together to encourage one another in the Lord! (Hebrews 10:25b) We need that. And though we may not be able to meet every day, we should meet as often as we can because the very life of the church is an assembling life. We come together to worship the Lord, to exhort one another, and to build up one another in love.

These believers in Jerusalem praised God and found favor with the people. They did not offend the general populace but they found favor with all the people. In other words, they bore a good testimony before the watching world. Hence, in reading the first chapters of the book of Acts we are given to see some demonstration of the life of the church in those early days. Oh, how true it is that the Spirit of God is living: He does not make everything uniform. Oh, let us not fall into the trap of thinking that because the early church was that way, therefore let us copy it. No, no, no! His ways are different in every place where the local church meets, but the principles which should govern are the same everywhere.

I am therefore not speaking here about a set form which we all must do or follow. Rather, I am speaking about the Holy Spirit showing us a pattern full of divine principles. Let us be led by the Spirit into practicing these principles. You will discover that every local place will be different and yet the governing principles are the same. So I do hope that the Lord will recover such life to us today.

Our heavenly Father, we do praise and thank Thee for the demonstration of Thy life in the church. Oh, Thy life is in us; may it be unhindered. And by the quickening of Thy Holy Spirit may there be the expression of it coming forth spontaneously to the praise and glory of Thy name. Father, we have shared these things, now it is left to You to work it out in us. We do not dare to stretch forth our hands and try to organize anything, but we simply commit ourselves to Thee for what Thy Spirit desires. In the name of our Lord Jesus. Amen.

Chapter Four

The Name of the Lord Jesus

Acts 3:1-16—And Peter and John went up together into the temple at the hour of prayer, which is the ninth hour; and a certain man who was lame from his mother's womb was being carried, whom they placed every day at the gate of the temple called Beautiful, to ask alms of those who were going into the temple; who, seeing Peter and John about to enter into the temple, asked to receive alms. And Peter, looking stedfastly upon him with John, said, Look on us. And he gave heed to them, expecting to receive something from them. But Peter said, Silver and gold I have not; but what I have, this give I to thee: In the name of Jesus Christ the Nazaraean rise up and walk. And having taken hold of him by the right hand he raised him up, and immediately his feet and ankle bones were made strong. And leaping up he stood and walked, and entered with them into the temple, walking, and leaping, and praising God. And all the people saw him walking and praising God; and they recognised him, that it was he who sat for alms at the Beautiful gate of the temple; and they were filled with wonder and amazement at what had happened to him. And as he held Peter and John, all the people ran together to them in the portico which is called Solomon's, greatly wondering.

And Peter, seeing it, answered the people, Men of Israel, why are ye astonished at this? or why do ye gaze on us as if we had by our own power or piety made him to walk? The God of Abraham and Isaac and Jacob, the

God of our fathers, has glorified his servant Jesus, whom ye delivered up, and denied him in the presence of Pilate, when he had judged that he should be let go. But ye denied the holy and righteous one, and asked that a man that was a murderer should be granted to you; but the originator of life ye slew, whom God raised from among the dead, whereof we are witnesses. And, by faith in his name, his name has made this man strong whom ye behold and know; and the faith which is by him has given him this complete soundness in the presence of you all.

Acts 4:5-12—And it came to pass on the morrow that their rulers and elders and scribes were gathered together at Jerusalem, and Annas the high priest, and Caiaphas, and John, and Alexander, and as many as were of the high priestly family; and having placed them in the midst they inquired, In what power or in what name have ye done this? Then Peter, filled with the Holy Spirit, said to them, Rulers of the people and elders of Israel, if we this day are called upon to answer as to the good deed done to the infirm man, how he has been healed, be it known to you all, and to all the people of Israel, that in the name of Jesus Christ the Nazaraean, whom ye have crucified, whom God has raised from among the dead, by him this man stands here before you sound in body. He is the stone which has been set at nought by you the builders, which is become the corner stone. And salvation is in none other, for neither is there another name under heaven which is given among men by which we must be saved.

The Jewish people had set times of prayer, usually three times each day—the morning prayer, the noon prayer, and the evening prayer. The morning prayer was about nine o'clock, and that was the time, we will recall, when the Holy Spirit came down upon 120 believers in the upper room and were filled with the Holy Spirit (see again Acts 2). The church, the body of Christ, was born at the time of morning prayer. People laughed and remarked, "These people are drunk." But Peter answered them, saying: "This is not the time for people to be drunk because this is the time of morning prayer." According to the custom of that time, Jews would not drink or eat anything before the hour of the morning prayer.

In the present chapter of Acts, however, the event recorded occurred at about three o'clock in the afternoon, with Peter and John going to the temple to pray. It was thus the time of evening prayer for the Jewish people. Peter and John lived in a transitional period between the Old and New Covenants. And accordingly, they and the other saints still kept the habit of going to the temple to pray at whatever the set hour, though at other times they would meet together as the church to remember the Lord in the breaking of bread. So as these two apostles of the Lord were entering the temple area, they saw a man lying there who was lame from birth. He was carried there daily by his friends and placed at the front of the gate called Beautiful for the purpose of asking alms from those who came into the temple to pray. What a contradiction! Here was the gate called Beautiful, but at this beautiful gate was an unattractive scene—a man lame from birth, begging.

This gate was called Beautiful because it had been made of a massive amount of brass and was greatly adorned. This was one of the three entrances to the temple. This man who was born lame was at the front of that gate. He was not allowed to enter the temple to pray, to worship, or to serve God; rather, he was kept outside the temple where the best he could do was to sit by the gate and ask for alms. When people went into the temple to pray, it was at a time of the day when their hearts would normally be soft and tender. So, psychologically speaking, this lame man was advantageously situated because those who were entering the temple to pray would surely be inclined to show compassion by giving some alms to the man.

Let us recall that when Solomon had built the temple, he had prayed along this line: "O God, heaven and the heaven of heavens cannot contain Thee. How, then, can I expect You to live in this temple?" Even though this temple was truly majestic, gorgeous, splendid, and made of massive stones and gold, yet if the heaven of heavens cannot contain God, how, by comparison, can God live in such a small place? Nevertheless, this temple had been built in order that God might set His name there. In other words, the temple was the one edifice on earth where God's name was placed.

Hence, the temple was different in one respect from all other houses erected on earth. It was not because it was more beautifully built, for there were probably other houses which were equally as beautiful. The only difference between this house and all the others lay in the fact that God's name had been set upon this one particular house. And because of that, His ears were there listening to the prayers offered up in that house. Moreover, the eyes of God were focused upon this house as well, and He therefore saw every one who came in. Consequently, it could be said that the preeminent characteristic surrounding the Jerusalem temple was the fact that the name of Jehovah was there; and hence, He himself was there.

By the time of Peter and John, of course, Solomon's temple had already been destroyed, but it had been rebuilt by those of the Jewish remnant who had returned to Jerusalem from their captivity in Babylon (Ezra 1-6). Much later, King Herod would spend 46 years enlarging and beautifying it (John 2:20a). So, outwardly, the Jerusalem temple was still a magnificent edifice, beautifully adorned. And we will remember that towards the end of the earthly life of the Lord Jesus, on the occasion of His last time in Jerusalem, His disciples had pointed out to Him how precious were the stones and the buildings which made up that temple (Mark 13:1).

Yes indeed, the temple was a beautiful object, a wonderful place of artistry, but was the name of the Lord really there? This was supposed to have been where the name of the Lord had been placed. And if this be factual, then it should be assumed that the Lord was there. And if the Lord was there, then every problem of one's life should be able to be solved: there should be no need for the lame man to be barred from entering the temple to worship God. He should be able to be brought into the temple, experience the powerful miraculous work of the Lord, and be able to pray and praise and worship.

We must acknowledge, however, that though the temple was there, and though everyone professed that it was God's temple where His name was set, unfortunately, there was no power and no reality associated with it; there was not a living presence of the Lord in that temple. On the contrary, it had become a house of merchandise, even a robber's den (John 2:16b, Matthew 21:13b). No wonder that all this temple could provide for a lame person with severe life problems was to grant him some alms by which to live. That was all. In fact, this beggar was not expecting anything more than that from the temple. All he was able to acquire was a little money to live on, beyond which he had no hope of anything better. That was the state and condition of both temple and man at that time. On the other hand, here came Peter and John into that disappointing situation, as recorded for us by Luke in Acts chapter 3.

In the preceding chapter we learned that the church had just then been born on the day of Pentecost. Consequently, when Peter and John entered the temple, they actually represented the real temple: the living house of God. Quite true, the physical temple was standing there in name, but it was not in reality. By contrast, here were two men, two living stones who, with other saints, had been built into a living house, and the name of the Lord was *with* these two and *in* these two. They came forward, and the beggar looked at them thinking that they were just the same as the other incoming worshipers. So the lame man was, as usual, expecting some alms from Peter and John. They in turn looked him over and then Peter said, "Look on us." He looked, expecting some alms; but Peter declared: "Silver and gold I do not have, but what I do have I give to you. In the name of Jesus Christ the Nazarene, rise up and walk." He took hold of that lame man, raised him up, and suddenly, the man's ankle bones and legs became strong. He stood, he leaped, he ran, and all the while praising the Lord. Then, with the two apostles, he entered the temple to worship God.

What did Peter and John have? Not silver or gold, but they had the mighty name of the Lord. And in the name of the Lord Jesus this man was healed. From being a longtime beggar he became a worshiper.

The church is a spiritual house, a holy habitation of God (Ephesians 2:19b-22). Like the temple of old, the church is where the name of the Lord has now been placed. Names are very important in the Scriptures. What is meant by a name? Webster's International Dictionary defines the word name as "a title by which a person or thing is known or designated, a distinctive appellation, a descriptive appellation." In other words, a name is a title which identifies a person. A name is not only distinctive, it is also descriptive—it describes that person and expresses the character or characteristic of that person.

The Bible places very much emphasis on the name of a person. In fact, we learn from Scripture that God often changed the names of people—for instance, Abram was changed to Abraham, Jacob to Israel, Simon to Peter. God puts great emphasis on names. And with respect to the name of God himself, we come to know Him by our being given to know His various names one after another. In fact, by means of the Bible God has revealed His name to His people in a progressive manner. For instance, when He disclosed himself to Moses in the incident of the burning bush, Moses had asked of Jehovah

God, "What is Your name?" To which God had replied: "I AM THAT I AM. That is My name" (Exodus 3:13-14). Throughout the Scriptures we learn how God revealed His name in toto to His people gradually. And by means of His progressive revelation of himself, God's people come to know Him a little better each time. Of course, this knowing of God by knowing His name is not that which comes to His people in a mechanical or technical way—in their minds; rather, they truly know Him in heart and spirit. So that, whenever God chose to reveal himself through this or that special name, that fresh name of His revealed further to His people who and what He is. And by their being given to know that fresh revelation about Him via a new name, God's people on each such occasion came to know Him somewhat more than before. This explains in part why in Scripture God has so many names.

Let us notice well that in the Bible Jesus, too, has many names. Even before He was born a special name was given to Him: "He shall be called Jesus, for He will save His people from their sins" (see Matthew 1:21). We are told in the Old Testament that He shall be called Immanuel—God with man; also, that His name is Wonderful, Counselor, Prince of Peace, Almighty God, Father of Eternity (Matthew 1:23 quoting Isaiah 7:14; Isaiah 9:6). The Lord Jesus has many, many names, and in knowing each of His names we come to know Him more and more.

A name identifies and describes a person if it is a right name—especially is this true when a person is absent from a given situation, for then that person's name stands in for himself or herself. Recall, for instance, that before the Lord Jesus would no longer be with His disciples, He had said to them: "Hitherto you have not asked anything in My name, but now, if you ask anything in My name, My Father will hear you" (see John 16:24). Jesus was soon going to the cross, and so He left His name with them. And when the disciples thereafter prayed in His name, it was as though He himself was praying before the

Father. His name therefore stands in for himself and represents Him; and that is why His name is so powerful. This is a most precious blessing which the Lord has left with us. Physically speaking, He is not with the church today, but spiritually speaking, He has left His name with the church. This is our heritage as the church. And whenever the church uses His name, that means that He himself is involved. Such, then, is the importance of a name.

What is the church and what is her relationship to Jesus' name? The Lord Jesus has himself explained it: "Where two or three are gathered together unto my name, there am I in the midst of them" (Matthew 18:20). The real meaning of the church in this regard is when two or three of Jesus' followers are gathered together to His name. Out of all the world's nations God has called one specific people to His name. In one very important respect these people are different from all the other people of the world because they have the name of the Lord Jesus. And by having that name they have the Lord himself.

Now if we measure the church by this measurement, where do we who constitute part of today's church measure up? Are we like the Jerusalem temple back in the time of Peter and John? Presumably we have the name of the Lord Jesus in us and among us, yet I am afraid that all we can do is give some alms to needy people: there is not the reality or power of that name present; and so, we cannot be instrumental in transforming those people into worshipers of the Father. Or, as the case might be, are we a people who really possess the name of the Lord Jesus? Which is to say, that the name is there, and He is there, and so He manifests himself as living by His being able—through the members of His body, the church—to bring people into the very presence of the Father and make them worshipers. They are not kept out of the Lord's house but are brought into the very presence of God.

There is a most telling story surrounding the statement and command which Peter uttered to this man lame from birth who begged at the temple gate. There was a famous theologian in the Roman Catholic Church by the name of Thomas Aquinas. He was one of the greatest theologians that institutional Church ever produced. And one day this esteemed theologian was visiting Pope Innocent II. And while visiting with the Pope the latter showed Aquinas all the much wealth and artistic treasures of the Vatican. And as the Pope was showing the theologian this wealth, he said to Thomas: "Today, we do not need to speak as St. Peter did: 'Silver and gold have I none.'" To which Aquinas responded with these words of friendly rebuke: "Yes, but neither can we say, 'In the name of Jesus Christ, rise up and walk.'"

Which is better for us who are in the church? What would you prefer to have? Would you prefer to have silver and gold and thus be able to give a few pennies to the needy beggars? Or would you prefer to have the powerful name of the Lord Jesus that will transform those beggars into worshipers? What is the actual meaning and mission of the church? She is not on this earth simply to perform some small but good, social work. By the grace of God we *should do that*, but we should do more. The very existence of the church on earth is to make people worshipers in spirit and in truth (cf. John 4:23). But do we have the power? Do we have the authority? Is the name of the Lord Jesus living and real among His people?

God has called us Christians out of every nation, every tribe, every tongue, and every people, and has gathered us together to His Son's name. Thank God for that. We are those who at one time in our lives had called upon the name of the Lord and were saved; indeed, as Peter and John would later declare to the Jewish religious and secular leaders, there is no name other than the name of the Lord Jesus whereby one can be saved because no other name has been given (Acts 4:12). We who believe in the Lord Jesus have been given His name, and we are called by His name, that is most true. So are you satisfied with being called with His name of Christian?

I do not know whether you have ever had any embarrassing experiences as I have had; but in many places where I have gone, people have come up to me and have asked, "Are you a Christian?" And when I simply say "Yes" and nothing more, they are not satisfied. They want to know what *kind* of Christian I am—that is to say, what denomination I belong to. In other words, the simple designation of Christ is not enough for them; instead, you must designate yourself as being something more in order to be recognized; for when I add, "I do not take upon myself any other name; I am just a simple Christian," they shake their heads in disbelief and say that that cannot be. This may seem to be a very small matter, but it says a lot about the thinking of people—even of Christian people! What is our attitude towards the name of the Lord Jesus? Is His name sufficient for us? Or do we need some additional designations in order to be understood to other people's satisfaction?

This sufficiency in the name of Jesus as simply designating oneself as a Christian is similar to what happens to a woman in marriage. Before a man and a woman are married they each have their own family name or surname, thus indicating that each of them belongs to a certain family having a specific surname. However, when a man and a woman marry, people observe that they are joined into one; but how is that oneness expressed to the world? I would say that something tremendous happens on the day of their marriage—at least according to the custom still observed in many countries today. For when a man and a woman marry, the wife takes upon herself the surname of the husband. She is no longer addressed as Miss so-and-so; rather, she is addressed as Mrs. so-and-so. Her own surname is submerged beneath that of her husband. She voluntarily gives up her family name and places herself under that of her husband. And that makes them one.

Henceforth the husband's name is hers, it is her possession. Whereas others cannot use her husband's name, she can, because she has a right to her husband's name. Everything which belongs to her husband is hers—even his debts! They are now one, and that underscores the importance of a name. Indeed, when this wife goes forth and does such-and-such in the name of her husband, the world recognizes the transaction as though her husband had done it. And even if her husband should explain that he had not told his wife to do such-and-such, and no matter how much he attempts to explain, it is understood that the matter has been done as though the husband himself had been the one who had done the such-and-such. This demonstrates the importance of a name.

Even so, upon our believing in the Lord Jesus, do we realize what happened? Well, among other things which happened, when we called upon the Lord's name, He gave us His name; which meant that from then on He is identified with us and we are identified with Him, and so we were now one. It further means that whatever we do, the Lord himself is involved. In fact, in this regard, I have many times thought that the Lord in heaven has been prompted to say to each one of us, "Well, now, you have really involved Me" in this or that uttered word or in this or that act of yours! I would therefore ask, Is the name of the Lord Jesus sufficient for you? Let us all realize that it is a tremendous privilege that we have the name of the Lord Jesus—that is to say, the name of Christian—it meaning Christ-one. We belong to Him and He belongs to us. Is not this wonderful name therefore sufficient for us?

Interestingly, for one of the seven churches in Asia Minor which the risen, ascended Lord Jesus had praised, that wonderful name of the Lord Jesus was quite sufficient for her members to identify with. As noted in chapter 3 of the book of Revelation, of those seven churches cited there, only the church in Philadelphia was praised, there not having been any reprimand directed towards that assembly. Now there were several reasons for the Lord's commendation of this church. First, it was because of the brotherly love which was there among her members: they really loved one another. And if

Christians love one another, as God's word tells us, the world will know that the Father has sent the Son (John 13:34-35, 17:21-23b). Second, these believers had kept God's word. Despite all the difficult circumstances and adverse environmental conditions confronting their lives, they had kept the word of God's patience. And third, these followers of Christ had not denied His name: no matter what happened in their lives, and though the name of Jesus may have been rejected by the world, and though they were persecuted and despised for holding to His name, they did not deny that name. On the contrary, these believers continued to identify themselves with His name, declared that they belonged to Christ, and bore the name of Christian—Christ-ones—faithfully.

Is there a lesson for us to learn here? Christ has given us His name. And since He has given His name to us, we have a right to His name, that is true; but though we may use His name, it may not be effective. We involve the Lord by using His name, but somehow He does not respond. Now if that should happen, then we shall find ourselves in a narrow, restricted place. To use His name is not something we can do in an automatic or mechanical way. He has given His name to us, but we should not use His name carelessly. Let us not forget that the third commandment of old is for God's people to not utter the name of the Lord in vain (Exodus 20:7a). We will not be considered innocent but guilty if we utter His name in vain (v. 7b). What does that mean? It means that because a person may employ the Lord's name in a careless or empty manner, such action misrepresents the Lord, since His name actually represents himself; and thus, to have His name is to be under His authority; for "where two or three are gathered together unto my name," said Jesus, "there am I in the midst of them" (Matthew 18:20).

If we truly want to use Jesus' name responsibly, there is a condition attached to such use. Peter and John had said, "Silver and gold we do not have, but what we have we give to you. In the name of Jesus Christ the Nazarene rise up and walk." And the lame man rose up and walked. When these two Christian men used the name of Jesus, why did the Lord honor it and positive things happened? It was because they had not employed that name in a mechanical or technical or vain manner; rather, it was that which was the result of two lives that were deeply spiritually related to the Lord himself. For let us take cognizance of the fact that before Peter and John had used the name of the Lord Jesus, these two men had first become fully committed to that name. For we must read carefully their spiritual history with the Lord Jesus from the beginning right up to this very moment: they were now not only *believers* in the Lord, they were fully-committed *followers* of the Lord.

One day, as Jesus was walking by Lake Galilee, He saw Peter casting the net. The Lord said, "Come, follow Me." Peter left everything and followed the Lord. Jesus went a little distance farther and saw John mending the net, and He said, "Come, follow Me." John forsook everything and followed the Lord (Matthew 4:18-22). "Silver and gold have we none," they had declared to the lame man. And that was a true statement. If we have too much, we may not be able to use His name too effectively. In order for these two disciples of Christ to have been able to use the Lord's name most effectively they had given up everything. By this time Peter and John had given up everything *for* that name, and they had likewise given up everything in order to have placed themselves *under* that name and its authority. In other words, they were fully committed to that name, and because of that, the Lord committed himself fully to their using His name.

One reason there is not that power when His name is used today is because we who are the Lord's have too much of other things. We are not fully committed to the Lord. To put it another way: we forsake too little of what we possess of the world; therefore, we possess very little spiritually. It is not a matter of entering into bargain with the Lord; it is instead a matter of observing a spiritual principle. To really be under His name requires that we forsake and deny everything, even ourselves. Otherwise, we cannot say we are actually under His name. Jesus had declared: "If anyone wants to be My disciple, let him deny himself, take up his cross daily, and follow Me" (see Matthew 16:24, Luke 9:23).

One day a young man came into the Lord's presence. Though he was a wealthy ruler, he was quite serious about spiritual matters. So he ran up to Jesus, and in front of the crowd he knelt before Him and said, "Master, Teacher, what should I do to inherit eternal life?" This was unusual for a wealthy young ruler to run up to and kneel before someone in front of a crowd. No wonder that Jesus, upon looking at him, loved him. Nevertheless, the Lord said in reply to the young man's question: "Go, sell everything, give to the poor, then come and follow Me." When that young man heard this response, he went away sad. And so the Lord commented thusly: "It is more difficult for a rich man to enter the kingdom, than for a camel to go through a needle's eye." The disciples were surprised and said, "Then who can be saved?" To which the Lord observed: "With man it is impossible, but with God all things are possible" (see Luke 18:18-27).

You may perhaps think Jesus was a little too hard on that young man, for he did have a real heart for spiritual things. So perhaps you think the Lord should have been a little more tactful and not to have said for him to sell *all* that he had, but to give *some* of what he possessed to the poor and then to come and follow the Lord. That would have been more tactful on Jesus' part. Yet, let us understand that Jesus realized that the young ruler's spiritual problem was not because he was *rich* but because he *trusted* in his riches.

I remember one brother asking: "Is there anyone who can really sell all, forsake everything he has?" That was a good question. We may assume that because that young man had *so much*, it was difficult for him to do what the Lord told him to do. Our thought may be that if a person does not have that much, it should not be that difficult to forsake all which one has. But I would say to you to try it; for is there anyone who can really sell all he or she has, give away all proceeds from that sale, and then go and follow the Lord—no matter how little or how much he or she possesses? I would say in truth that nobody can. The Lord knows that with man such a thing is impossible. So it is quite true that the Lord was asking the impossible from that rich young man. Jesus knows that no man in his own power can do it. Then why should Jesus have instructed this rich young ruler the way He did? The reason is that the Lord wanted him to realize and acknowledge that for him to do so was impossible but that *with God* all things are possible. If only that young man had said, "Lord, You know I cannot do what You have told me to do. I realize I cannot, but if You want this to happen to me, then You will have to do it in me and for me." Had he done so, Jesus would have done it in him. He would not have needed to go away sad. Instead, if he had only trusted the Lord, if he had only committed himself fully to Him, the Lord would have committed himself fully to that young man and great things would have happened.

Now if you do not believe what has just been said, then I would advise you to read the next chapter in Luke's Gospel. For in Luke the events recorded in these two chapters—18 and 19—come together. Let us therefore notice that in chapter 19 there is the account of another rich man. Probably this man was richer than the young man of chapter 18 because this man—Zacchaeus by name—was the *chief* of all tax collectors in his jurisdictional district. He was also an older man. A young man might have more likely inherited his wealth, but a much older man has worked hard and long to have acquired his much wealth. Humanly speaking, therefore, it was going to be more difficult for Zacchaeus to part with his wealth. The Lord said, "I must stay in your house today." And Zacchaeus—being short of stature, and having perched himself in a tree earlier in order to catch a glimpse of Jesus as He passed by—came down from that tree most happily, ready to receive the Lord; and the crowd began to murmur over the fact that He chose to lounge in the house of a great sinner. Interestingly, Jesus did not say or preach anything to Zacchaeus about his accumulated wealth. Nor did the Lord tell him what he should do with his riches as He had done with the rich young man. All which Jesus had said to this wealthy tax collector was this: "I must lodge in your house today." Nothing more!

Here is what subsequently happened. Probably as the Lord was dining with Zacchaeus, this notorious publican stood up at a certain point and declared the following without any prompting from his Guest: "Behold, Lord, I will give half of all that I have to the poor, and if I have extorted anybody, I will repay him fourfold." Now according to Mosaic Law, if anyone wanted to observe only the letter of the Law, all that that person was obligated to do was to add but one fifth as interest and that person would have fulfilled the Law's requirement. But the grace of God and the love of Christ by His very presence had so constrained Zacchaeus that when Christ came into his life, money and goods went out of his life! He said, "I will give half to the poor and what I did to others wrongfully I will repay four times" (Luke 19:1-10). In other words, he became poor by believing in the Lord Jesus. Though Zacchaeus lost everything, he gained Christ. With God all things are possible.

I am not suggesting that we all go back home and sell everything. But according to the spiritual principle involved here, this is what it is. If we want to use the name of the Lord with power there is a condition which must be fulfilled. We must be fully committed to that name; by which is meant that that name must make us poor of everything—not only of our wealth, but also of our opinions, our ideas, our self-will, our very all. We must lose everything. We must be able to say, like Peter, "Silver and gold I do not have. It is all gone. It is not mine; Lord, it is all Yours. I have no right over anything now. I am Yours; I am under Your name." If we are so fully committed in this way to His name, then He is fully committed to us. And, then, when we use the name of the Lord Jesus, there shall be power behind it. His name is power; His name is authority.

When the Jewish leaders—both secular and religious—had Peter and John brought in before them, they began to inquire by what name and by what authority they had been instrumental in healing the man lame from birth. Those leaders recognized that inherent in the name is authority. The wonderful thing is that this name—Jesus of Nazareth—once represented lowliness, even humiliation. That name—Jesus—is a humble, lowly name, but one day God the Father gave Him a name which is above every name, and that at the very sound of that name every knee shall have to bow and every tongue shall have to confess that Jesus is Lord (Philippians 2:9-11). Inherent in that name there is power and authority. And that name has been placed in the church, and it is meant for the church to use that name with the right spirit. It is not merely a nominal name, it is also quite real and living. Jesus stands behind His name, and His power and His authority are likewise behind that name. And please recognize that whenever that name was used by the church back then, things extraordinary happened (see, e.g., Acts 2:38 with v. 43, 3:16) because the brethren in the church in those early days were fully committed to that name, for they had forsaken all (Acts 2:44-45, 4:32-35).

We today also have the name of the Lord Jesus, but why is it that that name does not seem to carry with it the power and authority that it has? One reason is that today we are not fully committed to the Lord. That is the problem. We have not forsaken and given up everything to that name. We have not given up our name and come under His name—that is, under His authority. If we were to do so, we would have the same things happening in our midst as had occurred in the events recorded in the third chapter of Acts.

Having that name—the powerful name of Jesus—is such a privilege. There is such authority and power in that name, but of course, there is great responsibility as I have explained. But there is another facet to this matter which needs to be mentioned. We have to suffer for that name. And why? It is because that name is still being despised and rejected by the world today. Anyone who follows that name, who is serious about that name, must suffer for that name; and when the apostles suffered for that name, their attitude was to thank God that they had been considered worthy to have suffered for that name (Acts 5:41).

Is that our attitude today? The apostle Peter wrote the following: "… this is acceptable, if for conscience toward God a man endureth griefs, suffering wrongfully. For what glory is it, if, when ye sin, and are buffeted for it, ye shall take it patiently? but if, when ye do well, and suffer for it, ye shall take it patiently, this is acceptable with God. For hereunto were ye called: because Christ also suffered for you, leaving you an example that ye should follow his steps … For it is better, if the will of God should so will, that ye suffer for well-doing than for evil-doing" (I Peter 2:19-21a, 3:17 ASV).

From this passage it is clear that anyone who is fully committed to the name of Jesus will have to suffer for that name. Do not think that the day of suffering and persecution is over. Do not think that we who are in this land of America are spared from the suffering which our brethren in other parts of the world have endured and perhaps are still enduring. No. It may not be a matter of physical suffering for us here, but if we really mean business with that name, there will be suffering of some kind. Even so, our attitude should be, like those early apostles, that we are not worthy to suffer shame or dishonor for the name. Seeing that that name is above every other name—we are not worthy. Indeed, if we *are* counted worthy to suffer for that name, it is truly an honor. Moreover, the Bible holds out this hope for us: "If we suffer [with him], we shall also reign [with him]" (II Timothy 2:12a AV). That, then, should be our attitude.

In the book of Acts there are some 26 times when the following phrases referring to the name of Jesus appear: "the name," "his name," "thy name," and perhaps even more than 26 times. It shows what a special place the name of the Lord Jesus had had in the early church. Because of their respect and honor for that name, when those brethren prayed in that name or when they used that name, the Lord honored their use of it. It was all so real; it was all so living.

As we are approaching the end time to all things, the name of the Lord Jesus should be recovered in the church. There should be due honor and respect shown towards that name. And to show proper respect towards that name demands that we truly surrender our all and place ourselves under His name and under His authority. If we do, we shall find His presence and His power and His authority manifested among us in our day just as in the days of the early church, because He is the same yesterday, today, and forever (Hebrews 13:8).

Dear Lord, how we praise and thank Thee that we are a people called by Thy name. How we praise and thank Thee that Thy name is not merely nominal; Thy name is also most real. There is authority and there is power in that name. Oh, that we may honor Thy name, that we may realize what Thy name means, that we may really put ourselves under thy name and be fully committed to it. And Lord, may Thy name be so real among Thy people that there may be power and authority manifested when Thy name is used. Oh Lord, Thou hast put Thy name in the church. May Thy name be hallowed there. Lord Jesus, we ask all this, in Thy exalted name. Amen.

Chapter Five

The Presence and Authority of the Holy Spirit

Acts 4:32-5:11—And the heart and soul of the multitude of those that had believed were one, and not one said that anything of what he possessed was his own, but all things were common to them; and with great power did the apostles give witness of the resurrection of the Lord Jesus, and great grace was upon them all. For neither was there any one in want among them; for as many as were owners of lands or houses, selling them, brought the price of what was sold and laid it at the feet of the apostles; and distribution was made to each according as any one might have need.

And Joseph, who had been surnamed Barnabas by the apostles (which is, being interpreted, Son of consolation), a Levite, Cyprian by birth, being possessed of land, having sold it, brought the money and laid it at the feet of the apostles.

But a certain man, Ananias by name, with Sapphira his wife, sold a possession, and put aside for himself part of the price, his wife also being privy to it; and having brought a certain part, laid it at the feet of the apostles. But Peter said, Ananias, why has Satan filled thy heart that thou shouldest lie to the Holy Spirit, and put aside for thyself a part of the price of the estate? While it remained did it not remain to thee? and sold, was it not in thine own power? Why is it that thou hast purposed this thing in thine heart? Thou hast not lied to men, but to God. And Ananias, hearing these words, fell down and expired. And great fear came upon all who heard it. And the young men, rising up, swathed him up for burial, and having carried him out, buried him.

And it came to pass about three hours afterwards, that his wife, not knowing what had happened, came in. And Peter answered her, Tell me if ye gave the estate for so much? And she said, Yes, for so much. And Peter said to her, Why is it that ye have agreed together to tempt the Spirit of the Lord? Lo, the feet of those that have buried thy husband are at the door, and they shall carry thee out. And she fell down immediately at his feet and expired. And when the young men came in they found her dead; and having carried her out, they buried her by her husband.

And great fear came upon all the church, and upon all who heard these things.

The early church was in full possession of the wonderful name of the Lord Jesus. That name was very real and living and powerful in her midst. Even though these brethren did not have other things, they did have the name of the Lord Jesus. And in that name, great things were done. But in order that this name might be used rightly and backed up by the One who had that name, there needed to be a commitment on their part. As a matter of fact, they *were* a people fully committed to that name. They had no other name—they owned no other name—but that one name. Therefore, when they used that name, the One behind that name honored it. Hence, in this respect, such defines one of the real meanings of the church. In other words, the church is a people who are gathered together to the name of Jesus Christ, who have put themselves under the authority of that name; and in response the Lord Jesus declares, "There am I in the midst of them" (Matthew 18:20b).

Another facet to the life of the early church was the reality of the presence and the authority of the Holy Spirit. Let us recall that on the day of His resurrection Jesus, upon meeting with His disciples, breathed into them and said, "Receive [ye] the Holy Spirit" (John 20:22b). And after Jesus' resurrection the Holy Spirit was given; and ever since then, those who believe in Him receive the Holy Spirit. The Holy Spirit comes into them to dwell. He is the permanent Resident in us; and as such He is the Comforter, the Guardian, the Patron, the One who is fully responsible to bring us into God's full purpose. And He is in us forever—never leaving us nor forsaking us (cf. Hebrews 13:5b).

Now that was what occurred on the day of Jesus' resurrection and what has occurred ever since as its consequence in everyone who believes in Christ. On the day of Pentecost, however, something more happened: the Holy Spirit came down and baptized all those in the upper room into one body. The 120 individual believers were baptized into one body. And even more—the Holy Spirit came down to take up His abode in that body. So that we understand that whereas on the day of Jesus' resurrection the Holy Spirit came and dwelt in each believer, on the day of Pentecost the Holy Spirit came forth and took up His dwelling place in the body. I thus trust we can see the difference here. The Holy Spirit not only dwells in each one of us as the Comforter, Guardian, Patron, etc.; He also, in His capacity as representing the Head, dwells in the midst of us who together form Christ's body, the church.

Let us pause for a few moments and look back into Biblical history as a way of helping us to better understand what occurred on the day of Pentecost in Jerusalem. We learn from Moses' writings that after he had built the tabernacle and set it up, he placed in it all the pieces of furniture according to God's order. Then, when all was finished, the cloud of God's presence filled the tabernacle so that even Moses could not enter inside it (see Exodus 40). God had come in and had taken possession of the tabernacle. His presence was very real.

Similarly, after Solomon had finished constructing and furnishing the first Jerusalem temple, the glory of the Lord came down from heaven and filled the temple; so much so that even the priests could not remain inside. They had to make a hasty retreat because the glory of the Lord had overwhelmingly filled that house (I Kings 8:10-11; II Chronicles 5:11-14). In other words, God came and took possession of what became his dwelling place on the earth.

With that as typological background, we find that the same thing happened centuries later in Jerusalem on the day of Pentecost. A living temple, a living house of God, was formed on that day, and immediately the Holy Spirit came and filled that house and took possession of it. What, though, if the house were there, if the tabernacle—and later the temple—were built and made ready, but there were no cloud and no glory? This very scene occurred, as we read in the book of Ezekiel. God's prophet Ezekiel saw in a vision the glory of the Lord gradually leaving the temple. The glory of the Lord came out of the holiest place and rested on the threshold of the temple, as though lingering. Then the glory left, exiting through the east gate, and stood on the mountain opposite (Ezekiel 10:18-19, 11:22-23). When the glory of the Lord left the house, that house was made empty and was finally destroyed.

I would inquire again, what is the church? Is it not the house or earthly dwelling place of God in the Spirit? In Ephesians 2 we read that the body of Christ, the church, is being built up as a habitation for God in the Spirit (v. 22). That is the real meaning of the church. The Holy Spirit dwells in the church, yet not only in each member of the body individually, but also in the body as a whole. He comes in to take possession of the body, and He is in the body. The authority of the Holy Spirit makes the church. Whether an assembly of believers in Christ is the church of God or not depends mainly on the presence and the authority of the Holy Spirit. If He is not present, if His authority is not respected, if what occurs among the believers becomes a matter of human opinions or a matter of merely human-decision making or simply human activities—

in other words, all is arranged by man, then that assembly of believers has become an organization and is no longer a living organism.

How we need to revisit the early days of the church to discover her real meaning as the church of God! In doing so we shall discover that what makes the church different from all the other groups or associations of people on earth is the presence and authority of the Holy Spirit. And this is demonstrated quite vividly for us in the fifth chapter of the book of Acts. Sometimes in reading this chapter we may look upon what happened as having been a tragedy, and it was indeed a tragedy. And in our being occupied with that tragedy we may perhaps wonder for what purpose this particular incident was recorded. I would assert that there is a most positive lesson to be learned from it because the entire event illustrates one very important point, and that is how crucial the presence and authority of the Holy Spirit is in the church. When He is present and His authority is known, things will happen in one way or another. If nothing of positive consequence is happening, something quite necessary is missing. Let us therefore look into this incident positively, not negatively, and try to learn some lessons from it.

The Bible tells us that in those days the heart and the soul of the believers in the church were one. The grace of God was such that they were all delivered from that natural instinct of self-possessiveness. There is within us all an instinctual element of self-possessiveness. We like to possess things; we have a strong tendency to assert, "This is mine!" That makes us somebody; that gives us a sense of importance and even of security. But the grace of God was such that these believers in the early church were totally delivered from this native inclination at self-possessiveness. In fact, no one among them said, "This is mine." Instead, they shared all things in common. They really lived as members of one body. It was not a communal life as one might find in a commune; rather, it was a community life. They lived as one family. Yes, they lived as members of one body, but there is no evidence that they lived a communal life.

Why so? One brother has explained it this way: God lays emphasis very much on family life; yet in a communal arrangement there is no family life anymore; instead, family life is fractured. Yet the family is a basic unit before God, and hence, in the life of the church, family life is not broken but strongly supports the church life. In no way does church life eliminate family life. That is why I believe that the church life back then was not a communal but a community life. They really lived as one community. They loved one another; they shared everything; and nobody claimed that what he or she possessed was his or her own.

The believers in the early days of the Jerusalem church truly lived in the resurrection life of the Lord Jesus. Some who testify today concerning Jesus' resurrection lack the power behind their speech. These brethren, however, literally lived on resurrection ground, for humanly speaking, the way they lived was impossible apart from resurrection life. They were therefore delivered from self-possessiveness, shared everything, and they loved one another. In short, they lived on resurrection ground. And because the resurrection of the Lord Jesus was so powerfully demonstrated in the life of these people, no wonder that the apostles were mighty in testifying to the resurrection of the Lord Jesus.

Now some of these brethren who had land or houses noticed the need of other members in the body of Christ. Consequently, they sold their land and their houses and laid the money derived from such sales at the feet of the apostles to be distributed to each according to need. As an example of what had happened, one man in particular, Joseph, surnamed Barnabas, who was a Levite and was born on the isle of Cyprus, sold his land, and came and laid the proceeds from the sale at the feet of the apostles. He had been moved by the love of Christ and so he was willing to share what he had with his brothers and sisters. And after he had done that, it would appear as though the apostles had commended him for what he had done. Presumably, many also of the brethren may have commented favorably, perhaps saying something like this: "Look, he is a good brother who really loves the Lord and loves the church."

So another brother, Ananias, having seen what Barnabas had done and having observed the favorable reaction of the people towards Barnabas, probably desired to receive the same praise and glory from man. He was definitely not moved by the Spirit of God but was only attracted by the praise of man: he wanted to have a place of glory in the church by showing off and having people saying what a marvelous brother he was. And in order to accomplish that, Ananias sold something he owned. I noticed that in my Bible version it states that he "sold a possession." From this I have wondered if he had more than one possession, and if so, then he must have sold only a portion of his possessions. And hence, Ananias was not ready to part with all his possessions, but in his desire to have the praise of man, he was at least willing to sell one portion of his property. He having planned the scheme with his wife, she was therefore an accomplice with him in the matter. So Ananias sold the possession, put aside a part of the total proceeds gained, and brought the rest and laid it at the feet of the apostles—saying nothing and thus leaving the impression that that was the total proceeds gained from the sale. He mistakenly thought, of course, that he was simply dealing with man; he did not realize he was dealing with the Holy Spirit. All he assumed was involved in the matter was man.

Now having laid the money at the feet of the apostles, Ananias waited to be praised by the apostles and by all the brethren in the church as being such a marvelous brother. No such thing happened, for Peter, yet not because he possessed some sixth sense but because he was being used as the vessel of the Holy Spirit, said to Ananias: "Why has Satan filled your heart to lie to the Holy Spirit by your having kept back for yourself a part of the price of the estate you sold? While the property was still in your hands, was it not yours? Nobody forced you to sell it. When the property was still yours, it remained rightfully yours. There would have been nothing wrong with your continuing to hold onto it. And even after you sold it, the money was still under your control. You did not need to give any of it away. Why is it, then, that you purposed in your heart to do this? You have not lied to men but to God." And when Ananias heard these words, he fell down and died.

The reality was that Ananias met the Holy Spirit and not just man. So some of the young men in the church came forward, wrapped his dead body up, and carried him out and buried him. Someone has raised the question: "Why did they not notify his wife first?" Humanly speaking, it would seem as though some formality was not followed; for before they buried the husband, surely they should have notified the wife first, but they simply went ahead and buried him. I do not know why.

Some three hours later the wife came in but not knowing what had happened. So Peter asked her, "Is this all the money gained for that sold property of yours?" And the wife Sapphira, not knowing what had happened to her husband, replied, "Yes, that is all of it." So Peter said, "Why did you plan with your husband to deceive the Holy Spirit?" The result was that she, too, collapsed to the ground and died. When the young men who had carried out her dead husband came back inside and saw that the wife was dead, they wrapped up her corpse and took it outside and buried her alongside her husband. Now when the whole church heard all that had occurred, great fear fell upon all.

We need to look at this incident positively and not negatively. When the presence of the Holy Spirit is very real, when His authority is truly being manifested in the church, we realize we are dealing with God and not with man. Today people can do almost anything they like in the church and nothing happens. Is it because the time has changed? No, the real reason is that today the Holy Spirit is not manifesting himself in the church. If He were here, if His presence were living, if His authority were being respected, He would manifest himself in many ways. We are not dealing with man; we are dealing with God. If the Holy Spirit is present in the church, there will be His discipline, and He will make himself known to us in many ways. But today people seem to be able to get by doing whatever they like in the so-called church and nothing in the way of discipline happens. Even though we have the Holy Spirit dwelling in us individually, the presence of the Holy Spirit in the church corporately is missing. It is almost like that scene described in Ezekiel, and referred to earlier, wherein the glory of the Lord gradually left the temple. In that case, like the temple of old, the church becomes an empty house and man has taken over.

I believe there is a very deep lesson for us all to learn here. As we are approaching the end of all things in human history, this is the time that we should inquire as to what is the real meaning of the church. Why should there be a gathering of God's people? It is because such a gathering is the house of God; it is for God to dwell in by His Spirit. It is the place for the Holy Spirit to make His presence known, that His authority may be respected. The more we come together and learn to submit ourselves to the name of the Lord Jesus, the more manifest will be the Holy Spirit. There are many things we could get by doing before, and nothing happened. But when the Holy Spirit is very real and living in the body, anything that touches that body touches the Holy Spirit. So whenever we see the Holy Spirit engaged in discipline in the church, we should bow our heads and worship the Lord. This is not something negative but positive.

Let us realize that if the Holy Spirit had not been present in the early church that day, Ananias and Sapphira would not have died and they would have been looked upon by the other brethren as a marvelous Christian couple who loved the church so much. Moreover, we would have been left with a completely different picture (the kind of picture which, unfortunately, we see today). But we thank God that the Holy Spirit was present and that He manifested himself mightily on that day. That kept the church pure and living; moreover, that gave the true meaning to the church: there came over everyone a holy fear because the brethren were in the presence of God the Holy Spirit.

Is the Holy Spirit real and living with us today? Perhaps as individuals, more or less; if you live before God you know how real He is. You know He draws you. You know if you do or say anything wrong, He by His Spirit checks you and restrains you. On the other hand, if you are stubborn and continue to do wrongly, He disciplines you. You know that the Holy Spirit is very real in your individual life. But what if the Holy Spirit is not real in our individual lives? I believe our whole Christian life will be ruined. If we live our life on this earth doing things according to what we think are right or beneficial or profitable to us and we think that that is all so good, let me frankly observe that that is tragic.

Many believers complain, saying the following: "Why is it that other people can do thus-and-so but I cannot? Those other Christians over there can do many things and nothing in the way of discipline happens to them. They can get by very easily. But if I do those same things, God's hand comes down heavily upon me. Why is it that God by His Spirit is so strict with me? Oh, if only His hand would draw back from me so that I can do what the others do." Dear brethren, permit me to say that you do not know what you are talking about. Other people may but you cannot because you are specially loved by God. The closer you live with the Lord, the stricter the Holy Spirit will be with you. He will manifest himself to you. He will not let you go your way; rather, He will hold you to himself, chasten and discipline you, and in the process transform you (cf. Hebrews 12:5-13).

Now if this is true individually, how much more it ought to be true corporately. The Holy Spirit is not less present in the church than he is in individual believers. The authority of the Holy Spirit should not be less manifested in the church than in individual believers. But do we see this today? We may see the working of the Holy Spirit in individual lives—and thank God for that, but how much do we see the presence and the authority of the Holy Spirit in the church corporately?

This is the time, I believe, that we should go back to the word of God and discover how real this was corporately in the early church. Back then, when God's people came together, they dared not do anything they liked because the Holy Spirit was there. They were not dealing with man or with one another; they were dealing with the Holy Spirit. He was in charge and manifested himself in such a way that if they did anything amiss, they knew what could happen.

All this was very much manifested in the early church, and I do believe that as God's people come together today and put themselves under the name of the Lord Jesus, the presence and the authority of the Holy Spirit will be manifested. That will be a sign that the Lord is there. It will not be a negative but a positive consequence, and thank God for that. Everybody will know that the Holy Spirit is present, and brethren will have a holy fear not to dare to do anything amiss.

Now as we read on in Acts, we learn that the presence and authority of the Holy Spirit was not only known in the church, it was also known in the surrounding world through the church. By the hands of the apostles many signs and wonders were done among the people. And many new believers were added to the Lord, multitudes of both men and women (5:12a, 13-16).

Then the high priest and those with him, that is, those of the sect of the Sadducees, were filled with wrath. They laid hands on the apostles and put them in the public prison. But during the night, an angel of the Lord opened the prison doors and led them out, saying, "Go into the temple area and preach the gospel." So very early in the morning they all went to the temple area and started preaching.

That same morning when the entire religious council gathered, together with "all the elders of the sons of Israel," they sent men to bring the apostles from the prison to them. However, though everything at the prison was secure, there were no apostles there, and all were perplexed. Then someone came into the gathering and told them that those very same prisoners were at that very moment preaching in the temple. So they brought the apostles in before the council, who said to them, "Did we not forbid you to preach in that name?" These Jewish leaders thought they were dealing with people who were unlearned, unlettered, mere fishermen, etc. Peter, however, answered in the following manner: "God must be obeyed rather than men. What we have seen and heard we must preach. We are His witnesses of these things, and the Holy Spirit also bears witness with us" (see Acts 5:17-32).

The result was that the council did not know what to do with the Lord's apostles. They threatened them but they could not do anything. It was the council against the Holy Spirit in the church. What if the Holy Spirit had not been there? Those fishermen in and of themselves were no match for the council members and the elders because they constituted the highest Jewish authority in the land. They could not only crush these apostolic leaders easily, they could also crush the church very easily. Being innocent, unlettered men, certainly they would be frightened and intimidated. But those religious and secular leaders did not know they were dealing with the Holy Spirit in the church. The authority of the Holy Spirit was very real in the lives of these church brethren.

On the one hand, these apostles were submissive to the council: when they were arrested, they did not resist; when they were taken to the prison, they went peacefully. They did not rise up and rebel or revolt but they were very submissive. Even when they talked to the council, their spirit was submissive because the council was their ethnic authority on earth. And yet, they obeyed God because the Holy Spirit was in control of their lives. And when the Holy Spirit is in control of people's lives, none others can resist. If the people in the church are living right before God, the world does not know what to do with the church, not because her people are clever or different, but because the Holy Spirit is there among them.

I do hope that through these incidents God will show us something very real. Is the Holy Spirit real in our midst? Are we so living under His authority that even the people of the world are able to recognize it and that they find they are no match for the Holy Spirit?

As I have remarked earlier, we are now approaching the end and we find that history repeats itself. The world at large is trying to crush the church. In fact, though, if it were not for the Holy Spirit in the church, she would long ago have been eliminated. But no matter what the world does, the testimony of the Lord continues on. On the one hand, there is submission to authority; on the other hand, there is obedience to God in the power of the Holy Spirit.

I do believe that no matter what happens, the church will continue to exist. The testimony of Jesus will be maintained until He returns. So I hope that what has been said here today will be an encouragement to us to look to the Lord so that His Holy Spirit will be very, very real and living in the midst of His people.

Our heavenly Father, our hearts do rejoice because Thy Holy Spirit lives not only in each of us individually but also corporately in the church. This is Thy habitation. Thou art able to manifest thyself in many ways, proving that Thou art living, that Thou art here. Oh, our Father, we do pray that more and more of Thy people will enter into this reality. We pray that as we come together it will not be a formality but that we really put ourselves under

Thy name and that Thy Holy Spirit will be in charge. Oh, that Thou wilt manifest thyself in glory! We ask Thee that we may learn all these lessons and take them to heart. May the presence and authority of the Holy Spirit be known among Thy people everywhere. To Thee we give all the praise and glory. In the name of our Lord Jesus. Amen.

Chapter Six

The Unity and Coordination of the Body

Acts 6:1-7—But in those days, the disciples multiplying in number, there arose a murmuring of the Hellenists against the Hebrews because their widows were overlooked in the daily ministration. And the twelve, having called the multitude of the disciples to them, said, It is not right that we, leaving the word of God, should serve tables. Look out therefore, brethren, from among yourselves seven men, well reported of, full of the Holy Spirit and wisdom, whom we will establish over this business: but we will give ourselves up to prayer and the ministry of the word. And the saying pleased the whole multitude: and they chose Stephen, a man full of faith and the Holy Spirit, and Philip, and Prochorus, and Nicanor, and Timon, and Parmenas, and Nicolas, a proselyte of Antioch, whom they set before the apostles; and, having prayed, they laid their hands on them. And the word of God increased; and the number of the disciples in Jerusalem was very greatly multiplied, and a great crowd of the priests obeyed the faith.

It was mentioned last time how, as recorded in chapter 5 of Acts, the early church at Jerusalem had been confronted with a problem caused by a man and his wife who lied to the Holy Spirit in an attempt to get away with doing something amiss that would be favorable to themselves. However, the Holy Spirit was so real in the church that immediately the discipline of the Lord came upon that couple. It could be said, in fact, that this problem was like the proverbial fly in the ointment, but like the fly which is removed from the ointment before it can spoil the ointment, this problem was quickly removed before it could do damage to the church even in a limited way. Now because it was a personal problem, it was not that serious, for it did not affect the whole church; and so, that problem was dealt with and solved right away because the Holy Spirit was strongly present in the church.

In chapter 6 of Acts, however, we find that the early church was confronted with a truly serious problem—her first real one. In chapter 5 the problem had to do with a selfish couple, and therefore a more personal one in nature, but the problem described here in chapter 6 was the first truly real problem the church had had to face corporately.

I have wondered, Is there an expression of the church on earth that does not have any problems? On the one hand, we should never be satisfied with what we witness of imperfect assemblies of God's people. We should always strive for that in the church which will answer to God's heart. I do not believe that God wants us to sit back and harbor the attitude of, "Well, we are human; there will be problems. So what! We will close our eyes, sit back, and be content and satisfied with what is." Not so. God wants us instead to strive for that which will satisfy His heart. If His heart is not satisfied, let us, too, not be satisfied. That is very true.

On the other hand, let us recognize and acknowledge that in the church there will always be problems. If you are in search of the perfect church on earth, let me tell you that though you were to visit the whole world you would not find it. I know some people who are perfectionists, and they are constantly in search of a perfect church: they go to one place for a little while and discover some spots and wrinkles; so they travel to the next place, where at first it seems that this place is better, but within a few months they discover something amiss; and hence, they must move on elsewhere in their search for the perfect assembly of God's people. To state this matter succinctly: there is no perfect church on earth.

Though there will necessarily be problems, the early church thrived on them. Indeed, whenever faced with a problem, the church seemed to grow because of the problem. Instead of being defeated, instead of going under, problems served as opportunities for the Lord to elevate the church to a higher level. And this was what happened to the early church.

Today, let us not think that we can find a perfect church with no problems whatsoever. If the Lord has truly brought believers together, the closer they are and the more they are living as members of one body, the more problems they will find. If believers in a church visit but once a week for an hour or two and listen to a sermon, shake a few hands, and go home, there will be no problem. But let me say that that cannot be called true church life. If the Lord really puts you together as members of one body, you will see one another often, you will try to worship God together, you will try to serve God together, you will try to minister one to another; and in the process of doing all that, you will find plenty of problems. But the church which is according to God thrives on problems. If there are no problems there will be no growth. If there are no problems there will be no opportunity for the Lord to bring His people to a higher realm and to bring in His forethought. So let us not look for a perfect church without problems, but let us thank God that when there are problems, they are opportunities for God to accomplish His purposes. And such was the case with the early church.

The first real problem which arose in the early church was a problem created by both the Hellenists and the Hebrews. The church in Jerusalem was composed almost entirely of Jews; there were no Gentiles. Yes, there were some proselytes, but the church in Jerusalem was composed of people whose backgrounds were all Jewish. And hence, they had no racial problem, but they did have a cultural problem because these

Jews were of two kinds. Some were born and reared in the land of Judea and were Hebrew Jews who were exposed to the strict teaching and practice of Judaism. But there were other Jews who were born and reared in Gentile cities and whose parents had been dispersed throughout the world at that time; and thus they had been exposed to Greek culture. Though they were indeed Jews, they greatly imbibed the Greek culture. Their outlook and their views were affected by Greek civilization. And as a consequence, they were not as strict in keeping the Law as were the Hebrew Jews. They were more liberal because they had had more contact with the world, and probably they were more highly educated. So these were Hellenistic or Greek Jews.

Those, then, who were in the early church at Jerusalem were all Jews, but some were Greek Jews and some were Hebrew Jews. God had sovereignly put them together and had formed them into one body in Christ. Naturally, the twelve apostles, being Hebrew Jews, were more aware of the condition among the believers with Hebrew Jewish background. Therefore, in the matter of taking care of the widows among them it seemed as though the widows among the Christians with Hebrew Jewish background were well taken care of whereas the widows who belonged to the believers with Hellenistic background had been overlooked, yet not intentionally. Certainly the apostles would not intentionally have overlooked the Hellenistic widows and only taken care of the Hebrew Jewish ones. They would not have done that. It was not a matter of intention but simply one rooted in the circumstances of the situation.

I do not know why there were so many widows in those early church days. It would seem as though there were many widows in the Jerusalem church. Probably life was very hard in those days, and of necessity the church needed to take care of the widows. In Old Testament times God had commanded His people not to neglect the poor and the widows. Even when a man was reaping or harvesting his crops, if any produce had been accidentally left behind, he was not to return to the fields and collect what had been left behind. Instead, he was to leave it lying there for the widows, for the poor, the orphans, and the strangers to collect (Deuteronomy 24:19). We see in this that God was compassionate towards the widows and the other less fortunate ones: He is the Father of the fatherless and the Judge of the widows (Psalm 68:5). Moreover, in the New Testament, for example in I Timothy, we learn that if a widow was over 60 years old, she would be placed on a widows list of the church; which is to say, that the church would take care of these widows (v.9). Thank God for that. In the days of the early church the saints were truly one big family; but somehow in the Jerusalem church, and due to human limitations which were not intentional but circumstantial in nature, the widows among the Greek Jews were being neglected in the matter of food distribution; and as a result there arose some murmuring concerning it.

Thus there developed the first real problem in the church. Actually it was a problem which stemmed from a cultural difference. Even as there is today, back then there were many natural differences among people (see Colossians 3:11), such as racial differences—in this case, Greeks and Jews; cultural differences—those who were identified with Greek culture and those who were identified with Hebrew culture; social differences—some were masters and therefore freemen, and some were bondmen and therefore servants and slaves; educational differences—some were barbarians and some were the more sophisticated Scythians. Naturally speaking, in the world there are many, many distinctions. These constitute natural lines of demarcation between peoples. It is natural for the world to be divided through these demarcative lines because they are natural lines. It is thus very easy for people to be divided. But in the redemptive work of God through Christ, He does something tremendous. He brings into the body some from the Jews and some from the Gentiles and makes them one in Christ. He does the same thing with freemen and bondmen and makes them one in Christ, and the same with the Scythians and the barbarians. In Christ all these natural distinctions are eliminated: they disappear.

Therefore, the Bible declares that in Christ "there is neither Jew nor Greek or Gentile" (see Colossians 3:11a). So that, in the case of the early church, before you came into the church of the saved ones you may have been a Jew, but something happened: you were no longer a Jew, there being no Jew in the church. By the same token, before you came into the church you may have been a Gentile, but something happened: your Gentile identity was left outside and you became something else—a Christian, there being no Gentile in the church. Before you came into the church you may have been a freeman and had a high social position, but something happened: you were no longer a freeman, there being no freeman in the church but we all are slaves to Christ. Or you may have been a slave and had a very low social status, but when you came into the church, you were no longer a slave but you were set free in Christ (Galatians 3:28).

Even in our day, when we come to Christ and enter the church, God has done something in us. All these natural distinctions are eliminated. The old creation is finished and is left outside. We are now a new creation (II Corinthians 5:17a), we having become part of the body of Christ, with Christ being in us.

I always remember an incident having to do with brother Watchman Nee. He had a servant whom I knew, a dear brother in the Lord. Oh, he loved brother Nee very much, and he cooked for him. He loved brother Nee to such an extent that he used his own salary to buy food for brother Nee. If brother Nee said at any time, "I like this dish," he would then serve it every day. That brother loved brother Nee and served him so faithfully. Now because they were both brothers in the Lord, they would remember the Lord Jesus at His table; and this brother would always look to see where brother Nee sat. He felt he dare not sit near brother Nee but would always sit somewhere behind him. One day, however, brother Nee took hold of this servant-brother and had him sit immediately next to him. Why did brother Nee do this? It was because he recognized that in the church there is no freeman or bondman but all are brothers. In the early church, especially in the church at Rome, most of the brethren therein were slaves, but some were freemen. Yet, when they came together there were no sects of bondmen and freemen, but all were simply brethren in Christ together.

In the church all which is natural is left outside. We are all now in Christ and Christ is in us also. That makes us of one body, of one church. Nevertheless, our flesh is so subtle. Moreover, the enemy is also quite subtle, and he tries to bring into the church the old creation. And once we allow that which belongs to the old creation to gain entrance into the church, that will split the church if it is not dealt with. And if this problem surrounding the widows in the early church had been allowed to continue to fester, the whole church in Jerusalem would have been split along cultural lines: the Hebrew Jews would have begun to meet as one circle of brethren and the Hellenistic Jews would have created another distinct circle. The church would have been broken in two along the line of culture. In fact, it would have been a great temptation for brethren back then to have done so, for it is very easy for people to gravitate closely towards people who have the same cultural background or the same social position. Indeed, it is too easy for such to occur.

One day a brother who was a high official in the Chinese government talked to brother Nee. I knew him very well. He said to brother Nee: "I am thinking that there ought to be organized a church where all these high officials can come together and worship God, since these high officials will not attend any church. You need to organize a church for them." In response our brother said, "All right, if you want to have a church organized for high officials, then I think the rickshaw coolies who pull the rickshaws should also have a church of their own—a rickshaw church. Then they, like those high government officials, would likewise feel very happy because they are all rickshaw drivers. No! The church is above all these natural distinctions which belong to the old creation. Let us see that we are all one in Christ."

Oh how subtle is the enemy! Back in the time of the Jerusalem church the enemy had used that natural, cultural distinction between Jew and Gentile to try to bring a wedge into the life of the church. Again I say, so far as the apostles were concerned it was not an intentional oversight on their part; in fact, it could not be; it was circumstantial in nature. Even so, the murmuring about the overlooked widows began to rise and spread.

God does not like murmuring. From reading the Old Testament and the New we shall discover that God never likes murmuring, and sometimes when people began to murmur God would deal with them very severely. Why was this so? Murmuring is the beginning of strife and division. If the murmuring is not stopped, it will soon develop into something very serious. Being brothers and sisters in the Jerusalem church, why could they have not simply talked about the matter of the widows openly? The Bible says for Christians to speak the truth in love (Ephesians 4:15a). If the widows of the Hellenists were neglected, why did the Hellenists who knew the situation not go to the apostles and tell them? I believe the apostles would have appreciated it very much, for they were human like everyone else, and they too had their limitations. They did not see the problem even though they were very spiritual. Yes, the apostles were highly spiritual, but they were not perfect. But instead of going to the apostles and presenting the problem to them, the Hellenists murmured behind the apostles' backs and it began to spread. And if this had not in time come to the ears of the apostles, one day, suddenly the break would have come. It was dangerous, but fortunately the murmurs and complaints began to be heard by the apostles.

When the apostles finally heard the murmurs, what did they do? Here we find a problem which has arisen. Let us realize, however, that a problem is not a problem in and of itself. It depends on how it is handled. If the matter is handled rightly, it is not a problem but an opportunity. If the matter is handled wrongly, then it becomes a real problem. So let us notice that when the murmuring came to the ears of the apostles, what did they do? Instead of feeling hurt and offended, they brought the issue up openly before the whole body. It is much better if a matter that concerns the whole church is brought before the entire body of believers for fellowship rather than hide it and murmur behind the back of those in leadership. The apostles were humble and not proud as to think there was no difficulty which had arisen. On the contrary, they acknowledged it and were willing to lay everything about the matter before all the brothers and sisters, they observing that "it is not good for us to continue to serve the tables."

Actually, this so-called problem gave the apostles opportunity to reconsider their service to the Lord. Probably they were wondering during those days why they were so busy. They were so busy serving the tables that they did not even have time to pray or to minister God's word. Probably the apostles were perplexed. On the one hand, the tables had to be served and the widows had to be taken care of. They could not have the attitude, "Well, *these* tasks we must not and will not do, otherwise there will be *no* time for us to pray and minister God's word." No, they realized that they had to do those things; and yet, probably these apostles were wondering, "Why is it that doing those tasks have adversely affected our ministry of God's word and our prayer life?" They realized that there was something wrong but they could not explain why and how. Only after this matter concerning the widows had surfaced was their attention directed towards reconsidering their service to the Lord: they began to see the need for making a change.

What was the nature of this change which these apostles came to see was necessary? It was simply this: "We cannot do all the service required in the church." They began to see that in the church, which is the body of Christ, there is the need for each member to function—that there are diversities of ministry and service. They came to realize that as apostles they were not to monopolize all the spiritual service of the church. That, of course, was probably what they had been doing from the very beginning, for they did not know anything better. They thought that being called by God to be apostles and leaders, certainly they should take care of everything; not because they were ambitious to be at the head but because they were conscientious. They were innocent, so they tried to do everything for the church. They not only prayed, they not only ministered God's word, but they also served the tables in distributing the food. They in their humility tried to do everything; they were doing their best; and hence, we cannot blame them. In the end, however, they discovered that such an arrangement did not work. Though they were doing their very best to meet the needs of everyone, they learned that they had overlooked some of the brethren, and thus a problem had been created.

Nevertheless, as a consequence of this problem, these apostolic leaders now realized that they could not be responsible for everything in the church. Rather, they began to realize that every member of the body has his or her special ministry function. God calls the apostles to pray and to preach and to minister his word; He has not called them to serve tables. Indeed, it became clear that when they served the tables they did not serve the saints as a whole very well. We might think that if apostles serve tables, that would most certainly be their best service. Not so. When they ministered God's word, yes, that was true; but in serving the tables, they did not do very well, since though they successfully served many of the brethren in the church, they missed quite a few others. Thus, through this unintentional failure, these apostles discovered their limitations and began to realize that it takes other members of the body to complete all the service in the church.

It could be said, therefore, that this problem was an opportunity. If there had surfaced no such problem in the early church the apostles would have continued to serve the tables, with the result that they would have been so involved in social work that they would have had no time for preaching and for praying. But thank God for that problem, because it woke them up. They began to realize that this arrangement was not good and that this was definitely not God's way. God's way with His church is that different members have different ministries and that there is coordination among these serving members.

These apostles therefore suggested to the church that seven men be chosen—men with good reports, and who were full of the Holy Spirit and wisdom—and let them serve the tables. When the church members heard this proposal they were pleased and responded positively. That is the way to resolve matters like this. Anything that affects the whole body is not to be decided by a few leaders; instead, those in leadership should try to find out the feeling of the body. They should put ideas or proposals before the entire body and see how the brethren respond, since the solution to such problems will affect the whole church.

I would put before us this question: Is serving the table a lower ministry than serving the word of God? According to our human understanding, we would think that giving oneself to prayer and ministry of God's word is most certainly spiritual service, whereas serving tables is manual work and is therefore a secular work having nothing to do with spiritual work. But the Scriptures do not say so. Service to the Lord is defined or determined by what you are called to do. If you are called to minister God's word, then as you minister the word, you are serving the Lord and it is therefore spiritual service. Similarly, if you are called to do the work of serving tables, then as you minister in this way, you are likewise serving God and it is likewise considered to be spiritual service. There is no difference in the eyes of God. It is not because you serve with the word of God that you have to be full of the Holy Spirit, but that if you are serving the tables, you do not need to be full of the Holy Spirit. Not so.

We may think, What is the need of being filled with the Holy Spirit in serving tables, for anybody can do that. In response I would observe that it is quite true that in a restaurant a person can serve tables without being filled with the Holy Spirit; but in the church, if you are serving tables for the brethren, you must be full of the Holy Spirit. And why? Because serving tables in the church is a holy work; it is serving God and God's church; and hence, you need to be full of the Holy Spirit in order to do it spiritually.

Regarding our service or ministry in the church, the issue is not a matter of merely accomplishing the service. Some brethren may have the attitude, "I will do such-and-such a task, for all that matters is that it be done." That is not a right approach to performing spiritual service. No, in the church the issue is not a matter of *doing* a given ministry but that of *how* one performs it: Is it carried out with the Spirit of Christ in the person or is it accomplished merely because the service is to be done? If, for example, a brother preaches a sermon simply because it is something which must be done, such an attitude and approach is not commendable whereas if a brother serves tables with the Spirit of Christ, that is commendable.

Hence, when all is considered in this light, there can be no sense of a service done in the church as being superior or inferior: whether service to the Lord is so-called secular or spiritual in nature, all such service is the same: some brethren in the church are called to serve in one form and others are called to serve in another: yet all are spiritual ministries if they are carried out in a right spirit—even the Spirit of Christ.

After the apostles acknowledged their limitation and were willing to open up the services of the church to the other members of the body, the result was that those seven men who were chosen—who were full of the Holy Spirit, wisdom and faith—served the tables so well that there was no more murmuring. Furthermore, they did better in serving the tables than the apostles had done. And because these seven men did so well, the apostles were free to preach the gospel, and the word of God multiplied greatly. Through the cooperation and the coordination of the different members of the body, each fulfilling their ministry commendably, the result was that the body grew in love (Ephesians 4:16 ASV). That problem, which had been transformed into an opportunity, became a blessing because it was handled in the right way and in the right spirit.

It was explained at the beginning of this series of messages that in the New Testament the demonstration of what is the church, the body of Christ, is to be found especially in the book of Acts, whereas the teaching concerning the body is particularly laid out in the Epistles. And here in Acts chapter 6 we find a demonstration of the church as the body of Christ but no teaching. However, we learn from the epistolary teaching that the body is composed of many members, with each member having a function to fulfill (I Corinthians 12:7). We are further told in the Epistles that the Holy Spirit gives gifts to the members according to the purpose with which each one of them is called to minister (I Corinthians 12:4-11). It is not to be the case that a few prominent members are to monopolize the carrying out of all the responsibilities in and for the church. Were they to do that—as we have seen here in the account of Acts 6—the church will not grow, and those few leading members will not be able to perform those services well since they take upon themselves too many responsibilities; and the result is that nothing will be done right.

According to the Scriptures God in His wisdom has put every believer in Christ in the body (I Corinthians 12:12). We believers are all priests to God (Revelation 1:6a), and as a consequence there is a place, a service, a ministry for each one of us in the body. Moreover, it is God's will that all these members should learn to function coordinately, according to the grace and the gift God has given to each, they all not performing the same service. Everyone is to perform a ministry, and yet they do so together as members of one body. This which has just been said is what is to be found in Ephesians chapter 4. Yet, before the teaching of Ephesians 4 came into being, its practical demonstration was narrated by Luke in Acts 6. And as we have learned from Acts 6, those who are gifted more have the temptation to monopolize all the services or ministries in the church; whereas those who are little gifted or less gifted tend, so to speak, to bury their talent in the earth (cf. Matthew 25:15, 18); but according to the wisdom of God everyone in the church has a place for ministry. We need to be living members, functioning together coordinately as directed by Christ the Head through the Holy Spirit. And as was demonstrated in the account of Acts chapter 6, the result was that the preaching of the word of God increased greatly and many new disciples were added to the Lord during those days—including even "a great crowd of priests"!

We have seen from Acts 6 that the apostles brought this problem surrounding the overlooked widows to the whole church, and so they suggested that seven Spirit-filled men be chosen. In serving the Lord in whatever capacity it may be, even in serving the many tables involved, a person needs to be full of the Holy Spirit because that person will not be fulfilling such service according to his thought, by his strength, or in dependence upon his past experience. If a person fulfilling this ministry happens to be a waiter or waitress in a restaurant, he or she might think that he or she can quite easily serve tables in the church. Not at all! If a person who would assume the ministry of eldership in the church happens to be an executive in a large company, he might think he can easily be an elder in the church. Not at all! Such body members have to be full of the Holy Spirit and under the control of the Holy Spirit if they are to serve rightly. Any ministry or service carried out in the church has to be under the control of the Spirit of God, and any such ministry must be carried out by brothers and sisters who are under the control of the Holy Spirit. And if such be the case in the church, all service will be coordinated.

This problem of overlooked widows among the church's Hellenists having been brought before all the brethren, these brethren chose seven men who were well reported of. Now in reading the names of these seven men carefully, we are struck by the fact that they were all Hellenistic Jews; and lest we forget, they were in the *minority* in the church. None of them were Hebrew Jews, who were in the majority. But when the church's brethren as a whole chose these seven men, all of them turned out to be Hellenistic Jews. Is that not something wonderful?!

Let us recognize the fact that had the old creation been in control that day, most certainly the Hebrew Jews would have asserted: "We would like to choose seven men. Since we are the majority, we will choose Hebrew Jews, because we want to be sure *our* widows will still be taken care of." But no, these brethren with Hebrew Jewish background realized what the problem was. They loved their Hellenistic brethren so much that in order to comfort them, these brethren in the majority chose all of the seven from the opposite camp (if I may use that turn of phrase). Actually, they were not in the opposite camp from the Hellenistic Jews, for these Hebrew Jews realized that all of them—both Hebrew and Hellenist brethren—were all together in one camp, even the body of Christ. Since it had been the Hellenistic widows who were neglected, the majoritarian Hebrew element chose all seven from among the Hellenists in the church. They would know their widows' situation far better, and thus their widows would be well taken care of. These Hebrew Jewish brethren never thought of themselves: they were never afraid that "the tables would be turned upon them" and that their own widows would be neglected. No, they were not thinking of that at all.

We can readily discern here that love overcame all the natural fear within man. By the majority having chosen all seven men from the minority Hellenistic Jewish element in the church, they kept the unity of the Spirit (Ephesians 4:3). The church at that time had been faced with a truly serious problem. Had that problem been handled wrongly it would have split the church in two. It was that serious a problem. To keep the unity and the oneness of the body, however, those Hebrew Jewish brethren had such love that they forgot themselves and thought only of what would happen to those who had already been offended. In short, they went the second mile (cf. Matthew 5:41), and as a result the unity of the church was preserved. That is truly wonderful.

Let us not be afraid of problems. And when they do arise, that is the time when we should go before the Lord and seek His face. Probably the Lord has something to teach us, that out of the problems we may be raised to a higher spiritual level, and be brought nearer to the original purpose of God concerning His church. If we have that kind of spirit within us and are actually open to one another, if we truly love one another and strive to keep the unity of the Spirit in the bond of peace, and if we are really willing to forget ourselves and to think especially of our brothers and sisters, then by the grace of God the church will indeed be lifted to a higher level. And that is precisely what happened in the early church at Jerusalem.

As the Lord brings more of His people together, let us be prepared to encounter problems. We are still human; we are limited. But our limitations are God's opportunities as the means whereby we may know how we need one another. Otherwise, we may think we ourselves can bring it about. By means of God's problem-opportunities which are approached by us in the right spirit, we can learn to need one another and really learn to work together with humility, meekness, forbearance and love. If we truly do that, then the church, the body of Christ, will grow and be built up in love (Ephesians 4:16c ASV).

Our Lord, how we praise and thank Thee because Thou art working towards the completion of Thy body. We do praise and thank Thee that sometimes Thou dost allow problems to come among Thy people, that we may be given the opportunity to learn something more of Thee. Oh Lord, we do ask Thee that Thou wilt lead us on, that Thou wilt open our eyes so that we may see how we need to keep the unity of the Spirit in the bond of peace, how we need to bear and forbear with one another, how we need our brothers and sisters. We cannot do everything ourselves, but Lord, teach us how to be functioning members of the body according to that with which we each are called to serve Thee, and may we do so with humility and with faithfulness. Oh Lord, we do pray that Thy church may be built up in love. We do pray that it may soon be matured to the fullness of Thy stature so that You may return to claim Thy church as Thy bride. So we pray that these lessons may be deeply impressed upon us, and we pray that they will be worked in and worked out among us. We do worship Thee together. In Thy name we pray. Amen.

Chapter Seven

Stephen

Acts 6:8-15—And Stephen, full of grace and power, wrought wonders and great signs among the people. And there arose up certain of those of the synagogue called of freedmen, and of Cyrenians, and of Alexandrians, and of those of Cilicia and Asia, disputing with Stephen. And they were not able to resist the wisdom and the Spirit with which he spoke. Then they suborned men, saying, We have heard him speaking blasphemous words against Moses and God. And they roused the people, and the elders, and the scribes. And coming upon him they seized him and brought him to the council. And they set false witnesses, saying, This man does not cease speaking words against the holy place and the law; for we have heard him saying, This Jesus the Nazaraean shall destroy this place, and change the customs which Moses taught us. And all who sat in the council, looking fixedly on him, saw his face as the face of an angel.

Acts 7:54-60—And hearing these things they were cut to the heart, and gnashed their teeth against him. But being full of the Holy Spirit, having fixed his eyes on heaven, he saw the glory of God, and Jesus standing at the right hand of God, and said, Lo, I behold the heavens opened, and the Son of man standing at the right hand of God. And they cried out with a loud voice, and held their ears, and rushed upon him with one accord; and having cast him out of the city, they stoned him. And the witnesses laid aside their clothes at the feet of a young man called Saul. And they stoned Stephen, praying, and saying, Lord Jesus, receive my spirit. And kneeling down, he cried with a loud voice, Lord, lay not this sin to their charge. And having said this, he fell asleep.

According to the New Testament Gospel accounts of Jesus' earthly life Christ was born as a babe in Bethlehem. Because there was life in that babe, He grew up and waxed strong both physically and mentally (Luke 2:40, 52). He continued to grow until He reached the age of about 30—a mature age (Luke 3:23a). Then He began His ministry which lasted for some three years. If we use this analogy of birth and growth in Jesus and apply this principle of life to the corporate body of Christ that we find delineated in the book of Acts, we shall witness the fact that this same principle of life was effectively working in that body of Christ. When we think of a human body, we think of life; however, if there is no life present, then there is no body anymore: it is no longer a real body after its birth but a corpse. So when we think of a body, we think of life, and life is that which grows after its birth. Therefore, on the day of Pentecost the body of Christ began its existence: that is to say, the church of God was born on earth, and then she grew and grew and grew. So that by the time we reach the end of the book of Acts, the church, the body of Christ, has grown a great deal.

Now in applying this principle of life's growth to the book of Acts, we may divide its 28 chapters into three stages of growth.* By dividing this book in stages according to the growth of life of the body of Christ, we can see perhaps more clearly how God used this vessel in which and through which

* If, of course, we wish to divide Acts according to the spreading of the gospel in fulfillment of the commission the Lord has given to the church, then from chapters 1-7 it is a record of witnessing in Jerusalem. Next, chapters 8-12 are the record of the gospel's spread throughout all Judea and Samaria. And from chapters 13-28 until now it is a record of the spreading of the gospel to the ends of the earth.—*The Author*

the risen Lord could continue to speak and do. And hence, from chapters 1-5 it is an account of the babyhood stage in the growth of Christ's spiritual body. From chapters 6-15 it is the stage of adolescence. And from chapters 16-28 it is an account of the adulthood stage—or the reaching of maturity of the church as the body of Christ.

When we read the first five chapters of the book of Acts, what impression do they leave us with? I am speaking here of impressions which, though intangible, can nonetheless be very real. In those chapters this is what we learn: On the day of Pentecost 120 believers in the Lord Jesus were baptized in one Spirit into one body. Immediately thereafter, 3,000 more were added on that same day, and all those who believed in the Lord persevered in the teaching and in the fellowship of the apostles, in the breaking of bread and in prayer. And God was with them. Miracles were done and many more continued to be added. In spite of the rapid growth of the body, the whole condition was very healthy because all those who were together were of one mind and one soul. They loved one another, they having been completely delivered from self-possessiveness; for nobody among them claimed: "This object belongs to me"; on the contrary, they shared everything with everybody according to each person's need.

Though there were problems, there were not that many. Chapter 5 describes the little problem involving the deceitful couple, Ananias and Sapphira; but immediately God took care of the situation. So in the book's first five chapters what we see is natural, spontaneous growth. These saints were under the constant care of the heavenly Father. Also, the presence of the Holy Spirit was very real in their midst, and the blessing of the Lord was certainly upon them. They simply lived out their days most happily and joyfully, enjoying the Lord and enjoying one another, and there were almost no problems which arose. This was how it was in this initial stage.

In our natural lives, when we are babes we are taken care of by our parents. Those infant days of ours are days which are carefree and happy, with everything being provided for us. For us as babes and infants there is usually no problem of any consequence; and if there *is* any problem which arises, our parents will take care of it. So we may say that during the stage of babyhood and infancy we just enjoy and rejoice in the goodness of our parents.

Now the first five chapters of the book of Acts are like that in describing this initial stage of growth in the body of Christ. When this vessel of God, the church, was first born, it went through a period immediately afterwards of such blessedness and of such care by the heavenly Father.

When, however, a human being begins to outgrow babyhood and infancy and enters the adolescent period, it is a most difficult time. Conflicts begin to come in. There are struggles and problems. To say the least, this is an unsettled period, with everything seeming to be in turmoil and nothing seemingly settled. It can be the most unstable period in the lives of human beings. In fact, we call it the growing pain of life. As a person continues to grow there is some pain, and sometimes a person may not know to what it is due. He or she just feels there is something unpleasant there, yet it cannot be explained. Indeed, a person can become highly dissatisfied with everything, prompting the adolescent to try new thoughts, ideas and ways all the time, it sometimes resulting in all kinds of failures and defeats, yet the adolescent is full of wonder and amazement. But then again, it is a time of puzzlement and perplexity. Nevertheless, through all these various challenging circumstances, a young person's life grows. Such is a description of human adolescence.

Now in reading chapters 6-15 of Acts, I am left with the impression that the body of Christ—the church—is going through what we would term an adolescent period. There are numerous problems which have made their appearance. We find that quite a few adjustments had to be made, many new discoveries for accomplishing things had to be revealed, and because of that there were a number of conflicts which arose in the early church. Certain traditions and assumptions had to be questioned and perhaps shattered so that brethren could freely enter into entirely new realms of spiritual life together; and consequently, there were painful moments all along the way. But thank God, when believers can go through such a period together and come forth successfully, God's people realize they have grown a great deal in the spiritual life as members together of the body of Christ. That, then, is the substance of my impression of chapters 6-15.

Finally, chapters 16-28 reveal that the church was growing and spreading. And the church was not only present in Jerusalem and Judea and Samaria but she had been established in much of Asia Minor and even in European communities, and had eventually spread to the ends of the known world of that day. God's purpose was being carried out further through the body of Christ and farther in terms of the geographical expansion of the gospel.

Now the reason I have shared with you the foregoing impressions of mine is because there is that which I sense God wants us to learn with regard to the development and growth of the body of Christ. The church, which is Christ's spiritual corporate body, is an organism and not an organization. And because it is a *living* organism, therefore, there will be growth as such livingness goes on, and this positive circumstance of spiritual life we find laid out for us in great detail in chapters 6 and 7 of Acts.

As noted earlier, the church was first formed on the day of Pentecost, and after the martyrdom of Stephen the Roman Empire, as well as the Jewish society in general, looked upon this Way or this Life pursued by the followers of Jesus as just another sect of Judaism. At that time the term Christianity did not exist. We readily use that term today but the word

Christianity did not exist at that time, not even the term Christian. Today we who believe in Christ call ourselves Christians and everybody recognizes what we mean. But back then even the word Christian was not used yet because disciples of Jesus were first called Christians much later in Syrian Antioch. Hence, the people of the world who at the beginning observed those who followed the Lord Jesus did not know how to identify them.

Let us be reminded that there were well over ten thousand people in Jerusalem at that early time who believed in the Lord Jesus, who followed the Lord, who quite often spoke of the Lord, who also preached the Lord Jesus, and who, it must not be overlooked, lived a different way of life altogether. People observed them and commented among themselves, "Who are they?" Sometimes they were called followers of the man Jesus, and that is true. On other occasions they called them the people of the Way, because their way of life was so radically different from the other people in the world, but they did not know how to address them.

As a matter of fact, at that time people of the world looked upon these folk, these members of the body of Christ, as just another sect in Judaism. It must be noted as well that the Roman Empire did not persecute this group of people at that time because it had a policy of appeasing the various religions of the different peoples whom it subdued. So all the worldly people of that day considered these followers of "the Jesus religion" as part of Judaism since Jesus himself had been a Jew. Therefore, just as the Empire would protect the Jews, so they would likewise protect this group of people. Moreover, it must be noted that the unbelieving Jewish people themselves were confused because they discovered that these followers of Jesus were Jews; but because they were so different from the other Jews, the Jewish community in general did not know what to do with them.

In Judaism at that time there were different sects—for instance, the Pharisees and the Sadducees; and more recently we have discovered that there was another and highly righteous sect called the Essenes. But at that time people in Palestine considered the followers of Jesus as but another sect in Judaism. Consequently, for the time being the followers of Jesus were not persecuted, even though they were ideologically opposed by the unbelieving Jews. The Jewish community at large simply wanted to bring this "Jesus group" into conformity to Judaism. At first they were not thinking at all of wiping this group out as though it were an altogether different religious sect from themselves. That, then, was the situation in the beginning.

But Christianity (if I may use this term just for convenience' sake) is definitely not a sect of Judaism. Christianity is that which is totally different. What God has brought upon this earth is something entirely different from anything that has ever been on the earth. To consider Christianity as part of Judaism, as though it were *Judeo-*Christianity, is foreign to God's thought. Christ has come to this earth to bring forth a new life, and with this new life He is bringing into being that which is completely new and different from whatever has existed before. And if I may say so, it can be likened to new wine.

This new wine has come and for anyone to attempt to put this new wine into old wineskins will not only damage and even break the old wineskins but also the new wine will leak out and be lost. No one should ever put new wine into old wineskins because the new wine is full of expansive power; the fermenting action is still continuing to occur. And because of this, the old wineskin, having lost its elasticity and thus unable to expand anymore, cannot contain and hold the new wine if poured into it but will burst apart and be completely destroyed; moreover, the new wine would leak out and be lost. In view of this, Jesus observed that "you do not put new wine in any old wineskin" (see Matthew 9:17). New wine must be put in a new wineskin because of the latter's elastic quality: it can expand as the new wine's fermenting action continues, and thus the new wineskin can contain and hold the new wine. The Lord Jesus came to this earth to bring a new wine.

Now in one respect the people of Jerusalem were correct when they said of the 120, "They are filled with new wine." Those 120 disciples of Jesus, when baptized by God's Holy Spirit to form the body of Christ—even the church—on Pentecost day, became the new wineskin for the containing and holding the new wine—the resurrection- and ascension-life of the Lord Jesus—which was manifested in the upper room with the outpouring of the Holy Spirit. So when given this understanding of what *really* happened on the day of Pentecost, we should ask ourselves, How could God have ever put the new wine of the Spirit of Christ in the old wineskin of outworn, old, fixed, and therefore non-elastic Judaism? Indeed, how could Christianity ever be considered or made as just another sect of Judaism? Impossible!—on both counts!!

But historically speaking, before the martyrdom of Stephen everybody considered Christianity as merely an offshoot of Judaism, and probably even the early disciples were of this opinion. And why? Because those very earliest disciples who had traveled about with Jesus were all mainly Jews, and hence, they were confined within their Jewish mentality. Moreover, probably those early believers in Christ in Jerusalem had also considered themselves as part of Judaism. And that explains why they still went to the temple at the time of prayers even though during this same period they were also observing the breaking of bread in their homes. And because they did both, there was not that clear a testimony that what had happened in the upper room and subsequent events constituted a completely new departure: it had nothing to do with Judaism but represented, as it were, the pouring forth of new wine into the new wineskin known now as the body of Christ, the church.

Now how was this clear-cut departure—this unambiguous, undeniable break—from Judaism brought about? It was first effected by means of the deacon Stephen. He was that vessel through whom God was able to manifest the first evidence of an unmistakable separation from Judaism. And that is the reason Stephen is so significant in the growth of the church, the body of Christ. Furthermore, if we understand him correctly, Stephen is the forerunner of Paul the apostle. As a matter of fact, Paul began his life with Christ when present at the martyrdom of Stephen. Indeed, in studying more deeply the life of this apostle to the Gentiles you will discover that Paul's own vision and concept of the church as the body of Christ was actually a continuation of what Stephen had seen in a heavenly vision when being stoned to death as the first Christian martyr. This thus made Stephen to be the forerunner of the great apostle Paul. In fact, one could assert that Stephen was *the* pioneer of the heavenly way.

Who was Stephen? He was one of the seven deacons chosen by the Jerusalem church to serve the tables in the distribution of food, drink, and other necessities. As was pointed out in our last discussion together, the disciples in Jerusalem had greatly multiplied, and there were many widows among the Hellenistic believers who were being overlooked in their daily provision and care. In those early days the church at Jerusalem was composed of both Hellenistic and Hebrew Jews. And all twelve apostles were Hebrew Jews and who had somehow accidentally neglected the widows of the Hellenistic Jews, thus creating a problem. To solve that problem the apostles suggested that the church brethren select seven men of good report, and who were full of wisdom and the Holy Spirit, to serve the tables. And in the process of choosing these seven deacons the church chose Stephen as the first one. He was certainly full of wisdom and the Holy Spirit and who served the tables so well that he was able not only to carry out that service but also to minister the word of God. How true it is that if we are faithful in smaller matters we will be granted greater opportunities to serve God's people (cf. Luke 19:17).

Stephen was not only one of the seven deacons serving tables; evidently he in addition was one used by God in the ministry of His word especially towards the Hellenistic Jews. He was a man full of grace and power. In all which has been written concerning Stephen we find the word full being employed repeatedly. He was not one who knew Christ just a little; rather, he was one who was in the fullness of Christ. He was full of the wisdom, Spirit, grace, and power of God. Everything connected with Stephen was characterized by spiritual fullness.

Why was he so full? Probably it was because he was not in any way fettered or bound by Jewish tradition. Had Stephen been a Hebrew Jew he would have been prone to have been bound by the tradition of the fathers, but being a Hellenistic Jew he was freer in his spirit. Not being bound by the tradition of the fathers he was open and free in his spirit to receive more of the fullness of Christ. He was a man who knew and experienced the fullness of Christ.

He ministered Christ and His gospel primarily to the Hellenistic Jews who resided in Jerusalem, and because of that, the synagogues of these Hellenistic Jews rose up to persecute him. The persecution did not come from the Jewish synagogue as a whole but from the synagogues of the Hellenistic Jews, those synagogues which had been established for the Hellenistic Jews currently residing in the Jewish capital and who had hailed from Africa, Asia Minor, and Cilicia. So the Jews in these particular synagogues rose up and began to persecute Stephen. And ultimately they brought him before the Jewish council—the Sanhedrin or council of the seventy, the highest Jewish court—where they accused Stephen of speaking words against the holy temple and the Law. They accused him of the same things which the Jewish leaders had accused Jesus of; for recall that those leaders had accused the Lord Jesus of being one who had said He would destroy the temple and in three days raise it back up. They, of course, had not understood that the Lord had been referring to His own body, but they falsely accused Him of declaring that the temple would be destroyed. And here with Stephen was the same accusation: they accused him of saying that this same Jesus would destroy the temple and change the customs Moses had taught them.

Here, then, was a man full of Christ—that is to say, a man full of the new wine—and he accordingly came into direct conflict with the old wineskin of Judaistic tradition. These Jewish accusers would have liked to have seen this new wine contained in the old wineskin of Judaism. But if this new wine refused to be contained in their old wineskin, then they must persecute these "new-wine" people. Conform, or else be destroyed.

At this juncture we realize that a very serious crisis had now arisen. Was God going to be able to keep His life pure on earth or would there emerge a destructive compromise? Would the body of Christ be a new-wineskin vessel that can contain and hold the new wine of the Spirit of life or would the body of Christ degenerate into an organization, institution, or a sect of Judaism? That was really the issue here. Or to describe the issue another way: should Christianity be Judaized or should it be free according to God's pattern? This was the crux of the crisis.

What at its core is Judaism? What are its main features or characteristics? They are four in number. First, it is a code of law; second, it is a system of priesthood; third, it requires and has a particular place of worship; and fourth, it is a set of earthly promises. These four features comprise Judaism.

Judaism is first of all a code of law—the Mosaic Law, which consists of the Ten Commandments plus all the statutes, ordinances, and precepts. This code of law was given by God and not invented by man. Its origin was divine, it having been given to Moses as God's human intermediary by the hand of angels who were believed to have been present at Sinai; and thus the Law came from God (Galatians 3:19b).

Why was the Law given in the first place? The book of Romans tells us that the Law was given to mankind because only through the Law comes the knowledge of sin (3:20b ASV). And in Paul's Letter to the Galatians we learn that the Law "was added for the sake of defining transgressions" (3:19a NASB mgn).

In other words, by means of the Law we humans know what sin actually is. Or as the Phillips New Testament translation of this verse in Galatians reads, the Law "was an addition made to underline the existence and extent of sin." People do not really know themselves. They assume they have the ability to do what is right, that there is that in them which is good and which can please God. Because people do not know themselves they incorrectly think they have God-pleasing merits. Therefore, God gave the Law to man to enable him to have a true knowledge of sin. If there were no Law we would not know what sin is. This is not meant to indicate that there is no such thing as sin but that there was no *knowledge* of sin; to the contrary, sin was still there; in fact, from the day of Adam until Moses sin was already there, but people did not have the knowledge of sin until the Law came.

For example, the Law says, "Thou shall not covet"—which informs you that you are capable of coveting; and that hence, if and when you covet, you are being greedy, and so you know you have sinned; and thus by means of the Law you have been given the knowledge of sin. Accordingly, by means of the Law we come to know that we have not done what we should: by means of the Law we realize we have failed, bringing us to our extremity and thus shutting us up to Christ. In other words, the Law is meant to lead us to Christ—that is the ultimate purpose of the Law (Galatians 3:23-24 NASB). But with regard to the Israelites, instead of learning and benefiting from the real purpose of the Law, they self-confidently asserted: "All that

God has said we will do. We will obey and do them. Most surely we will do them." Throughout their history they repeatedly tried to be justified by their good works, but because of that they were condemned by the very Law they desired to keep. Thus Judaism's first and primary characteristic is a code of law of which Judaism greatly boasts. Indeed, we must acknowledge that there is no law under the heavens nobler and higher and more divine in origin than the Law of Moses. Yes, the adherents of Judaism boast of that Law, and yet they are condemned by it. Such, in part, is Judaism.

Is it not true that from the very beginning of the history of the church up to the present, people have tried to turn Christianity into a religion like Judaism? By which is meant their attempt to reduce the Bible to a mere system of theology, or by putting out a rule-book of doctrine or a rule-book of discipline or reducing Christianity to simply a creed of faith. All is to be reduced to rules and regulations—albeit with good intentions, and simplifies everything in an attempt to make all things very clear—as in the Ten Commandments. But in doing these things people are actually guilty of Judaizing Christianity. And in doing so, believers are placed under the bondage of law—under the bondage of a legal system. But the truth is that though we Christians are not *under* law we are not *without* law: we do have a law; but it is the law of the Spirit of life in Christ Jesus (Romans 8:2). God has not summed up and reduced everything in Christ and in the church to a code of rules and regulations. Not so; instead, He has given us the Spirit of life, and the Spirit of life in the church is her law. So Christianity is not a dead entity; rather, it is a living reality. And that is the new wine which has been poured into the new wineskin: the church, the body of Christ.

Stephen's accusers viewed him as one who had been speaking against the Mosaic Law, for they were those who kept the Law in the physical, material sense and according to the letter. But Stephen saw that the real purpose of the Law was to lead people to Christ and to God's true resting-place on earth, His church (Galatians 3:24a NASB; Acts 7:37 quoting in part from Deuteronomy 18:15-19; Acts 7:44-50 quoting Isaiah 66:1-2). But Stephen's accusers could not accept that.

A second feature of Judaism is its system of priesthood—the Levitical priesthood. God's intention in the beginning was to make of His people, the Israelites, a nation of priests. In Exodus 19 we read that God had told Moses to say to the Israelites: "I have borne you on eagles' wings and brought you to myself … and ye shall be to me a kingdom of priests" (vv. 4b, 6a). What is meant by the phrase, a kingdom of priests? It means that every Israelite was intended by God to be a priest serving Him. But when soon afterwards Moses was receiving the Law on the summit of Mount Sinai, down below, the children of Israel had made for themselves a golden calf idol and were worshiping it (Exodus 32:1-10); and because of their failure, they disqualified themselves to become God's priests. Consequently, out of the twelve tribes of Israel's people God was forced to select one tribe, Levi, for the priesthood, and of that tribe only the family of Aaron was able to serve as priests (Exodus 40:12-15). Judaism is thus a religion wherein the people in general cannot serve God; *they* are not able to serve Him because they are not allowed to serve Him. Service to God was limited exclusively to but one tribe and to but one family within that tribe. That was another characteristic of Judaism—a limited priesthood.

Is it not true that throughout the centuries-long history of Christianity right up to the present time, people in Christendom have tried to Judaize Christianity? Instead of seeing all believers are priests, they have often succeeded in limiting service to God in the church to a certain class, and only those of that class can serve God. The rest of the church people are deemed to be the laity who know nothing and that even if they wanted to and were allowed to serve, they would not know how to serve God. Spiritual service is hence monopolized by a few belonging to a special class. This is probably the meaning of the proper name, Nicolaitans, mentioned twice in Revelation 2 (vv. 6, 15). In the history of Christianity we do not find any clear definitive reference to such a sect other than in Revelation. So we are limited in discovering who and what this group of people may have been by searching out the meaning of their name as it appeared in the original New Testament Greek. And here is what we learn: Nikao = overcome or conquer, laitan = laity—and therefore meaning, conquer(ing) the laity. In other words, they were a special class of people in the church of that day whose aim was to monopolize all the spiritual service for themselves and thus to leave the rest of the brethren to being the laity whose place was to be the audience. And that is a form of Judaized Christianity.

The apostle Peter tells us in his first letter that when we come to Christ we are as living stones, being built up into a spiritual house and serving as a holy priesthood (2:45). We all as Christians are not only a spiritual house that is being built up but at the same time we are also a holy priesthood who serve in the house of God—the church. In other words, every believer is a priest. And the apostle John in Revelation has echoed this same truth in his having declared that the Lord Jesus has "washed us from our sins in his blood, and [has] made us a kingdom [of] priests to his God and Father" (1:5b-6a).

Why, then, are we saved? We are saved to serve God as priests. We do not need an intermediary class between ourselves and God, for there is already a mediator between God and man—Jesus Christ the Lord (I Timothy 2:5 ASV); but there is no mediator between ourselves and the Lord. Such an understanding is known as the universal priesthood of the believers, which constitutes the new wineskin. But how often in the history of the church people have tried to put the new wine into the old wineskin of a limited priesthood! You and I as believers have the divine life in us as priests and yet in some church groups within Christendom you and I would not be allowed to serve because you and I would not have been trained and ordained by man. That is putting the new wine of the Spirit of life in the old wineskin of a limited and limiting priesthood. It will most surely break up and burst the old wineskin.

The temple as the required and particular place of worship is most important to Judaism and constitutes its third feature. Yes, the temple site was chosen by God, and the pattern of the temple was revealed to man by God. The temple was built as a physical house of God on earth for God to dwell in by His Spirit. Therefore, the temple was and still is everything to the Jewish people. As a matter of fact, when the temple was destroyed by the Romans in AD 70, Judaism's existence was nearly finished, and has remained so even up to the present. Why do I say that? My reasoning can be traced out as follows: If there is no temple in Jerusalem, there can be no sacrifice; and if there is no sacrifice, there is no remission of sin; and if, in Judaism, there is no remission of sin, there can be no salvation.

I have attended several of my Jewish friends' funerals, and after listening on each occasion to what the rabbi has said, I go away with a sense of hopelessness. If, as is the case in Judaism, there is no temple, no sacrifice, no remission of sin, and therefore no salvation, then there is no hope. Hence, what can the rabbis do? The only thing they can do is try to comfort their people with this: "Perhaps your merits will go before you and be God-pleasing and thus may speak well on your behalf." That is all. Nevertheless, despite this apparent hopeless state, the place of worship remains a very important feature in Judaism today: a Jew must go to Jerusalem to the last remaining vestige of the temple—its wailing wall—and there the Jew can worship God. Otherwise, in reality he cannot.

Let us recall what happened when Jesus met a Samaritan woman by the well of Jacob at Sychar in Samaria. On that occasion the religious feeling of this Samaritan woman was stirred up by the Lord's words with her. So the woman said to Jesus: "You Jews say a person must worship in Jerusalem—that there is no other place. But we Samaritans worship here on Mount Gerazim. Now what is right: should we all go to Jerusalem or should we all go to Mount Gerazim?" Jesus replied: "Woman, an hour is coming when neither in Jerusalem nor on Mount Gerazim shall anyone need to go to worship the Father; on the contrary, the time is coming and now is, that the Father is seeking for true worshipers, those who shall worship Him in spirit and in truth" (John 4:20-24). People today—even many Christians—put much emphasis on a building, as though that is the holy place where God is to be worshiped and nowhere else, the emphasis being so strong that it even borders on superstition.

In this connection I need to relate an incident I experienced many years ago. At the outset of World War II's Pacific theater of conflict, which began in late 1941, I was in Singapore, and of course bombing by the Japanese was occurring there every day. The bombs were falling here, there, and everywhere. One day, early in the morning, a brother in the Lord ran to my house to speak to me about something urgent, and as soon as I saw him I could see the great agony on his face. He ran up to me and said, "Brother Kaung, did you see it? A bomb fell right through the roof of the assembly hall. If God does not protect His church, then where is our protection?" I could see that He was lost.

Oh, how we too often have that Judaizing concept in our mind! We think that God is to be worshiped in a physical place. No, we worship the Father in spirit and in truth. The place is secondary. If the Lord is here, even if it be a garage, thank God for that. If the Lord is not present and even if the place be a magnificent cathedral, what is that? To God it is just another building. But throughout the centuries people have tried to Judaize Christianity to such an extent that when we say, Let us go to church, we mean to a building, a place. From this kind of talk one can see how far we have moved already in the direction of the old wineskin of Judaism. The Judaizers of his day accused Stephen of blaspheming the temple, but they saw only the physical; Stephen saw the real, the spiritual.

Finally, with regard to Judaism's four main characteristics, we need to see that it also embraces a set of earthly promises. God promised Abraham and his seed many earthly blessings. For instance, the Lord said to the Israelites: "If you keep My word, then your sheep or oxen or cows will not lose their calves or lambs. Your fields will be prosperous and you will have many children" (see Deuteronomy 28:1-14). All the promises to the people of Israel were a set of earthly ones which the Jewish people are still looking and waiting to be fulfilled. For example, when the Messiah finally comes, they believe, then Israel will become the head of the nations and shall no longer be the tail (cf. Deuteronomy 26:19a, 28:13), and that is one very significant reason why they rejected Christ at His first coming to the earth; for after closely examining and observing Christ for some three years, they in the end concluded that He was not going to make Israel the head; and therefore, in their minds He could not have been the promised Messiah. Judaism holds to a set of earthly promises which still remain to be fulfilled.

How people today attempt to transform one facet of Christianity's teaching into that which promises believers that they shall be prospered with earthly blessings of all kinds. Perhaps you have heard of the teaching of prosperity. This teaching holds that if you love the Lord and if you do this and do that, then you will prosper. God promises you to be prosperous. If, for instance, you want to own a Cadillac motor car, you will get one if you observe the requirements of this teaching.

In this context, what is Christianity? God does not promise us *earthly* blessings, but He has assured us in His word that He has already blessed us with every spiritual blessing in the *heavenlies* in Christ Jesus (Ephesians 1:3). Today people are looking for earthly blessings. You do not find that in true Christianity. Yes, God does bless us physically, even materially, that is true, but that is not Christianity. God can bless us and does, but that is not Christianity. God has blessed us with every spiritual blessing in the heavenlies in Christ Jesus; and that is true Christianity. What are we Christians looking for? If we are looking for earthly blessings, we transform Christianity into a form of Judaism. If, however, we are looking forward to apprehending more of the spiritual blessings in the heavenlies in Christ, that is true Christianity.

Here before us, then, is the conflict between Stephen on the one hand and the high Jewish council and the various synagogues on the other. These ultra-traditionalists wanted to reduce Christianity to becoming merely another part of Judaism—which would be a returning to the old wineskin of the Mosaic Law, the limiting priesthood, the temple, and so forth. But Stephen, full of wisdom and the Holy Spirit, in tracing the history of Israel from Abraham on down to his day saw that history *in God's light*. Which is to say, that in the narrative of Israel's history Stephen saw that whatever God had been doing was a leading up to the coming of Christ, and that with the coming of Christ all the foreshadows have disappeared because the reality—even Christ himself—had now arrived. He thus saw most clearly the real meaning of the history of Israel. Stephen therefore stands as one who has seen and understood that which is spiritual, that which is heavenly, that which is eternal and real. And he realized that it is all in Christ, the Son of man, who lives in glory. That in essence is what Stephen saw. What a contrast between that glorious vision of his and the outworn concept of the Jewish leadership and much of the Jewish people at that time. It was, and still is, at its core a conflict between heaven and earth.

In truth Stephen was a pioneer of the heavenly way. He refused to accept the notion that Christianity was merely another sect of Judaism; rather, He saw that Christianity—that is, the church of Jesus Christ—is the new wineskin for containing and manifesting the new wine of the Spirit of life in

Christ. What Stephen saw and embraced is that which is completely different from Judaism. It is heavenly and spiritual in nature, not earthly nor physical. And because of his embrace of this new wine and because, further, of his fearless proclamation of it in the grace, power and wisdom of the Spirit, Stephen was stoned to death. Yet while being stoned, he testified before his murderers that in looking upward he saw the heavens opened and the Son of man standing at God the Father's right hand. That, then, was the heavenly vision which this first martyr of the church, the body of Christ, beheld that day.

Now if the Head of the body of Christ is in heaven, then His body on earth—the church—is heavenly in nature. And if the Head is at the right hand of God, then the body has all the power and authority of the Head. And here in his martyrdom Stephen exhibited a spirit not unlike the spirit of Christ; for let us recall that when Christ was facing His death on the cross, He prayed, "Father, forgive them for they do not know what they are doing" (see Luke 23:34a). And here we witness the same spirit in Stephen, for near the end of his being stoned, he prayed, "Lord, lay not this sin to their charge." In other words, he prayed for God to forgive them. Yet let us realize that, symbolically speaking, the spilled blood of Stephen was like a seed which was at that moment sown in the heart of Saul of Tarsus who witnessed this cruel martyrdom first hand. For much later this same Saul (then to be known as Paul the apostle) took up the cause of Christianity's clear-cut departure from Judaism just where Stephen had in death left off.

Let us thank God that as the body of Christ grew, and though it went through certain pains and conflicts, nevertheless, out of all those various experiences God was able to keep Christ's body on earth pure from the contamination of Judaism. Yet let us never forget that the events surrounding Stephen and his death marked the beginning of what would ultimately be the definitive clear-cut separation of Christianity from Judaism.

And as one continues on in reading and studying the book of Acts, the separation becomes clearer and clearer until finally in the ministry of Paul one sees in practical expression the pure, new wineskin with the new wine within.

Hence, in order to see and fully understand the conflict which we even in our own day are in, we need to return to God's word, and in that light, we shall realize that it is an unceasing conflict between heaven and earth, a conflict between the advocates of the new wine of the Spirit and the advocates of the old wineskin of a Judaistic-type of religion. As we have come to realize, the new wine of the Spirit of life in Christ can never be contained in, nor expressed through, the old wineskin. Instead, the new wine must find a new wineskin; and according to the Scriptures, the church is that new wineskin. She is entirely different from any organization, but is a living organism that is elastic and capable of ongoing expansion with the Spirit of life in Christ within.

Our heavenly Father, we do thank Thee for Thy word. Thou dost reveal to us Thy mind through Thy word. We thank Thee for giving us a new life, even the Spirit of life in Christ Jesus Thy Son; and it is Thy will that that new wine should be contained in a new wineskin, never in an old one. Oh Father, we do pray that we may not be foolish by trying to put Thy new wine into old wineskins but that we may offer ourselves to Thee as the new wineskin so that Thy life may be preserved and that Thy life may grow. So, Father, we pray that Thou wilt use these simple words to help us to see that Thy divine life must not be in any way inhibited but that Thy life may be preserved and be useful and beneficial to many. In the name of our Lord Jesus. Amen.

Chapter Eight

Paul

Acts 7:58-8:3—And having cast him [Stephen] out of the city, they stoned him. And the witnesses laid aside their clothes at the feet of a young man called Saul. And they stoned Stephen, praying, and saying, Lord Jesus, receive my spirit. And kneeling down, he cried with a loud voice, Lord, lay not this sin to their charge. And having said this, he fell asleep.

And Saul was consenting to his being killed. And on that day there arose a great persecution against the church which was in Jerusalem, and all were scattered into the countries of Judaea and Samaria except the apostles. And pious men buried Stephen and made great lamentation over him. But Saul ravaged the church, entering into the houses one after another, and dragging off both men and women delivered them up to prison.

Acts 9:1-22—But Saul, still breathing out threatenings and slaughter against the disciples of the Lord, came to the high priest and asked of him letters to Damascus, to the synagogues, so that if he found any who were of the way, both men and women, he might bring them bound to Jerusalem. But as he was journeying, it came to pass that he drew near to Damascus; and suddenly there shone round about him a light out of heaven, and falling on the earth he heard a voice saying to him, Saul, Saul, why dost thou persecute me? And he said, Who art thou, Lord? And he said, I am Jesus, whom thou persecutest. But rise up and enter into the city, and it shall be told thee what thou must do. But the men who were traveling with him stood speechless, hearing the voice but beholding no one. And Saul rose up from the earth, and his eyes being opened he saw no one. But leading him by the hand they brought him into Damascus. And he was three days without seeing, and neither ate nor drank. And there was a certain disciple in Damascus by name Ananias. And the Lord said to him in a vision, Ananias. And he said, Behold, here am I, Lord. And the Lord said to him, Rise up and go into the street which is called Straight, and seek in the house of Judas one by name Saul, he is of Tarsus: for, behold, he is praying, and has seen in a vision a man by name Ananias coming in and putting his hand on him, so that he should see. And Ananias answered, Lord, I have heard from many concerning this man how much evil he has done to thy saints at Jerusalem; and here he has authority from the chief priests to bind all who call upon thy name. And the Lord said to him, Go, for this man is an elect vessel to me, to bear my name before both nations and kings and the sons of Israel: for I will shew to him how much he must suffer for my name. And Ananias went and entered into the house; and laying his hands upon him he said, Saul, brother, the Lord has sent me, Jesus that appeared to thee in the way in which thou camest, that thou mightest see, and be filled with the Holy Spirit. And straightway there fell from his eyes as it were scales, and he saw, and rising up was baptized; and, having received food, got strength. And he was with the disciples who were in Damascus certain days. And straightway in the synagogues he preached Jesus that he is the Son of God. And all who heard were astonished and said, Is not this he who destroyed in Jerusalem those who called on this name, and here was come for this purpose, that he might bring them bound to the chief priests?

But Saul increased the more in power, and confounded the Jews who dwelt in Damascus, proving that this is the Christ.

The church, the body of Christ, was born on the day of Pentecost, and after the church was born she began to grow. In the process of growing, the church was gradually being formed according to the heavenly pattern. But in the process of growing there was bound to be conflict, and this is part of the growing pains of life.

First, we find the conflict manifested surrounding the person of Stephen. Stephen was the one who had a vision of the Son of man in glory, and to him the church was not an earthly, physical, material entity but was that which is spiritual and heavenly in nature. Because of that understanding, he came into conflict with the Judaism of that day.

Then, in the process of the church growing further, Philip was used of God to break through the prejudice of the Jews against the Samaritans, because the very nature of the church is her universality. Yet there was that Pentecost unity which must be preserved, and for this reason the Holy Spirit was withheld in His outpouring until the apostles came from Jerusalem and laid hands upon these Samaritan believers.

But I think no one has made more of a contribution to the early church's formation than the apostle Paul. In the process of that formation God used Stephen, a Hellenistic Jew, and Philip, another Hellenistic Jew; and here with respect to Paul, God used another Hellenistic Jew. Probably the reason for this is the fact that they were not as bound by the traditions of the fathers as were the Hebrew Jews of that era. Yet it must be observed that though in one sense Paul was the same as Stephen and Philip in their flexibility, we shall see that in another sense he was not. Nevertheless, when the church was in its formative years, it seems as if God used certain vessels that were more suitable for Him to break through the obstinacy of the Hebrew Jews in Jerusalem. And in the case of Paul, in one respect he was an entirely new vessel: he was not one of the twelve apostles, he was not one of the seven deacons who served the tables, he was not even a follower of Jesus. Moreover, he was a blasphemer, and a persecutor of the church. And hence, it can be said that in Paul God used an entirely new vessel for the ongoing formation of the church according to the heavenly pattern, and I think that was the wisdom of God.

In this regard, then, I believe that Saul of Tarsus (who later became Paul the apostle) continued where Stephen's testimony ended in death. For let us recall that when Stephen was stoned, he gave testimony to what he saw in glory. He saw the Son of man standing at the right hand of God in glory, and then he fell to his death in martyrdom; and that was where his testimony ended and where the converted Saul continued on with the same testimony in his subsequent ministry of the gospel. For on the road to Damascus he experienced the implications of that same heavenly vision. So in a very real sense, what God began through Stephen was continued through Paul.

Now the first mention of Paul in Scripture occurs in Acts 7 in Luke's narrative about Stephen being stoned to death; there he is referred to as "a young man called Saul." We know that Saul was born in the city of Tarsus in Cilicia, a Roman city (Acts 21:39a, 22:3a). The Roman Empire had conquered the whole known world of that day and had made certain strategically located cities Roman cities. All those who were born in those cities enjoyed the privilege of possessing the citizenship of the Roman Empire. Whereas most people in the Empire were conquered slave people, only Romans themselves and those people who were born in those Roman cities were Roman citizens. Hence, Paul's Roman citizenship was gained by reason of birth and not through purchase, which was another means of gaining such citizenship (Acts 22:27-28).

When Saul of Tarsus was not quite in his teens—that is, probably at the age of twelve—he was brought to Jerusalem to learn the Mosaic Law. At this time twelve was considered to be the proper age for a Jewish boy to experience the ceremony of Bar-mitzvah—thus signifying that the lad was to be made a son of the Law. So young Saul was now to be reared in Jerusalem and to be taught in the strictest sect of Judaism, he becoming a Pharisee. In so doing he sat at the feet of Rabbi Gamaliel who was the grandson of famed Rabbi Hillel of Israel. So as a youth and young man Saul was taught by Gamaliel, perhaps the greatest teacher of his time. Though young as he was, he was nonetheless a very zealous and earnest Pharisee, and he told us himself that he was far more advanced than any of his contemporaries in Judaism, and he therefore lived as a very strict Pharisee (for all this biographical data, see Acts 22:3, 26:4-5; Galatians 1:14a).

In thinking of the Pharisees today we usually do not have a very good impression of them; but the truth of the matter is that the sect of the Pharisees had begun with a very good aim and objective in mind; for the Law was actually preserved by the Pharisees, even though most of them eventually descended into being Pharisees in name, not in reality. In fact, it was because they had become rank hypocrites that Jesus had felt it necessary to denounce the Pharisees most strongly. What they taught was right, He said, but He declared that they would not lift a finger to live by what they themselves taught (Matthew 23:4). They placed a huge burden upon others but did not bear that burden themselves.

However, the young man Saul was different. As we have already learned, he himself was not only educated as a Pharisee, he was also a true Pharisee because he *lived* the life of a Pharisee. In other words, he was very strict, very honest, and very real. Hence, he once wrote: "According to the righteousness of the Law, I was blameless" (see Philippians 3:6b). He was most zealously that kind of person. And, of course, being a highly-taught Pharisee Saul was very deeply involved in the traditions of the fathers. That could not be avoided because all Pharisees studied the Law according to the traditions of the fathers (see again Acts 22:3b, 26:5b).

So that by the time of Jesus Saul manifested the fact that he was very honest, very sincere and very real, but he was also deeply occupied with the traditions of the fathers (Galatians 1:14b mgn). He looked at and judged all matters and people in the light of those traditions, and according to that outlook he considered Jesus an impostor (cf. Acts 26:9). Consequently, Saul deemed the followers of Jesus worthy to be persecuted, and in persecuting them he thought he was serving God (I Timothy 1:12-13; cf. Romans 10:2).

When we first read of Saul in the Scriptures, we learn that he was watching over the robes of those who stoned Stephen to death. As a matter of fact, he was believed to be numbered among the 70 members of the Jewish Council called the Sanhedrin, which in Judaism was the highest judicial authority among the Jews in Israel. And even though Saul was only a relatively young man at this time, he was believed to have been one of this Council's members, since he would later testify that whenever the Council condemned anybody, he gave his consenting vote (Acts 26:10c). Saul had a vote, and evidently he was made the executioner of the Council's decisions. And with regard to Stephen, the Council had decided that he must be stoned to death because in their view he was a blasphemer, thus worthy of death. And Saul as executioner was present at the place of stoning and was watching over the garments of those who stoned Stephen to death.

We can therefore recognize from all this that by this time Saul had truly advanced quite far in Judaism. However, even before the foundation of the world God had chosen this man for His purposes; for Paul himself testified that God had set him apart from his mother's womb (Galatians 1:15a). And though until his rendezvous with the ascended Lord Jesus on the road to Damascus Paul was not called by God's grace (Galatians 1:15b), nevertheless, in God's sovereign election he was chosen from before the foundation of the world. He was set apart from his mother's womb without his ever knowing anything about it till much later. He was chosen and called by God for a specific purpose: to be a master builder in the house of God on earth (I Corinthians 3:10a ASV).

Saul's spiritual life with God actually began at the hour when he witnessed the testimony and death of Stephen. When this first martyr of the church bravely testified before the Sanhedrin, he was heard to say at the end of his testimony: "I see the heavens open and the Son of man standing at the right hand of God" (Acts 7:56). And even before Stephen, standing before the Council members, had begun his lengthy testimony, they saw that his face was like that of an angel (Acts 6:15). Now Saul as a member of the Council certainly did not see that heavenly vision of Stephen's, but he certainly heard all of what Stephen had said. And, again, though Saul did not see that vision, yet, by seeing the angelic-like face of Stephen and by hearing what Stephen said, he could not get away from the spiritual reality that was present. At the very minimum Saul of Tarsus was a sincere, honest person. People who are insincere and false might listen to those words, but nothing would register in them. Saul was misled, that is true—misled by the traditions of the fathers; nevertheless, he was honest and sincere in everything he experienced.

So when Saul was faced with such a dramatic spiritual reality as this involving Stephen, he ultimately could not escape from its implications. He did not see the vision but he subsequently witnessed Stephen dying, giving up his spirit to God and praying that He would forgive those who were stoning him to death. Hence, it is not too much to say that the young man Saul could not escape from this event's spiritual impact. So I would say that the blood of Stephen germinated as a seed in the life of Saul (cf. Acts 22:20).

On the very day Stephen was stoned, persecution of the church in Jerusalem broke out. Who was the chief persecutor? Saul of Tarsus. He persecuted the people of the Way with such vehemence that he would enter every synagogue and beat and then imprison all who had believed on the Lord Jesus (Acts 22:19a, 26:11a) and even enter every home and drag out both men and women and have them put in prison (Acts 8:3, 22:4). That was not like the action of a gentleman, and certainly Saul was brought up to be a gentleman. A true Pharisee should be a gentleman, but the way he now acted was almost like to that of a madman (Acts 26:11b ASV). He would not only drag the men out of their homes, he did the same with the women. There was no kindness, sympathy nor gentleness in Saul.

Now I wonder why he had persecuted the people of the Way in such an ungentlemanly-like manner? Could it be that his conscience had been bothering him? When a person's conscience is troubled he will do all he can to fight against it. And in fighting against his conscience that person will do things which he would not ordinarily do. I believe Saul was trying to drown out the voice of his conscience by perpetrating these cruel acts. He was attempting to convince himself that this activity of his was serving God (cf. I Timothy 1:13).

So most likely the martyrdom of Stephen had on the one hand triggered the beginning of something spiritual in Saul's life and from which ultimately he was not able to avoid its implications, but on the other hand had forced Saul to try to drown the voice of his conscience and which caused him to act cruelly against the people of the Way with a double intensity. Moreover, Saul persecuted believers not only in Jerusalem but also in the villages and cities throughout Judea. He even pursued believers in Jesus to the extent of asking for, and receiving, documents from the high priest authorizing him to go to foreign (that is, Gentile) cities and accomplish the same evil purpose there (Acts 26:11c). Damascus, for example, was a Gentile city in Syria, and so he was intent on going there with those documents obtained from the Jewish authorities authorizing him to seize anyone of the Way and bring them to Jerusalem to be condemned. So evidently the Spirit of God was striving with Saul at this time, but he was fighting and fighting furiously against his conscience.

Let us notice that Saul did not have his encounter with the risen and ascended Lord Jesus until he had nearly reached the gate of Damascus. This is evidence that sometimes God is never in a hurry; He allowed Saul to go as far as he could; but then at noontime a great light brighter than the sun shone down upon him and his associates, and they all fell to the ground (Acts 26:13-14a). Right then and there he experienced the heavenly vision, and that was the turning point in the life of Saul. That turning point had actually had its beginning with the death of Stephen, but had its completion on the road to Damascus and inside that city, and which brought about a complete change in Saul. Even towards the end of Paul's life, his testimony before King Agrippa was worded in this manner: "I was not disobedient to the heavenly vision" (see Acts 26:19). His whole life and ministry was explained by the heavenly vision, and that vision was in reality the same vision which Stephen saw when he was about to be stoned to death. That is why I say that Paul continued on from where Stephen's testimony ended due to his death. Actually Paul's ministry—the work of his contribution to the formation of the church—was along the same line as Stephen's.

What is this heavenly vision which Saul, who later came to be named Paul, saw on the road to Damascus? I think there are at least three essential elements comprising that heavenly vision of Saul's which he would long afterwards refer to as the gospel which he had received neither from man nor from having been taught but was received "through a revelation of Jesus Christ" and which God had been "pleased to reveal His Son [to] me" (Galatians 1:12, 15b-16a NASB). The first essential element began, of course, with a great light which shone down upon him, causing him to fall upon the ground. All his companions saw the light and heard the sound, but they did not understand the voice. Only Saul heard it, and which said: "Saul, Saul, why do you persecute Me? It is hard for you to kick against the goads" (see Acts 22:6-7, 9; 26:13-14).

When Saul heard these words about kicking against the goads, he knew exactly what they meant for him spiritually; but let us first be clear what they meant physically. When Jewish farmers plowed their fields, they did so, using a plow and an ox or horse. They would put an ox, or perhaps two oxen, under a yoke and attach the yoke to the plow. The farmer would place one hand on the plow to guide it as it was being pulled by the ox or oxen under the yoke, and in his other hand he would have a sharp-pointed instrument called a goad. Now in plowing his field the farmer must keep the plow going straight ahead so that the furrows for planting will be straight instead of zigzagging. But sometimes the ox would exercise its own will by not following the direction of the farmer and moving itself instead to the right or to the left, thus requiring the farmer to use the goad to prick the leg of the ox gently but firmly enough so as to cause the ox to feel the goad's pointed spike sufficiently so that the ox would learn to be obedient and submissive. However, the ox might sometimes be very stubborn and instead of learning the lesson it would kick against the goads and be hurt. And this might occur more than once until, having been wounded enough times by one pricking of the goad after another, the ox had learned the lesson of obedience.

I believe that what was being portrayed here by the use of these words of God the Son regarding the goads was simply this: "God has a purpose for your life, Saul. Even before the foundation of the world He had already chosen you. When you were in your mother's womb God had set you apart for a specific purpose, but He first has had to put you under a yoke for pulling a plow—that is to say, for doing His will and work. However, you, not knowing this, have rebelled against it, you wanting to go your own way and doing your own desires. But because of that, God has had to prick you very gently from time to time. Instead of learning the lesson, though, you have kicked and kicked and continue to kick, even though you have been wounded time after time. So God has had to say to you: 'Saul, I have apprehended you for my purpose, but you insist on kicking against the goad of My will for your life again and again because you have desired to go your own way. Nevertheless, I must tell you that you will not succeed, for I shall continue to goad you repeatedly, Saul, until you learn the lesson of obedience and submit yourself to Me and to My purpose.'"

Now when Saul heard the words about how hard it was for him to kick against the goads, he instantly knew that it was no use to fight—to kick—any longer against the will and purpose of God. The only response for him to make was to surrender. So Saul responded with: "Lord, who are You?" He knew that he had met a Man in glory against whom he could no longer strive and struggle and fight. He knew that before *that* Man he was defeated. Saul was able to defeat everybody else whom he had been persecuting, but before that Man he knew he had to surrender. So he addressed that Man as Lord: "Lord, who are You?" In these few words Saul was saying the following: "Though I do not know who You are, I know that You are my Lord. Against You, I am no match. From this moment forward You have a hold upon my life and so I must surrender myself to You, but exactly who are You, Lord?" To which the Lord responded, "I am Jesus of Nazareth whom you are persecuting" (Acts 22:8). At that very moment Saul acknowledged for the first time in his life one very essential fact, that the man whom he had called an impostor—Jesus of Nazareth—is Lord of all. And that constitutes the very first essential element in one's understanding of this heavenly vision which came to Saul the unbeliever.

Sometimes our conversion from unbelief to belief in the Lord Jesus is not complete at the beginning. When we first believe in Jesus we accept Him as our Savior, but it may take several years more before we acknowledge Him as our Lord. Because of that, our Christian life can oftentimes be very weak because we only receive Him as our Savior and do not recognize and submit to Him as our Lord. In the case of Paul, however, it was quite different. When he was converted and saved, he surrendered himself and his life completely to Christ.

In that connection, I would like to mention Watchman Nee's conversion which was almost like Saul's. In 1920 he was seventeen years old. He was brought up in the Methodist Church in China and studied in the Anglican Mission School, but he had absolutely no interest in Christianity. He had his own plan for the future. Young Watchman was very, very brilliant and could have been a success in any field; there is no doubt about that.

In 1920 a lady evangelist came to Watchman's native city. Her name was Dr. Dora Yu, a medical doctor, and when she was conducting a gospel campaign, brother Nee's mother got saved. His mother was a strong character, very domineering. And Watchman Nee at this period hated his mother because she had at one time mistreated him. But after the mother got saved, she approached brother Nee's father and asked him for forgiveness. In the family she had dominated everything, but after she was saved she asked forgiveness from her husband. That touched Watchman's heart very much; so when he was invited to hear this lady evangelist at one of the gospel meetings, he went, he acknowledging that anyone who could convert his mother was worth a hearing.

Nothing happened in Watchman's life during the first two nights, but on the third night the Spirit of God began to convict him. Nevertheless, he did not accept the Lord that night; instead, he struggled inwardly for several days thereafter. In fact, brother Nee later told us himself that the reason he struggled during those days was not because he was not ready to accept the Lord Jesus as his *Savior*. To do that he was most ready; rather, it was because he was not ready to give his life over and acknowledge Jesus as his *Lord*. That he could not do, for he knew that he could not accept the Lord as his Savior without completely giving his life to Christ and making Him his Lord. Brother Nee knew that that would not be right. For him it had to be both: either both or neither. But young Watchman could not do that because he had a great future already planned out for himself, and thus he was not ready to give up everything along that line and surrender his life to the Lord.

So he struggled during those few days until, finally, brother Nee later reported, while he was in his room one night the Spirit of God began to put before him all his sins. He stated that he saw the blackness of his sins but at the same time saw the redness of the blood of Jesus Christ. It was at this moment that the love of Christ constrained him to accept Jesus as his Savior and simultaneously to accept Him as his Lord. That was how Watchman Nee's conversion took place.

Now the conversion of Saul occurred in the same manner. It was not only Saul's receiving of forgiveness from God. Thank God we do receive forgiveness when we believe in His Son Jesus Christ, but if one's conversion is solely that, such a conversion is very weak. Unless we also see and receive Him as the Lord of all and can say to Him, "You are my Lord and Master now," our beginning as a believer in Christ is very shallow.

Hence, in the conversion of Saul, the first essential element of the heavenly vision which this future apostle of Christ understood and embraced was to see and accept Jesus as Lord of all aspects in one's life. While He was on earth in humiliation Jesus was crucified but rose from the dead and is now at the right hand of the Father, having been made both Lord and Messiah-Christ. And this is what Saul discerned in that heavenly vision.

Then there is the second essential element or feature of this vision. In Saul's asking—"Lord, who are You?"—he was saying that he saw that Man in glory, but he did not yet recognize Him. So he asked, "Who are You?" And that Man in glory responded, "I am Jesus whom you are persecuting." When that Man in glory had first asked—"Saul, Saul, why do you persecute Me?"—had Saul used his mind at that moment, he could easily have answered in self-defense, "I have never persecuted You. You are well beyond my reach; how, then, could I possibly persecute One in heaven's glory? I can only persecute people on earth." Saul could easily have defended himself in that way, but no, when one is confronted with a heavenly vision, it is not an occasion for trying to figure it out with one's mind.

"Saul, Saul, why do you persecute Me?" That assertion by the Man in glory greatly puzzled Saul because he could not at first understand. Had that Man said—"Why do you persecute My followers?"—Saul would have readily understood. But in asserting to Saul—"Why do you persecute *Me*?"—the risen and ascended Jesus the Nazarene was wanting to show Saul there on the road to Damascus that in his persecuting the followers of the Way on earth it was the same as doing so to the Man in glory. And thus Jesus was desirous of having Saul see that the Head and the body are united into one—that should anyone touch any part of the church, the body of Christ, the Head would complain and say, "Why do you touch Me?"

Suppose someone were to strike or kick your leg, would you say, "Why do you kick my leg?" No, you would say, "Why do you kick me?" So when Saul was persecuting the people of the Way, he was actually touching the members of the body of Christ the Head in Jerusalem, in the cities of Judea, and now he was on the road to Damascus to do the same thing there. And so the Head in heaven complained to Saul, saying, "Why do you persecute *Me*?" So in that heavenly vision on the road to Damascus it was not just the Head whom Saul saw; he saw as well the one new man, with Messiah Jesus of Nazareth as the Head in heaven and the church as His body on earth. He thus saw that the body and the Head are one, and all this he commenced realizing there on the road to Damascus.

God therefore dealt with Saul in this manner on the very first day of his conversion from vehement unbelief to belief in Jesus of Nazareth, and showing him the body of Christ. Anyone who interacts with or touches any part of the body touches the Head because the Head and the body are one. Hence, we may say that on the road to Damascus Saul met a universal man; everywhere he had gone he had met that man. He had met that man in Jerusalem, in the cities of Judea, and, he would very soon meet that man in Damascus itself. That man is a universal man who fills both heaven and earth. And that was the second essential feature of the heavenly vision which Saul saw on the very first day of his spiritual walk with God: he saw the church, the body of Christ, she being one with the Head as the one universal man who is to be found everywhere wherever the followers of the Way are to be found.

There is yet one other essential element comprising the heavenly vision which God revealed to His sovereignly chosen vessel on the road to Damascus and which needs to be presented in some detail. We read in Acts that Saul then asked this question: "Lord, what shall I do?" (22:10a) Now most certainly he was expecting the Lord to give him a direct answer. Saul, of course, had been his own master; he had known exactly whatever he had wanted to do. Up to this point in his life and career Saul had been the head of every undertaking and activity, but here he was completely shattered, broken and even blind. So now he had surrendered himself to a new master in his life; and, therefore, Saul at this helpless moment could only say, "Lord, what do You want me to do? You are now the Lord in my life; so please give me Your command." Given this attitude in Saul he would certainly have the mindset to expect the Lord to tell him what to do. He may even have thought, moreover, that for the Lord to have such a great Pharisee serving Him would surely add honor and glory to the Lord. But the strangest thing was that the Lord did not tell Saul directly what He wanted him to do. Instead, He said to him: "All right, arise and go into Damascus, and there it shall be told you what you must do."

Had the Lord directly told Saul on the Damascus road what to do, here is what would have happened thereafter. Saul of Tarsus would have instantly become Paul the greatest apostle, but he would have turned out to be the most independent apostle since he would have received his commission directly from the Lord and Master of all the apostles. And thus he would not have needed anybody else. Saul as Paul would have gone forth to build up the church, the body of Christ, and yet he would have violated every principle of the body. Indeed, because he was so great, Saul as Paul would have become, as it were, the body himself. Therefore, the wise Lord needed to teach Saul a most practical lesson from the very outset of his commission: "Yes, you are going to become a great member in the body of Christ, but you must constantly bear in mind that you are but one single member. You will need other members of the body of Christ if you are to rightly fulfill the commission I am about to issue to you. You will have to learn relatedness, you must learn submission to others in the body when necessary or helpful. You have to learn to have fellowship. Yes, it is quite true that you cannot live and do God's work without Me, but neither can you live and do His work without your brothers and sisters."

Such was the practical lesson Saul had to learn, and learn from the very beginning. Otherwise, being such a big member and being so gifted, he would most assuredly have turned out to be a very independent member of the body. And he would most certainly have violated every principle of the body which he would be used to build up. Therefore, the Lord Jesus had to teach Saul some very practical lessons and which could only be learned *in* Damascus. So Saul, having been given the vision and the Head's instructions, would obey and enter Damascus and learn there some very important practical lessons and which could only be learned *in* Damascus. So Saul, having been given the vision and the Head's instructions, would obey and enter Damascus and learn there some very important practical lessons as well as some less significant lessons before he could properly launch out in wider ministry elsewhere.

Is that not the problem with many of us? Should God give us a vision, and especially if it be a great vision, immediately our attitude and intention would be this: "All right, I shall go forth and bring it about," without our first learning some practical lessons concerning that vision. If the vision cannot first be worked into us, we shall not be qualified to go forth and work that vision out.

Furthermore, it needs to be pointed out that Saul had been blinded by the light of that vision and that for three days and nights after entering Damascus he remained blind while fasting and praying. Yes, that Man in glory told Saul to enter Damascus, and so he went there, but in a totally blind state and not at all sure of what to expect next. In this connection I often hear people say concerning the light God has given them regarding some vision or indication of His will for them: "I saw the light and I know exactly what it is which God wants me to do." Permit me to say, however, that if you have seen God's light, you will, like Saul, have been blinded by that light. And hence, you ought only say, "I think I see something, but actually I am not sure I know." You have really only seen the light. So, the Lord Jesus instructed Saul to go into Damascus, and he did so in a totally blind condition, where he waited to know for certain that he had seen and understood all the implications of the heavenly vision he had received out on the road.

We realize, then, that the heavenly vision did not cease its revelation on the road outside Damascus but continued its unfolding *inside* Damascus. While Saul was fasting and praying he saw in a vision a man by the name of Ananias coming to where Saul was and laying hands on him so that his sight would be restored. Do realize, therefore, that this further revelation was part of the entire heavenly vision which Saul as Paul would much later speak about (see Acts 22:6ff., 26:19a). Many of us make the mistake of confining the heavenly vision to what Saul received on the road outside Damascus, but that was only part of the vision. Outside that city Saul had heard the voice of a great universal man, the Man in glory, and that lifted him up. Yet that was not the whole of the heavenly vision God was giving him. For upon entering the city Saul received another part of the heavenly vision.

What was that other part? It was not this time a vision of that great and glorious universal Man who had met him on the road outside Damascus, but a small man by the name of Ananias. Whereas Ananias was unknown in Jerusalem Saul was not only known there but known elsewhere in the world as well. Ananias was a very pious believer, probably a leading brother of the church in Damascus (cf. Acts 22:12), but he was unknown in Jerusalem and elsewhere. Yes, he was well known in Damascus because he was a pious man, but in comparison with Saul he was a small man. Saul now saw in the extended vision that that great Man whom he had encountered outside Damascus had seemingly condensed or reduced himself into a small man. And it was that small man who came to Saul and laid hands on him and was used by the Lord in restoring his sight.

Thus we need to recognize and acknowledge the importance of both parts of the heavenly vision received by Saul. On the one hand, the church as the body of Christ is universal in scope, in that the church universal is to be found throughout the ages and generations of Christianity's history. All people everywhere since the day of Pentecost who have believed in the Lord Jesus Christ are in that body of Christ and therefore the church is to be found wherever believers have met in the past, and are meeting today, to worship and serve the Lord. Indeed, we can touch that body everywhere, for it is universally present on earth with the Head seated in heaven. We therefore continually need to see this part of the vision because it will enlarge our capacity to observe what God is doing worldwide.

He is doing a great work through a great and large body with a great Head. This we must constantly see and recognize; otherwise, we shall be very narrow in outlook and involvement.

On the other hand, we need to see and appreciate the content of the other part of the heavenly vision, which part Saul received inside Damascus. There he realized that the body universal which was revealed to him outside Damascus has been condensed or reduced to being a local expression of that body in every place where believers in Christ meet. And in touching the local expression—that is, the local church—it appears, by comparison, to be a small man. Nevertheless, that small man is most practical since it was that small man—brother Ananias—who came and laid hands on Saul to restore his sight and to inform Saul of the will of God for his future life and spiritual service (see Acts 9:15, 22:14-15). Consequently, to appreciate the practical side of the universal body of Christ, we must take into account the continuation of the vision which was revealed to Saul inside Damascus by means of that small man—brother Ananias.

During recent years I have met many believers in America and have read the writings of various Christian authors, all of whom have indicated that many of God's people are beginning to see and to talk about the body of Christ, and for this I thank God. However, a great mistake which many are making is the fact that they have only seen that big man—the body universal; they fail to see the small man—that body in local expression. For when they speak about the body of Christ, it is only in terms of its universality, they failing to see and enter into the practical side, which is to be experienced in its local expression—which is to say, in the local church. Yet, whether it be the big man or the small man, it is not a different man but only the big man condensed or compressed down to the local level where brethren in Christ need to learn all the practical lessons inherent in body life. It is no use for anyone to say, "I have fellowship with all the body of Christ." To the contrary, we have to learn to be related to our brothers and sisters in Christ who live and work next to us. If we cannot relate to those who live next to us, how can we declare, "I am in relationship with all those in the universal body of Christ"? That is most impractical. That, I believe, poses a real problem for many brethren today.

We are here speaking about the body of Christ, that which is so glorious! But for many believers, relating to the body of Christ at the local level may be a problem. For them it is difficult to enter into the practice of body life together with other brethren in Christ in the church. If, for example, they happen to be what I would call big members, as was the case with Saul of Tarsus, they, like him, may perhaps find it very humiliating—as big members in the church—to receive help from a small member as indeed happened to big-member Saul in his being greatly helped by the relatively unknown Ananias. But the Man in glory had a purpose in orchestrating that encounter between these two. He refrained from telling Saul outside Damascus what He wanted him to do but instead used another and little member to convey to Saul the purpose for why he was called. And why? Because that Man in heaven's glory wished to teach Saul a very important lesson from the very outset: that though Saul was to be one of the most prominent vessels for the upbuilding of the body of Christ, he must first learn that essential lesson himself. And what was that lesson? That he needed a little member!—that he could not be alone, that he could never see without his smaller brother's help, that he would never know certain things of God without the assistance of his brother—whether that brother be small or big, and that he could not do without his brother. Hence, in a very real sense, Ananias represented the local expression of the body of Christ in Damascus.

Let us not overlook the fact that the vision which Saul had received outside Damascus was confirmed by the vision which Ananias subsequently received inside the city. For in this latter vision the Man in glory instructed this smaller brother to go to the street called Straight and find in the house of Judas there a man named Saul of Tarsus. Upon hearing this, however, Ananias replied: "Lord, I have heard about this man and about the evil he has done in Jerusalem; and he has now come here with letters from the chief priests, authorizing him to seize all of us who call upon Your name." Ananias realized that he being one of the leading brothers in the Damascus church would be one of the primary targets of Saul's evil intentions. Let us realize that these two men could never, naturally speaking, meet each other without one of them ending up being seized and murdered. Which is to say that given the circumstance and situation of that day, these two men could not co-exist. And hence, in so many words, the response of Ananias to the Lord's instruction to go find Saul of Tarsus was this: "Lord, I cannot do what You have told me to do because that man has come here with the purpose of seizing all followers of the Way, and I will therefore be the very first one whom he will be seeking here in Damascus."

Nevertheless, the Man in glory said to His servant, "Go, for this man is My chosen vessel to bear My name among the Gentile nations and before kings and the children of Israel. Moreover, he shall suffer much for My name's sake." So, instead of relying on his logic and reasoning, Ananias trusted the Lord and went as he had been told.

Though these two men could not safely meet on earth under natural circumstances, the beautiful result in this scenario in the Spirit was that Ananias went into that house and laid his hands on Saul. Ananias identified himself with Saul, for he said, "Brother Saul." What a beautiful phrase that is! Heretofore, they had been enemies, but by the grace of God they were now brothers in Christ. "The Lord Jesus, who appeared to you on the road, sent me to you in order that you may see and be filled with the Holy Spirit." Immediately, scales as it were fell from Saul's eyes, and when Saul opened his eyes, what he first saw was a fellow brother in the Lord. So he remained with the disciples in

Damascus for a few days. And that is how Saul began his spiritual journey with the Lord.

The heavenly vision which Saul of Tarsus experienced was not only something tremendous, spectacular, glorious and very uplifting; it also had another aspect to it which was equally significant and essential. And that other aspect is most practical and very much down to earth. Because of that, Paul's entire life and ministry was for the building up of the body of Christ along that most practical line. He testified that he was willing to suffer that which is lacking of the afflictions of Christ in his flesh for the sake of the church, that is, for the sake of His body (Colossians 1:24). Paul's whole life and ministry was to build up the body of Christ, that vessel through which the risen, ascended Head is able to continue to do and to teach. But when he was performing that ministry, he was never independent; he was always related to someone. Even when he wrote his epistles he always had someone with him: Paul—and Timothy or Silas or Sosthenes.

Paul went back again and again to Jerusalem to seek for fellowship. Wherever he went he sought for fellowship. He was never an independent agent. The heavenly vision Paul received on the Damascus road and in Damascus was very real to him. It was worked out in his own life first, and because of that, Paul was able to be used of God to build up the body of Christ. Even towards the end of his life he could testify, as was noted earlier: "I was not disobedient to the heavenly vision" (Acts 26:19). Having seen the vision, it was henceforth a matter of obedience for Paul. And I would emphasize again that the vision not only included what was given him on the road to Damascus but also included what was given him within the city of Damascus. And thus those two parts of the vision formed a complete picture.

I therefore hope that in our tracing together today the formation of the body of Christ we have seen how God was leading his church into taking a heavenly, spiritual position through Stephen, then towards understanding her universal character through the ministry of Philip among the Samaritans, and finally through Paul, thus completing the heavenly pattern on earth of the body of Christ. All that, as is traced for us by Luke in the book of Acts, is what was happening during the formative years of the church, the body of Christ.

Dear Lord, we do praise and thank Thee that Thou art forming Thy body according to the heavenly pattern. Thou dost use various vessels to bring that body into the reality of that pattern. We thank Thee for these servants of Thine. We ask Thee, Lord, that we may see Thy pattern; that we may not only see it but we may experience it ourselves. And in seeing and experiencing it we may be able to be used by Thee for the furtherance of Thy purpose. Oh Lord, during these last days Thou dost desire to see Thy body—the church—fully grown, matured, so that Thou mayest come back and claim her as Thy bride. Oh Lord, great is the task! We humble ourselves before Thee and ask Thee to show us and to bring us into that practical experience of it and to use us for Thy eternal purpose. To Thee we give all the praise and the glory. In Thy name we pray. Amen.

Chapter Nine

Peter

Acts 9:43—And it came to pass that he [Peter] remained many days in Joppa with a certain Simon, a tanner.

Acts 10:1-48—But a certain man in Caesarea,—by name Cornelius, a centurion of the band called Italic, pious, and fearing God with all his house, both giving much alms to the people, and supplicating God continually,—saw plainly in a vision, about the ninth hour of the day, an angel of God coming unto him, and saying to him, Cornelius. But he, having fixed his eyes upon him, and become full of fear, said, What is it, Lord? And he said to him, Thy prayers and thine alms have gone up for a memorial before God. And now send men to Joppa and fetch Simon, who is surnamed Peter. He lodges with a certain Simon, a tanner, whose house is by the sea. And when the angel who was speaking to him had departed, having called two of his household and a pious soldier of those who were constantly with him, and related all things to them, he sent them to Joppa. And on the morrow, as these were journeying and drawing near to the city, Peter went up on the house to pray, about the sixth hour. And he became hungry and desired to eat. But as they were making ready an ecstasy came upon him: and he beholds the heaven opened, and a certain vessel descending, as a great sheet, bound by the four corners and let down to the earth; in which were all the quadrupeds and creeping things of the earth, and the fowls of the heaven. And there was a voice to him, Rise,

Peter, slay and eat. And Peter said, In no wise, Lord; for I have never eaten anything common or unclean. And there was a voice again the second time to him, What God has cleansed, do not thou make common. And this took place thrice, and the vessel was straightway taken up into heaven. And as Peter doubted in himself what the vision which he had seen might mean, behold also the men who were sent by Cornelius, having sought out the house of Simon, stood at the gate, and having called some one, they inquired if Simon who was surnamed Peter was lodged there. But as Peter continued pondering over the vision, the Spirit said to him, Behold, three men seek thee; but rise up, go down, and go with them, nothing doubting, because I have sent them. And Peter going down to the men said, Behold, I am he whom ye seek: what is the cause for which ye come? And they said, Cornelius, a centurion, a righteous man, and fearing God, and borne witness to by the whole nation of the Jews, has been divinely instructed by a holy angel to send for thee to his house, and hear words from thee. Having therefore invited them in, he lodged them. And on the morrow, rising up he went away with them, and certain of the brethren from Joppa went with him. And on the morrow they came to Caesarea. But Cornelius was looking for them, having called together his kinsmen and his intimate friends. And when Peter was now coming in, Cornelius met him, and falling down did him homage. But Peter made him rise, saying, Rise up: I myself also am a man. And he went in, talking with him, and found many gathered together. And he said to them, Ye know how it is unlawful for a Jew to be joined or come to one of a strange race, and to me God has shewn to call no man common or unclean. Wherefore also, having been sent for, I came without saying anything against it. I inquire therefore for what reason ye have sent for me. And Cornelius said, Four days ago I had been fasting unto this hour, and the ninth I was praying in my house, and lo, a man stood before me in bright clothing, and said, Cornelius, thy prayer has been heard, and thy alms have come in remembrance before God. Send therefore to Joppa and fetch Simon, who is surnamed Peter; he lodges in the house of Simon, a tanner, by the sea who when he is come will speak to thee. Immediately therefore I sent to thee, and thou hast well done in coming. Now therefore we are all present before God to hear all things that are commanded thee of God. And Peter opening his mouth said, Of a truth I perceive that God is no respecter of persons, but in every nation he that fears him and works righteousness is acceptable to him. The word which he sent to the sons of Israel, preaching peace by Jesus Christ, (he is Lord of all things,) ye know; the testimony which has spread through the whole of Judaea, beginning from Galilee after the baptism which John preached—Jesus who was of Nazareth: how God anointed him with the Holy Spirit and with power; who went through all quarters doing good, and healing all that were under the power of the devil, because God was with him. We also are witnesses of all things which he did both in the country of the Jews and in Jerusalem; whom they also slew, having hanged him on a cross. This man God raised up the third day and gave him to be openly seen, not of all the people, but of witnesses who were chosen before of God, us who have eaten and drunk with him after he arose from among the dead. And he commanded us to preach to the people, and to testify that he it is who was determinately appointed of God to be judge of living and dead. To him all the prophets bear witness that every one that believes on him will receive through his name remission of sins.

While Peter was yet speaking these words the Holy Spirit fell upon all those who were hearing the word. And the faithful of the circumcision were astonished, as many as came with Peter, that upon the nations also the gift of the Holy Spirit was poured out: for they heard them speaking with tongues and magnifying God. Then Peter answered, Can any one forbid water that these should not be baptised, who have received the Holy Spirit as we also did? And he commanded them to be baptised in the name of the Lord. Then they begged him to stay some days.

As we have come to see in our previous times of fellowship together, God raised up a few key persons through whom He was able to lead and direct the church, the body of Christ, to become the new wineskin as He had ordained. And that is what we continue to be interested in as we look further more closely into the book of Acts and other related Scriptures.

Earlier we had considered together concerning Stephen, Philip, and Paul. God first raised up Stephen, who pioneered the heavenly new way on earth. He saw that the church born on the day of Pentecost is not a part of Judaism but is a new creation, a new vessel—indeed a new wineskin. And because he was found courageously pioneering this truth, Stephen became the target of Judaism's fanatical persecution and became the church's first martyr. This truth was then furthered forward somewhat more by Philip in being used by God in joining the half-Jew, half-Gentile Samaritans with the full Jews. For centuries past there had been tremendous prejudice exhibited between these two, but through Philip and the two apostles who arrived on the scene of his gospel ministry, the Samaritans were joined to the Jews and the Jews to the Samaritans (Acts 8:5-17). Then God raised up a most unusual vessel in the person of Saul of Tarsus, later to become Paul the apostle to the Gentile nations. He had been the very symbol of strict Judaism, but God shattered his Judaism completely and used him as one of the great master builders of the body of Christ.

We come now today to the fourth key person, Simon Peter. Peter came to the Lord through his brother Andrew who was with John the Baptizer. And when Jesus passed by one day, John the Baptizer said of Him, "Behold, the Lamb of God." But when the next day John testified to this a second time as Jesus once more appeared, Andrew and his companion left John and followed Jesus. They stayed with the Lord that night, and the next morning Andrew went to find his brother Simon, to whom he reported, "We have found the Messiah."

So he brought Simon to Jesus and it was wonder, adoration and trust at first sight on the part of Simon towards the Lord. For when Jesus saw Simon and Simon saw the Lord, they did not merely cast a glance at each other, because the word in the Greek original and translated in the Gospel account as "Jesus looked carefully at him" meant a viewing or gazing carefully and thoroughly (John 1:42a). It was actually a mutual sizing up of each other. After carefully looking at Simon, Jesus said to him: "You are Simon, son of Jonah; you shall be called … Peter" (see John 1:29, 35-42 Darby and ASV).

And in the light of another passage elsewhere in Scripture we are assured that on this same occasion when Simon first met the Lord, he received a revelation of Jesus as the Messiah from the heavenly Father and that it was not by means of flesh and blood; for immediately after Simon had confessed to the Lord that He is the Messiah, the Son of the living God, Jesus responded to that by saying to him: "You are blessed, Simon son of Jonah, because this understanding of Me as the Christ did not have its source in flesh and blood but has been revealed to you by My Father in heaven" (see Matthew 16:15-17). Thank God for that revelation!

And according to another passage elsewhere in Scripture, Jesus made clear that this revealing by the Father to Simon concerning His Son was that which was well-pleasing in the Father's sight. In fact, added Jesus, "No one knows the Son but the Father, and no one knows the Father but the Son, and those to whom the Father or the Son is pleased to reveal Him" (see Matthew 11:25b-27). In other words, the Father is indeed the One who revealed the Son to Simon, enabling him to confess and declare to Jesus: "Oh, You are the Christ, the Son of the living God."

However, this revealing by the Father concerning His Son constituted only the first part of the revelation given Simon Peter during his first encounter with Jesus. There was a second and equally important part; and this was what the Son proceeded to reveal after the Father had revealed His Son to Simon. What, then, did the Son reveal to Simon Peter? It is what we are told in the very next verse of Matthew chapter 16 already cited: "I say to you that you are Peter [a living stone], and upon this Rock I will build my church and Hades' gates shall not prevail against it" (see v. 18).

Yet how is the foundation of the church to be laid, how can the church be built upon this Rock? Jesus revealed and explained from that moment forward how this was to be accomplished. Said the Lord to Peter and the other disciples: "I must go to Jerusalem, suffer many things there, and be killed; but on the third day thereafter I shall be raised from the dead" (see 16:21). What a tremendous revelation this second part was! It was as tremendous as the first part had been. The Father had revealed the Son to Peter and the Son had revealed His purpose in coming to the earth.

Why did the Son come to this world? He came to build His church. In order to build His church, however, He had to go to the cross because death and resurrection is the essential governing principle for building—not only for laying the foundation but also for building up the house of God. Did Peter understand? Did Peter "get it"? He "got" the first part, but he missed the second part. When the Lord Jesus said, "I will build My church upon this Rock, but I must suffer and die before that can happen," it went in Peter's one ear and out the other. What registered in his mind? All that registered was that it was going to be too costly. Said this disciple to his Master: "You have to go to Jerusalem and die? You do not need to do that!" So Peter took hold of the Lord physically and said, "Lord, do not do that. Be good to yourself; be kind to yourself" (cf. 16:22). This disciple was not ready for the cross, and because of that, he was not ready for the church.

It has often been said that if you preach the church you get the cross; and if you preach the cross you get the church. The Lord Jesus had revealed to Peter concerning the church, the body of Christ—meaning the new wineskin He is going to establish; but He made it clear that it has to come by the cross. However, at this time Peter rejected the cross; and therefore, the vision of the church evaporated in Peter's thinking. Consequently, he had to be tested beyond measure. For in a sense, when the Lord was crucified on the cross, Peter died with Him (cf. Romans 6:3-11; Galatians 2:20a), he having at that moment hit the bottom. For when Christ was standing trial just prior to going to the cross, Peter denied Him three times (Luke 22:54b-62). Having struck bottom, Peter went into death. Nevertheless, at the resurrection of the Lord, he too was raised from the dead (again, Romans 6:3-11). And on the day of Pentecost, God was able to use him as *the* spokesman, not only on behalf of the Head but also on behalf of the body (Acts 2:1, 14).

Peter's ministry was mainly centered among the Jews, he being an apostle to them. And he was very faithful. At the outset he moved exclusively among the Jews and nobody else. On one occasion he was sent to Samaria (Acts 8:14-17), that is true, but the Samaritans were partly Jews and therefore not completely Gentiles. So as was indicated previously, at the beginning, the church, the body of Christ, was composed mostly of Jewish believers. And even though some might not have been Jews, at least they were proselytes: they endorsed Judaism and were thus Judaized. For instance, the eunuch from Africa was most likely a Gentile proselyte who came to Jerusalem to worship; and hence he was connected with Judaism (Acts 8:27ff.).

Even the apostles at this early stage thought that the church, the body of Christ, was just part of Judaism, perhaps a reformed expression of Judaism. In fact, the Judaistic concept and character of God's house was very deep and strong in those early days. If anyone not a Jew wanted to be a believer, that person must become a Jew as well: he must be circumcised and become a Jew, and only then could he become a Christian (see, e.g., Acts 15:1, 5). They could not yet see that the body of Christ is the new wineskin; that it is different from any "ism." Because they could not see that at first, they thought that the church could only be composed of Jews and proselytes to Judaism. But God in His sovereignty began to move.

The movement of the Holy Spirit during this early period in church history is most fascinating. Had God told Peter in Jerusalem that He was going to send him eventually to the house of Cornelius, probably he would have behaved like Jonah, attempting to flee in the opposite direction from God's will (Jonah 1:1-3a). But He did not tell him anything. In fact, it appeared as though Peter was moved by God through various circumstances from one place to another until finally he was in Joppa. God had orchestrated Peter's movement in such a way that he ended up at Joppa (Acts 9:32-43) without his totally knowing why: God's purpose was to use this apostle to open the gospel to the Gentiles.

It needs to be understood that the Jews had nothing to do with the Gentiles. They were completely separated from them. They would not even enter the home of a Gentile. This was because they could not eat at the same table with a Gentile due to the requirements of the entire chapter 11 of the Old Testament book of Leviticus. God had there issued numerous ordinances to the Jews according to which there were certain things they could eat: the meat of animals God had deemed to be clean: creatures with split hooves and which also chew the cud. Animals which do not chew the cud or have split hooves were deemed by God to be unclean and therefore could not be eaten. What was the reason for that? Well, according to Leviticus 11, God had twice declared, "Ye shall be holy, for I am holy" (vv. 44a, 45b). That is the reason the Jews could only eat of the clean animals, fish and fowl and not of the unclean ones. Yet, throughout the Old Testament there is not any commandment to the Jews that they should not enter the house of a Gentile; no such commandment exists. The Jews became separated from the Gentiles completely only because they could not eat unclean food, as was enunciated in Leviticus 11.

This understanding is still true today among orthodox Jews, who cannot eat any food that is not kosher (Yiddish term from the Hebrew meaning that which is fit, proper, clean). Therefore, an orthodox Jew cannot enter any Gentile home and dine with that family because their food would not be kosher. It is mainly because of this matter of eating and the law governing what can and cannot be eaten which gradually caused the Jews to become completely separated from the Gentiles. And thus they considered themselves as clean and the Gentiles as unclean because the latter prepared and ate non-kosher foods. Jews could do business with Gentiles, but they could not enter their homes and eat at the same table.

Such was the implications of the Levitical law of cleanness and uncleanness. Now why did God give His people such a detailed ordinance of the Mosaic Law as outlined in Leviticus 11? God was preparing a people for the coming of Christ. And after Christ would come, then all various ordinances of the Law, especially the ceremonial law, would be fulfilled. With the coming of the reality (Christ) the typological shadow would necessarily pass away. Therefore, we read in Colossians 2:14: "Having effaced [blotted out] the handwriting in ordinances which stood out against us, which was contrary to us, he has taken it [the handwriting] also out of the way, having nailed it to the cross."

With the coming of the Lord Jesus He has blotted out the handwriting in ordinances which stood out against people. Some observers (as is found, for example, in the footnote of Darby's Bible translation) tell us that the meaning of the word handwriting here is an "obligation to which a man is subject by his signature." It is like a bond—a person signs his name under an above-stated obligation, thus indicating that that person is going to fulfill the obligation. When the Law of God was given on Mount Sinai, the children of Israel, as it were, signed their name, thus stating: "All that God has said, we will do" (Exodus 19:7-8, 24:3, 7; Deuteronomy 5:25-29, 26:16-18). And because they had signed their name, they were obligated to fulfill the Law. And if they did not fulfill the Law they were condemned. However, with the coming of Christ and His dying on the cross, He has blotted out the handwriting in ordinances that had stood against or had been hostile to people. Not only that, He has taken that handwriting of ordinances and laws out of the way, having nailed it to the cross.

Some people tell us that it was the custom in the olden days that when anyone signed an I.O.U. document, that paper was kept by the creditor until the debtor, obligated eventually to pay it back, would do so later. And on the day when the debtor did pay the debt, he received back the I.O.U. paper and would then hang it upon a doornail to demonstrate to everyone that the debt was now paid. This, therefore, is what has taken place with the coming of the Lord Jesus to the earth and His being crucified: He has taken, or removed, out of the way the handwriting of the ordinances of the Mosaic Law which had stood out against mankind by His having nailed that handwriting to the wooden beam of His cross. In other words, this particular I.O.U. has been taken away, it having been nailed to the cross of Calvary. And hence, mankind is no longer under the Law but, for those who believe in Jesus, are under God's grace. Or to explain the matter further by means of the New American Standard version of the Bible: When Christ came, He fulfilled the Law by His "having cancelled out the certificate of debt consisting of decrees against us and which was hostile to us; and He has taken it [the certificate of debt] out of the way, having nailed it to the cross." Especially have all the ceremonial ordinances found their fulfillment. Henceforth, it is the spirit, not the letter, of the Law which is to operate and govern in one's life.

Now it is very difficult for a Jew to accept that the Law has passed. All his life Peter had kept the Levitical Law of cleanness. Then one day God said to him—in a vision of a great sheet lowered from heaven containing both clean and unclean creatures—"Rise up, Peter, kill and eat" (Acts 10:11ff.). Was God contradicting himself? Usually our reaction would be to say, "Lord God, You say one thing at one time, but now you are saying the opposite thing. You have said in the past that we should not eat the meat of any unclean thing because You are holy and You want us to be holy; now, however, You say, 'Rise up, kill and eat' of both the clean and unclean things. You appear to be contradicting yourself." Do we not sometimes find ourselves in an apparent similar situation?

Thank God that He is the living God. The Law was given as a temporary emergency measure as the means of shutting us up to Christ; for when He came to the earth, these things of the Law were intended to recede and were replaced by Christ himself. It is not that God was contradicting himself but that there would come a time when He would henceforth work according to His permanent design. To separate the Jews from the Gentiles was God's temporary measure, but now that Christ has come, God was thereafter intent on bringing believing mankind into His permanent design.

Let us here recall what Paul wrote relevant to this intention of God's: "Now the promises [of God] were spoken to Abraham and to his seed. He does not say, 'And to seeds,' as referring to many, but rather to one, 'And to your seed,' that is, Christ" (Galatians 3:16 NASB). God's permanent design has always been that in and through this one seed—Christ Jesus—all the nations (i.e., the Gentiles) shall be blessed (Galatians 3:14a NASB). Nevertheless, how easy for human minds to hold onto the old—in this case the ceremonial ordinances of the Law, especially if a person bases that position of holding onto the old upon the fact that the old had come from God. Yes, the Law did emanate from God, but it has all been fulfilled in Christ. And as Paul's Letter to the Galatian believers further states, "… if you belong to Christ, then you are Abraham's [seed], heirs according to promise" (3:24 NASB).

Now Peter happened to be in Joppa where he stayed with a man named Simon, who was a tanner. A tanner is one who tans animal skins by applying any of several kinds of chemical mixtures to the skins for preserving or hardening them, and which are then used, among other purposes, for making wineskins; and in the process of this being done, the resultant odor can be terrible. Therefore, the local authorities did not allow a tanner to live in the city but he had to live outside the city; so he lived by the seashore where there was a good sea breeze and plenty of water. Simon Peter nonetheless stayed with this tanner.

As a matter of fact, when I was in Joppa, which today is called Haifa, I found that house. I went there because I remembered that the Bible mentioned Joppa and all the things which occurred there involving Peter. When I went to this city, nobody seemed to know where the place of Simon the tanner was located. I saw a great cathedral but that was not situated on what was once the tanner's house. However, nearby to that cathedral I saw a house with a sign on it—"Simon, the tanner's house." I do not know whether it was the original house or not, because this house has now gone commercial. You knock at the door, and when somebody comes, you have to pay an entrance fee. Upon entering the place one can see some dye urns. I went up the stairs to the roof that overlooks the sea where—if this is the original house—Peter had prayed. It is quite interesting, but there was nothing more to see.

Now at a certain point on this day when Peter had gone up onto the flat rooftop of the tanner's house to pray, it happened to be at about the sixth hour, that is, at about noontime; and he suddenly grew hungry and desired to eat. And it was while he was hungry and praying that God gave Peter the now famous vision, an ecstasy or trance having come upon him. Permit me to pause here to observe that no one ought to feel bad if one becomes, under certain circumstances, hungry while praying: such is quite natural. But I wonder, when you are hungry, can you pray? Probably when you pray and are hungry, you are thinking of food, and that was what Peter was doing. So as he was praying, and because he was hungry, he naturally thought of food, and the Lord gave him a vision remarkably appropriate for that moment.

Sometimes when the Lord reveals things, the revelation taking place comes quite naturally. You can hardly believe it, for you would normally think a revelation or vision has to be so spectacular and supernatural that it shocks you. However, very often a vision or revelation from God will simply come upon you when you least expect it—in the midst of the most common occurrence of things happening in your life.

Consider, for example, what happened to Moses. He was in the desert and saw one day a burning bush. That is a most common sight in the desert and happens every day; but because God was present, something was quite different about this particular common occurrence in Moses' life (Exodus 3:1-6). And now here Peter was praying and yet he was thinking of food because he was hungry—a quite common circumstance in anyone's life. So, as he was praying, he saw in a vision a vessel, but he could not exactly describe it. He said it was a vessel like a sheet coming down from heaven with its four corners tied. It was lowered down to earth far enough so that he could look and see inside the sheet. It was filled with all kinds of quadrupeds, creeping things and fowls, both clean and unclean, all mixed together. Then he heard a voice: "Peter, rise up, kill and eat." And he said, "No, Lord, I have never touched or eaten anything common or unclean." But the voice said, "What God has cleansed let no man make common." This happened three times, and three times Peter said, "No, Lord; no, Lord; no, Lord." Then the sheet was taken back up into heaven. Indisputably, that was a most dramatic vision.

Let us not forget that Peter had been an expert fisherman all his adult life up to the time of the Lord's call to him; yet in this vision he was not shown a net nor did he see any fish. God was here taking him out of his own familiar realm in order to show him that which was altogether new, because what God was wanting to teach him by means of this vision was far more than even preaching the glorious gospel of Christ. Yes, having become God's ministering servant, Peter was called by the Lord Jesus a "fisher of men" (Mark 1:16-17) whose work for God called for him to throw out the fisherman's net in preaching the gospel, closing the net full of souls, drawing them up out of the sea of this world's kingdom, and bringing those rescued souls into the kingdom of God. That in fact was the usual service this fisherman-apostle had been undertaking ever since, in particular, the day of Pentecost. Even so, God was now wanting to reveal to Peter something further by means of this remarkable vision.

Instead of the centerpiece of the vision being a familiar net being cast into the sea and gathering up fish, the centerpiece was a vessel like to a great sheet tied at its four corners and descending from heaven to the earth. And if one were to invert this vessel as it is being let down to earth, what will it appear like? Will it not appear to be a tent or tabernacle? And because it originates in heaven, it is that which, coming down to the earth, will rescue and gather up all the so-called clean and unclean souls and be taken back up into heaven. Is that not a vision of the church?

The church is not earthly in origin but heavenly, even as the apostle John reported what he saw revealed to him in an end-time vision: "I saw the holy city, new Jerusalem, coming down out of the heaven from God" (Revelation 21:2a). The church is a heavenly body, and according to God's original purpose and design that heavenly body came down from heaven. The church is not that which has its origination in man nor that which is organized by man, nor is she an invention of human ingenuity. No, the church, like the vision of the sheet, comes down from heaven from God and touches the earth. And why? For the purpose of cleansing and gathering together into the church both the clean and unclean of mankind. The church comes down from heaven and it will go back to heaven.

What, however, is the meaning which lies behind the word of God to Peter to "rise up, kill and eat"? It simply means this: Have fellowship. Eating together with others is an act of fellowship. Therefore, God was saying to Peter: "Have fellowship with that which is in the sheet; make no distinction." Peter's first, second and third response was: "No, I cannot. I am a Jew. I must keep a Levitical law, the ceremonial law of purity. I must observe that." But the Lord countered with these significant words: "What God has cleansed, let no man consider common." This refers not only to what the Levitical law said was *un*clean, but also to what that law said was clean. Both Jews and Gentiles are cleansed by the blood of Christ.

Levitically speaking, according to ceremonial law, the Jews are clean, the Gentiles are unclean. But in coming into the presence of God we are all unclean (Isaiah 64:6a). There is no difference whatsoever: All Jews must be cleansed by the blood of the Lord just as the Gentiles must, and they are; indeed, that is the argument to be found in Paul's Letter to the Galatians.

Even Jews are to be saved exactly like the Gentiles—saved not by works of law but by faith in the Lord Jesus (see chs. 2-3, esp. 2:16). What God has cleansed, let no man call unclean or common.

In his letter to the Ephesian believers, many if not most being Gentiles, Paul has described in the following manner the formation process in the making and the building up of the body of Christ without there being any distinction between Jew and Gentile:

> Therefore remember, that formerly you, the Gentiles in the flesh, who are called "Uncircumcision" by the so-called "Circumcision," which is performed in the flesh by human hands—remember that you were at that time separate from Christ, excluded from the commonwealth of Israel, and strangers to the covenants of promise, having no hope and without God in the world. But now in Christ Jesus you who formerly were far off have been brought near by the blood of Christ. For He Himself is our peace, who made both groups into one and broke down the barrier of the dividing wall, by abolishing in His flesh the enmity, which is the Law of commandments contained in ordinances, that in Himself He might make the two into one new man, thus establishing peace, and might reconcile them both in one body to God through the cross, by it having put to death the enmity. And He came and preached peace to you who were far away, and peace to those who were near; for through Him we both have our access in one Spirit to the Father. So then you are no longer strangers and aliens, but you are fellow citizens with the saints, and are of God's household, having been built upon the foundation of the apostles and prophets, Christ Jesus Himself being the corner stone, in whom the whole

> building, being fitted together is growing into a holy temple in the Lord; in whom you also are being built together into a dwelling of God in the Spirit (Ephesians 2:11-22 NASB).

What, then, is the church? Well, since the church is designed by God, she has her origin and roots in heaven. Moreover, the church includes all who are cleansed by the Lord, both Jews and Gentiles. Hence, the Lord said to Peter, "Have fellowship with all; make no distinction." But Peter said, "No, I want to have fellowship only with Jews. I want a Jewish church. Let the Gentiles have their own church." Despite Peter's objection, God's word declares that He has one sheet, not two sheets, that He has mixed both groups together inside the sheet—the church. Peter was so bound by the traditions, so bound by the Law, so bound by the past; he just could not at the beginning obey God's word in the vision even though he knew it was God who was talking to him and instructing him along a new path. Instead, Peter insisted: "No, Lord; no, Lord; no, Lord."

None of us should think that it is very easy to break away from tradition or to break away from the past; on the contrary, it is very difficult. It is very difficult to let the old pass and enter into the newness that is in Christ. God was leading Peter into the fullness of Christ and he found himself unable. Three times and the sheet was taken up into heaven. And at that very moment the messengers from Cornelius, the Roman centurion in the city of Caesarea, arrived at Simon the tanner's house door. They knocked at the door and said, "We are here to see a man, Simon surnamed Peter. Is he here?" Meanwhile, upon the rooftop Peter was pondering over the vision and what it meant. And as he continued pondering, God's Spirit said to Peter, "Go with those men who are seeking you downstairs, for I have sent them, and do not doubt."

So Peter went with those messengers to the house of Cornelius; and upon entering the home he said the following to all those gathered there with Cornelius: "You all know that it is not lawful for a Jew to associate or visit with a Gentile, but God has shown me not to call any person common (profane, unholy) or unclean. And that is why I came here without saying anything against it." Thank God that in the meantime Peter had had time during his final overnight lodging at the tanner's home and while traveling to Caesarea to reflect and to realize his error. And so, through Peter's preaching before all those gathered in this home, the gospel came to the Gentiles and the Holy Spirit sealed the matter with His approval; for the gift of the Holy Spirit was poured out upon the Gentiles also, because Peter and all those Jews who had accompanied him from Joppa heard these believing Gentiles speaking in tongues and magnifying God just as had happened with those Jewish believers back in Jerusalem on the day of Pentecost.

The body of Christ is a heavenly body, but it touches the earth. All the principles which govern the church are heavenly in character, but they are very practical in their outworking on earth. And one of the foundational principles is that in the church as the body of Christ, "there is no distinction between Greek and Hebrew, Jew or gentile, foreigner or savage, slave or free man. Christ is all that matters, for Christ lives in them all" (Colossians 3:11b Phillips). So if it is Christ, can anybody make any distinction? All such natural distinctions have all been effaced, erased, blotted out, nailed to the cross. There being no more I.O.U.'s, we are free in Christ to have fellowship with all brothers and sisters, regardless. Because the church is a new creation all the old discriminations and distinctions have been consigned to the cross. That is the church. And so God says to all of us who bear the name of Christian, "Rise up, kill and eat: have fellowship."

There is another aspect to what happened with Peter in Caesarea which is truly wonderful. Cornelius was a Roman army centurion who was the leader of a cohort or battalion whose name was Italic or Italian; which meant that all his soldiers were Italians who came from Rome; and they were garrisoned in the Judean seaside city of Caesarea some 30 or so miles north of Joppa. And though Cornelius was not a proselyte to Judaism, he, being a very pious man, admired the purity which he found in that religion. And thus he regularly practiced giving alms and praying much. Now regardless whether a person is a Jew or Gentile, if that person is truly seeking after God, He who knows the heart will in some way meet that person's spiritual need. And in this case God had an angel appear and speak to Cornelius in a vision.

However, the strangest thing is that God did not have the angel preach the gospel to him that he might be saved. Instead, God had the angel instruct Cornelius to send messengers to Joppa to have the apostle Peter come and tell him and his household how to be saved. Yet would we not look upon that way of handling the matter as being rather troublesome, awkward, or perhaps even inconvenient? But God never acts according to convenience or expediency but always according to principle. Had He had that angel preach, the angel might well have delivered a most perfect gospel message; nevertheless, his having no experience of salvation as would we human beings, the result would have been the emergence of a very orthodox church but without possessing life.

Another observation needs to be made regarding this matter of principle governing God's way of handling situations pertaining to the church. And here I would ask if anyone knows who was probably already in Caesarea and who could have easily been the one to evangelize these Gentiles? The great evangelist Philip was most likely present in Caesarea at this very time. For we read in two chapters earlier in Acts that "Philip was found at Azotus [some 25 miles south of Joppa], and passing through he announced the glad tidings to all the cities till he came to Caesarea" (Acts 8:40, cf. 21:8). Hence, if God had wanted Cornelius to hear the gospel, Philip was right there almost next door, as it were, to the centurion's home.

Why, then, not send Philip instead of having people sent on at least a two-days' journey to Joppa and fetch Peter, thus involving a minimum of four-days travel back and forth! This again points up what we humans would deem to be a strange, inconvenient and cumbersome way of handling this matter.

Yet God by His Spirit never acts in a certain way because it is convenient or most direct; He always acts according to principle. Philip was a highly experienced and proven evangelist greatly used by God. Most certainly, therefore, had the Spirit of the Lord God told him, "Go next door to Cornelius and present the gospel to him," Philip would have been most happy to do so. But no, God had Cornelius send two servants and a faithful soldier to Joppa to bring Peter to Caesarea. And why? It was for the purpose of ensuring that the oneness of the body of Christ would be maintained which body had first been formed by the Holy Spirit in that upper room in Jerusalem on the day of Pentecost.

We can ask the same question this way: Why did God use Peter to open the door to the Jews and use that same person to open the door to the Gentiles? It was to keep the unity of the body of Christ. Had He used Philip, probably there would have been a Gentile church established there. But no, regarding the formation of the body of Christ, we will notice how God in His word stresses again and again its oneness—that "in this new man of God's design" (Colossians 3:11a Phillips) there can be neither Jews nor Gentiles but that Christ is all and in all. Let us thank God that though Peter previously had been so prejudiced and bound by tradition, God was able to break through this apostle's obstinacy a great deal. Yes, he would later have a relapse in Antioch (Galatians 2:11-16); nevertheless, God did break through at Joppa/Caesarea and at the Jerusalem Council (Acts 15:7-11).

So we find that the Gentiles and the Jews were all baptized by one Spirit into one body, wherein there is neither Jew nor Gentile, but all have been made to drink of the one Spirit

(I Corinthians 12:13). That, then, is the church of God, the body of Christ, the one new man of God's design.

Our heavenly Father, we do worship Thee because Thy ways are always higher than our ways. Thy mind is always higher than our minds. How often we would act according to our way, thinking that we are wise; but Father, Thy ways are better. How we praise and thank Thee for preserving the nature of the oneness of the body of Christ. How we praise and thank Thee because Thou hast cleansed us in spite of what we are. And Thou hast made us one, and Thou dost desire that we fellowship one with another in the spirit of love. O Father, we do pray that this vision may not be lost to Thy people today so that Thy body may be that vessel specially designed and chosen to contain thyself and to express thyself. Father, we do worship Thee. Thou art great. In the name of our Lord Jesus. Amen.

Chapter Ten

Barnabas

Acts 9:26-27—And having arrived at Jerusalem he [Paul] essayed to join himself to the disciples, and all were afraid of him, not believing that he was a disciple. But Barnabas took him and brought him to the apostles, and related to them how he had seen the Lord in the way, and that he had spoken to him, and how in Damascus he had spoken boldly in the name of Jesus.

Acts 11:19-26—They then who had been scattered abroad through the tribulation that took place on the occasion of Stephen, passed through the country to Phoenicia and Cyprus and Antioch, speaking the word to no one but to Jews alone. But there were certain of them, Cyprians and Cyrenians, who entering into Antioch spoke to the Greeks also, announcing the glad tidings of the Lord Jesus. And the Lord's hand was with them, and a great number believed and turned to the Lord. And the report concerning them reached the ears of the [church] which was in Jerusalem, and they sent out Barnabas to go through as far as Antioch: who, having arrived and seeing the grace of God, rejoiced, and exhorted all with purpose of heart to abide with the Lord; for he was a good man and full of the Holy Spirit and of faith; and a large crowd of people were added to the Lord. And he went away to Tarsus to seek out Saul. And having found him, he brought him to Antioch. And so it was with them that for a whole year they were gathered together in the [church] and taught a large crowd: and the disciples were first called Christians in Antioch.

Acts 13:1-2—Now there were in Antioch, in the [church] which was there, prophets and teachers: Barnabas, and Simeon who was called Niger, and Lucius the Cyrenian, and Manaen, foster-brother of Herod the tetrarch, and Saul. And as they were ministering to the Lord and fasting, the Holy Spirit said, Separate me now Barnabas and Saul for the work to which I have called them.

The formative years of this new vessel called the body of Christ, the church, are very, very important years. Whether this new vessel would be formed according to the heavenly pattern and become a vessel fit for the Master's use or whether it would degenerate into something other than what God wanted depended very largely upon those formative years, as can be learned from Acts chapters 6 to 15.

But thank God, He raised up certain key men and used them to help in the formation of this body of Christ, thus finally achieving what He had wanted. We have mentioned several of those key men already: Stephen, Philip, Paul and Peter. This morning I would like for us to continue on to Barnabas, because this man had a very special place in the body's formation. He served as a kind of bridge, for it is not too much to say that he joined Peter and Paul together; and for that reason alone Barnabas had a very special ministry which contributed greatly to the formation of the body of Christ.

We see this man mentioned in Scripture for the first time in Acts 4, and during the period covered there regarding the early church's history God was increasing the number of those who had believed in the Lord; and all those who believed were together and were of one spirit and one soul. Moreover, they loved one another and were delivered from avarice and possessiveness; instead, they wanted to share everything of theirs with one another. They were truly one body. And it was during this same period that some of the members of the body realized that there were quite a few poor people in their midst—those who were in need. In noticing that a substantial number of their brothers and sisters were in need, they could not simply say to them, "May the Lord supply all your needs." Not so; to the contrary, these more well-off brethren felt constrained by the Lord to supply the needs of those needy saints. As a consequence, some of them began to sell their property and place the proceeds of those sales at the feet of the apostles for them to divide and distribute such to all who were in need.

Now numbered among these concerned brethren was one who stood out from the others and whom the Holy Spirit inspired Luke to mention by name. He was, of course, not the only one who performed this act of charity, but he was the only one the Holy Spirit mentioned in particular as an example. Here, then, was a man by the name of Joseph, a Levite, a Cyprian from the isle of Cyprus who now being a resident of Jerusalem sold his property and laid the proceeds at the feet of the apostles. And the apostles were moved to attach to him another name, that of Barnabas, which means "son of consolation," "son of encouragement," or "son of comfort." His former Jewish name was Joseph, which means "He will add," or "God will add." But that other name of his, Barnabas, meaning "son of encouragement" or "son of consolation," was most appropriate, as we shall soon discern.

This man was a Levite who had originally been born and reared on the eastern Mediterranean island of Cyprus, and so he was a Hellenistic and not a Hebrew Jew. In Barnabas was to be found the combination of not only the Greek or Gentile culture but also that of the Hebrews, and in that sense he was very much like Paul. He loved the Lord and expressed that fact not only in words but also in deeds such as that deed already mentioned of selling his property and giving the proceeds to the apostles for the needy among his Christian brethren in the body of Christ. He did all this in relatedness with the church, not independently.

Sometimes in doing good things we would rather do them independently. But in the early days of the church, as brethren were moved by the Spirit of God to do certain things, they never did anything independently. It was always in a spirit of relatedness to the church. Everything done—whether within or without the church—was in relationship to the church. Even in this matter of ministering to the poor, such action was always taken in relation to the church and not undertaken independently, as would have been the case had Barnabas, for example, divided and distributed the proceeds to the needy privately instead of it being done by the church leadership. Now that was something most beautiful and praiseworthy.

Now it will be recalled that before Saul of Tarsus was converted he was at Jerusalem where he became infamously well known as the chief persecutor of the church, dragging both men and women out of their homes and placing them in prison. Then he went to Damascus and was converted through his encounter with the risen, ascended Lord on the road there. Then, following his conversion Saul went off immediately to Arabia (Galatians 1:16b-17b), probably remaining there for some three years (Galatians 1:18a) where he was continually before God in coming to a fuller understanding of what had happened to him spiritually. After those years he went back again to Damascus and was with the saints there for a time (Galatians 1:17c); but because his witnessing was so effective, Saul could not stay in Damascus, he having to flee for his very life by being let down in a large basket which his fellow believers helped lower over the outside of the city's walls. And so he escaped (Acts 9:19b-25).

Saul next went to Jerusalem to seek out fellowship with the brethren there, but nobody believed that he had truly become a member of the Way. Even after three years the impression of him as a vengeful persecutor was just too deep. The believers in Jerusalem were afraid of Paul, who at that time was still called Saul. For though he had come back to Jerusalem a truly changed man, nobody believed him. Hence Saul of Tarsus was stuck in Jerusalem, rejected by the Jews, and not accepted by the believers. He as it were was all alone, and it must have been a terrible experience for him. But thank God, of all the disciples in Jerusalem there was one man among them whose heart was big enough to be moved by the Spirit to reach out to him in a ministry of encouragement and comfort.

Let us not forget that Barnabas was a Hellenistic Jew, and when persecution first broke out in Jerusalem it was actually focused mainly on the Hellenistic Jews, of whom Stephen was one of the most prominent, and he was stoned to death. Certainly Barnabas, who also was a Hellenistic Jew, was likewise a target; so he must have remembered Saul's persecution efforts against those of the Way quite well. Yet Barnabas was a man of such a big heart that he was able to forgive and to forget the past involving Saul's evil actions. He was able to discern what God had done in this persecutor's life, and so he was able to believe in what God had done. He had faith not only in God but in man too.

Sometimes it is very difficult for us to change our view of a person. Once you come to a conclusion, it becomes a settled opinion. Very often people will inquire of others: "Brother, what do you think of this brother or that sister, this man or that woman? Do you think there is any hope?" When you are trying to figure out a person, in the beginning you do not know exactly what kind of person he or she is, but then you have some contact, and you begin to form an idea, an opinion. And once your decision is made, it usually remains fixed. But do you believe God? Can you not believe He is able to change a person, to transform someone? If you believe in God, then you can believe in man; not that man can change himself but God can bring it about.

Do consider this: All the other disciples in Jerusalem could not believe that Saul could be changed. They probably thought it was merely another trick he was playing. He was simply trying to find out who these followers of the Way were by joining with them and then he would persecute them. Nobody would believe Saul had changed. But Barnabas was a man of faith with a big heart. He saw what God had done in that person, and so, at the risk of damaging his reputation, he took Saul in and introduced him to the leading brethren in Jerusalem (Acts 9:26-27). Saul met Peter, for example, through the introduction of Barnabas (cf. Acts 9:26-27 with Galatians 1:18). And hence, because of Barnabas's helpful intervention, Saul was able to be with the Jerusalem disciples for a certain period until his witnessing there became so strong once again that he had to leave the city and Judea as a whole. The church therefore sent Saul away, he returning to his native city, Tarsus, where he spent a number of years in Cilicia where Tarsus is situated and in Syria (Acts 21:39, Galatians 1:21).

Now the disciples in Jerusalem were widely dispersed elsewhere because of the great persecution which had broken out there as a result of Stephen's strong testimony; and as they traveled along the way elsewhere they ended up in such places as Phoenicia, Cyprus and Antioch. And as they went forth they announced the glad tidings, yet only to the Jews; but there were some among them who were Cyprians from Cyprus and Cyrenians from Cyrene in North Africa who, upon entering Antioch, began to witness also to the Gentiles, resulting in the Lord adding many of them to the church. Eventually the news began to be known in Jerusalem that in these Gentile cities many were converted to Christ, they being not only Jews but Gentiles. The brethren in Jerusalem decided to send forth one person to visit all these places, who turned out to be none other than Barnabas. The choice of this brother was most fitting for this kind of ministry. Having been sent forth as such, he ended up at Antioch. Did Barnabas go out as an investigator or inspector? Not at all! In the early church there was no thought at all of one church controlling another church. Jerusalem was not considered to be the mother church during this early period in church history, with all the other local churches being deemed to be "offspring" churches. That was a concept which came in much later.

In those early days, as the church began to spread to different places, every local church that was established maintained its independence in government; nevertheless, there was always carried on in those days the fellowship in the Spirit among all these local churches. Consequently, when the brethren in Jerusalem heard that God had done a good work in these different places, they sent Barnabas out to these new local assemblies which had sprung up, yet not with the purpose of investigating or inspecting and then bringing them under the control of the Jerusalem church. No! They sent Barnabas forth to seek for fellowship, that they all might be joined in one and to strengthen one another. God in His word never conveys the concept of there being a mother church and children churches. Never! What the Bible teaches is the concept of *sister* churches. The Scriptural basis for that is to be found in the little letter of II John verse 13, that letter being little in size but not in essence: "The children of thine elect sister greet thee."

The relationship between and among the churches is that of sisterhood. One local church is a sister to another local church. Some are bigger sisters, some are smaller sisters, but they all are nonetheless sisters to each other. It is not a relationship between parents and children, because if it were, then the parents would be in control and have rule over the children, with the children having to obey the parents. But if the relationship be that of sisterhood among these local churches, then their relationship is one of equality and of mutual fellowship. So in the formation of the body of Christ which is the church, we will find that the Holy Spirit is guiding and leading the way in the most practical expression of the church.

Having been sent out, Barnabas was the kind of person who, being a Hellenistic-Jewish believer and a "son of consolation," has a big heart; and so, he did not go forth to these places with the intention of overwhelming all these churches that God had raised up and bringing them into the fold of the church in Jerusalem. That would be the human way, not the divine way. The Holy Spirit had started all these churches, and then Barnabas was sent out to join all of them in fellowship with one another in the Spirit, but not to bring them under the control of the local church in Jerusalem.

The whole structure of the church today is unscriptural. Every local assembly is independent in the sense that she is governed directly by God. No one church governs another church, and yet they all are bound together in fellowship between and among them so that they really are one. The body of Christ is one universally, and yet in its practical outworking back then there were various local churches to be found here and there throughout the known world of that day. Even so, all these local churches were expressions of the body of Christ; therefore, they had fellowship one with another, and in doing so they demonstrated the fact that they were really one. And that is a most beautiful reality.

That, then, was the reason Barnabas was sent out, and as he traveled about he saw the grace of God manifested among the believers in these places. It is very easy for us, when going about visiting various local expressions of the body of Christ, to see all the faults and weaknesses and shortcomings. If we have a very keen ability to observe, we can go to any place and within a few hours, we can recognize the weaknesses and the faults in God's people. And if we are not careful, we could end up going there as a judge and not as a fellow brother. But Barnabas was such a man that when he went into the midst of these so-called Gentile believers, instead of noticing their weaknesses and their immaturity, and possibly looking down upon them and even judging them, he witnessed the grace of God in their midst (Acts 11:23).

Oh, how easy it is for us to view things negatively. We do not need to look too deeply to observe the negative things because they are all there for people to see. But it is very difficult for us to see that which is positive because our very nature is negatively oriented; our sinful nature is negative in character. But this brother, Barnabas, was full of the Holy Spirit. He was truly under the control of God's Spirit, so that when he came into the midst of these brethren in Antioch he harbored no thought of dominating them. He had no intention of judging them. He simply came as a fellow brother ready to help. Having seen the grace of God in their midst Barnabas rejoiced. He could rejoice in what God had done apart from himself and any other servant from the Jerusalem church. He therefore encouraged them to serve the Lord with one purpose and to abide in the Lord.

In other words, his ministry was that of establishing the believers. Barnabas was not too much of an evangelist; his gift was instead more like being a pastor. He would come in and help them, strengthen them, and establish them in the Lord. And because of his labors among these brethren in Antioch, the Lord added many more to the church there. It was a ministry of establishing the believers. How we need such a ministry in the churches today! And as he stayed over time with the Antiochan church brethren Barnabas began to realize the potential in this particular church. He came to realize that what God would be able to do in the church in Antioch was that which he could not do by himself. It was bigger and greater than he could handle; Barnabas therefore went to Tarsus to get Saul.

Now let us pause and consider for a few moments this that Barnabas did in seeking out Saul. Humanly speaking, it is quite often a temptation to servants of the Lord that if they should go to a place and God begins to use them, they would consider that as their kingdom. With the frequent result that here and there this servant of the Lord will carve out a kingdom for himself here and that servant of the Lord will carve out a kingdom for himself over there. Furthermore, such a servant will guard his kingdom very carefully; he considering the church as his personal property and prohibiting anybody else to touch it, saying: "This is my territory." That is the human temptation. And such a development happens in many places.

Each servant of the Lord needs to ask himself or herself this question: What am I building?—Am I building my own kingdom or am I building the body of Christ? As a missionary tactic the different missionary societies operating in various regions of the world have had to come to an agreement among themselves by dividing up a given region this way: "You go to the east, I will go to the west, he will go to the south, and the other will go to the north. We each will carve out a territory and work in it. You are not to come to my territory to work, and I am not to go to your territory to work." This is to keep peace. As God's servant, what are you building? Are you building your own kingdom or are you building the body of Christ? If it is the body of Christ you are building, know and acknowledge that it belongs to Christ. If it is the body of Christ you are building and not your own kingdom, then the local expression of the body of Christ should be allowed to benefit from all the ministries of God's servants whom He has bestowed upon the church.

Barnabas was a person who was not seeking his own gain. He did not come down to Antioch from Jerusalem to be a king in Antioch. On the contrary, acknowledging that what he was witnessing among the brethren in Antioch was verily another local expression of the church, the body of Christ, he realized that it had to be taken care of and helped. Furthermore, he recognized the growing potential in this Antiochan expression of the church; and in realizing that it was more than he could handle, he went forth in search of brother Saul. Thank God for Barnabas!

If God's servant can realize and acknowledge his limitation, that is something for which to be thankful. Barnabas was only thinking of the welfare of the church—he was not thinking of his position and power. Had he been thinking of his position he would never have gone to find Saul, because he knew from the very beginning that Saul was more gifted than he was. That is why he went to find Saul. He realized that this was a work which he could not handle by himself. He was able to establish the disciples in Antioch at the beginning, but he ultimately reached his limit. Yet Barnabas was determined not to confine the church in Antioch within the boundary of his limitations; rather, he wanted them to be what God wanted them to be. All the servants of God today should learn this lesson.

Barnabas therefore went forth to find Saul who by this time had relocated himself somewhere in Syria and Cilicia for a number of years already. For let us recall that because Saul could not remain in Jerusalem out of fear for his life, the brethren there had sent him away to his native area Tarsus (Acts 9:30); and hence, he was to spend quite a number of years thereafter in that area. In his Letter to the Galatians he had later written that he had spent some time in Cilicia and Syria laboring for the Lord (1:21). Moreover, those churches of Judea had only heard that the former persecutor was currently announcing the glad tidings where he now was situated but that he was still unknown by sight to them (1:22-23). In other words, Saul had been in that area for a number of years all alone, totally forgotten about up to this point. In fact, it has been estimated by one Bible commentator (Halley) that Saul had remained in and around the Tarsus area for some six or seven long years. And it is my belief that had this isolation continued for much longer, one of two eventualities would most likely have occurred. Either Paul would have gotten so discouraged that he would have given up, he concluding with the thought: "They sent me away from Jerusalem and there has been no more contact. I have been forgotten." Or he would have become so infuriated by the treatment he had received that he would have concluded with the notion by saying to himself: "All right, if you brethren in Jerusalem have no more concern for me, I shall have no further concern for you. I will establish God's work in my area and that will be my territory and my own kingdom. I shall have nothing more to do with the church in Jerusalem or with anybody else."

Saul could indeed have gone to either of these two extremes, for he was that kind of person. If he had not had someone to balance him (such as a Barnabas) he would have indeed gone to those extremes. But let us thank God, for in His divine wisdom Barnabas went forth to find him. Even so, in reading the relevant Scriptures more carefully one discovers that it took Barnabas some effort in looking for and finding Saul, who at this moment was back in his home city of Tarsus some 100 miles northwest from Antioch. It was not that he knew Saul was definitely in Tarsus, and so he simply went there and knocked at his door. Not so; he did not know specifically where Saul was, he had to find him. We can therefore see from this that Barnabas was willing to spend time and effort in finding where Saul was; and when at last he found him, he brought him to Antioch. There Saul labored with Barnabas for a whole year, and because of their much laboring together, something remarkable happened: the followers of the Way were for the very first time mentioned in Scripture as having been called Christians in Antioch.

Through the joint labor of these two servants of the Lord, the disciples of Jesus had grown so much in the Lord and the church was manifesting Christ in such fullness, that people of the world around, in noticing what was happening with these followers of Christ, wondered about them and saying among themselves: "Who are these people? They are certainly not part of Judaism because most of them are pure Gentiles." Let us recall that at the beginning most of the believers in Christ had been Jews, so the people of the world could understandably look upon the church as being just a sect of Judaism. But in

Antioch the situation was considerably different, in that here the disciples were mostly Gentiles. No one could reasonably say, therefore, that the church in Antioch was a sect or part of Judaism because she definitely had no part with Judaism. The church in Antioch was something entirely new.

And in attempting to explain what accounted for this that was new and totally different in these people, those people outside the church at least realized that it was because of the Person whom these church people followed. And so, in wondering what to call these ones in the church there, they coined the name Christian as their way of identifying who these people were. The outsiders therefore began saying, "They are Christians"—with the plural Latin suffix of the name, *ians*, meaning partisans of or followers of; and thus designating these church people as Christ-followers or Christ-ones. The character of Christ was so manifested in the midst of these brethren that they had earned that nickname of Christian. And it must be observed that these Christians were able to arrive at this level of spiritual growth mainly because of the love, the humility, and the labor of Barnabas.

We read in Colossians 2 that we are told to hold fast to the Head, "from whom the entire body, being supplied and held together by the joints and ligaments [or, bands], grows with a growth which is from God" (v. 19 NASB). We as members of the body of Christ are to hold fast to the Head who is Christ. And if we do that, then, just as in the human body, the whole body of Christ can be supplied and held together by its various joints and bands. We realize that the human body needs both: the joints being those parts which supply the blood, the very life of the body; and the body also needs bands because they hold all the parts of the body together. And thus, by means of those brethren in the body of Christ who are either joints of supply or bands of uniting, Christ's body, the church, can grow with that growth which is from God.

Now in the local expression of the body of Christ in Antioch one could look upon Barnabas as a ministering band, whereas Saul, who was probably greater in ministry, was a ministering joint; nevertheless, Barnabas could justifiably be said to be a great band. And without such bands the church's growth cannot be increased.

We often emphasize, do we not, the ministry of the joints in Christ's body, but for some reason we overlook the ministry of the bands. We mistakenly assume that for the building up of the body of Christ we only need people who are like joints and can supply Christ's life. We must certainly thank God for all the joints He provides. But there are church brethren who do not seem to provide much of the supplying and yet they are engaged in a quiet ministry of binding, joining, or uniting members of the body together. Such a ministry is just as essential as that of the joints in the church. Usually they are not seen, even perhaps overlooked by others; yet, without these more or less hidden bands, the body cannot properly reach its intended growth by God. But through both the bands and joints that were in the church at Antioch, she reached her fuller growth in God. And the result was that a wonderful testimony emerged there: the followers of the Way were now called Christians.

Now it is in this manner that the church, the body of Christ, is formed. It is by recognizing the need for, and encouraging such ministries—those of both joints and bands—that the body of Christ can grow and be built up. Wherever the church is to be established, wherever there is going to be the manifestation of body expression locally, joints and bands shall be necessary for growth in God. Saul and Barnabas are both needed.

With the passage of time God raised up five prophets and teachers in the church in Antioch. Barnabas was apparently the leading one since his name is mentioned first, and Saul was the last one of the five mentioned, since he was relatively young in the Lord—he was still learning. We are told that these five prophets and teachers were ministering to the Lord with fasting and praying. Before they ministered to the people of God in the church they first ministered to the Lord, and that is the right order. They ministered to the Lord's need first, and then to the church. And as they were ministering to the Lord, He said, "Set Me apart Barnabas and Saul for a special apostolic work to which I have called them." Because they had been faithfully ministering in the local church, God would next increase their ministry by giving them a wider ministry—even an apostolic ministry. And consequently God sent Barnabas and Paul out to undertake that apostolic ministry. We can see from this that the manner and place wherein God trains His servants is always in the local church.

Very often people will wonder, "If a person wants to serve God, what should he or she do?" Naturally, when young people have a desire to serve God, immediately they think of the distant place. That is natural because there is a sense of adventure in such a prospect. Indeed, you never think that you will serve God here at home. Young people—and even older ones—are generally thinking of serving God somewhere else. That is quite natural. And in order to serve God somewhere else, what should you do to train to be prepared? Answer: attend a Bible school; for where else is there to go?

Now I cannot criticize people who had opted to follow this choice because I did so myself. When I was saved, I was on fire, and I wanted to serve God. I asked myself, Where should I go? Distant Mongolia, of course! Certainly not in Shanghai, my native place. And how should I prepare myself to go to Mongolia to serve? Of course, I should attend a Bible school. Yet, according to Scripture, where can a potential servant of God be trained?

From a careful perusal of both New and Old Testaments one clearly gains an understanding of where and how God had trained His future workers during Biblical times: it was where these prospective servants were spiritually raised up. If God puts a desire in you to serve, the church where you are is the training ground. It is not a school; it is the church, the body of Christ. There is no school where you can better learn Christ and learn how to serve Him than in the local expression of the body of Christ. You may counter by observing that everybody knows you there. And I would respond by saying, Thank God that everybody knows you. That is the very circumstance where the training ought to begin. And if you are faithful in the place where God has put you, and you minister to the Lord, one day He will say, "Set Me apart; and then go out." And thus you are able to enter into a larger and wider ministry. But it should always begin in the place where you are.

If you cannot be used by God among the people where you are, how can you expect to suddenly be able to be greatly used by God among the people whom you do not know? Many would-be servants of God state that they cannot win any souls here, but if they should be called to go, for example, to Africa, they believe they will suddenly be able to win many souls to the Lord. No, your calling has to be proven here first, and out of faithfulness shown here first God will enlarge your ministry for elsewhere.

So Barnabas and Saul were set apart to go forth in wider service to God. Barnabas was such a man of big heart that he was always trying to help people. He was always looking out for those he could encourage and help build up. He did that to Saul. Without Barnabas we would not have had Paul. Though God had revealed himself in such a dramatic way to Saul, without Barnabas, Saul who later became the great apostle Paul would have been lost. It was Barnabas who had brought him to the fellowship of the saints back in Jerusalem (Acts 9:26-27); and it was also Barnabas who brought him into the work at Antioch. In fact, Saul was actually trained under him. Barnabas had always had his eye on Saul, for it was after several years following Saul's conversion that Barnabas met Saul for the first time in Jerusalem, where they were together for a period of perhaps two years; and then after several years more Barnabas still remembered him. Saul was still a relatively young man who was very promising, and hence, Barnabas sought to help him and build him up to be someone greater than he himself was.

Now when God set Barnabas and Saul apart for an apostolic work, immediately Barnabas set his eyes on another young man, his cousin John Mark (Colossians 4:10b). However, it was not because John Mark was his cousin, for I believe that Barnabas was mature enough in the Lord not to let fleshly considerations enter into the work. He was much better than that. Barnabas realized that in the work of God fleshly relationships must not be allowed to enter in. No, it was simply the fact that the big heart of Barnabas was continually on the lookout for those young people whom he could assist in building up to be a fit vessel for God to use. And for this trait in Barnabas we need to give God thanks.

This is what the church is in great need of today. There are young people who really have a desire to serve God and who truly want to learn. Yet who will help them? Who remembers them? Probably the older brethren are afraid of the young people out of fear that perhaps one day those young people will destroy them. But not Barnabas. Whenever he saw the grace of God in a person he sought to help and build that one up. He therefore set his eyes on his cousin, John surnamed Mark (Acts 12:12b), and Saul agreed with him (Acts 12:25). And because Saul agreed, we can be fairly confident that Barnabas's suggestion that his cousin accompany them was not put forth due to a fleshly relationship. Accordingly, these three went forth together to the work (Acts 13:5b).

Now it is important to notice that the Holy Spirit through Luke's narrative concerning this first apostolic journey out from Antioch made it clear at its beginning that Barnabas was the leader of this team of three. For recall that the Holy Spirit had said, "Separate me now Barnabas and Saul for the work …" And so these three—Barnabas and Saul, with John Mark serving them as their attendant—had gone out as a company.

And the Holy Spirit, again through Luke's narrative, continued to say, "Barnabas and Saul," for instance in Acts 13, verse 7. However, two verses later we read these words: "Saul, who also is Paul …" And by the time of verse 13, instead of the account stating that it was Barnabas and his company, Luke's narrative reads this way: "Paul and his company came to Perga …," thus indicative of the fact that the leadership had changed. But that very same verse also adds this: "… and John [Mark] separated from them and returned to Jerusalem." It is my belief that the reason John Mark left this apostolic company was because he could not agree to the fact that his cousin was no longer the leader, that at this point in his young life John Mark was, spiritually speaking, still a person full of the flesh.

Let us now, though, consider Barnabas. Did he utter any word of disagreement, did he object saying, "I'm the leader leading this team"? Not at all; instead, Barnabas yielded to the dictate of the Holy Spirit. None of us in Christ has any fixed position in the work to which we have been called, since it is the Holy Spirit who determines who should be in the lead and who should follow. Yes, at the beginning the order was, Barnabas and Saul; but then, Saul who has now become Paul had apparently gone ahead spiritually; and in recognizing this, the Holy Spirit, once again through Luke, now said, "Paul and Barnabas" (e.g., in Acts 13:43, 46, 50, etc.). And Barnabas gladly assumed the secondary place in the apostolic team, whereas the young brother John Mark, disappointed and offended, departed from the work and returned home.

On the other hand, Barnabas continued on with Paul who was now more prominent than his associate: people recognized Paul, heard Paul, talked with Paul, and talked about Paul. The consequence of which Barnabas was henceforth under the shadow of Paul; yet he accepted all of this graciously as though nothing had happened. Such was the mark of humility in this man of God.

Oh, how I long to see something like this today among God's servants! Very often they strive for position and for prominence against one another. That is like those who strive for authority and power in this world. It is sad. If we only knew how to really surrender ourselves to the Head, and that whatever the Head says, that is where we should want to be, even if humanly speaking it may be difficult and humiliating. Yet let us be willing to be like Barnabas, who was not at all seeking to undermine Paul's position but who was supporting Paul's ministry. Nowhere in Scripture is there the slightest indication that Barnabas was outwardly going along with Paul's position and ministry but that secretly he had sought to undercut Paul in any way. On the contrary, Barnabas fully supported Paul with his whole heart as "a true son of encouragement." That is the kind of man Barnabas was.

It is true that when Paul and Barnabas were considering to go forth on a second apostolic journey, Barnabas had proposed taking John Mark with them once more (Acts 15:36-37). After this young man had abandoned the apostolic work the first time and had returned home to Jerusalem, somehow, most likely through the ministry of the apostle Peter (cf. I Peter 5:13), he had been restored to such an extent that Barnabas and Paul had apparently brought John Mark with them back to Antioch following their attendance at the Jerusalem Council of the church as discussed by Luke in Acts 15. (This bringing him back to Antioch again can be fairly confidently assumed from the fact that verse 37 there presumably meant that John Mark was already present in Antioch at the time when Paul proposed to Barnabas for them to go on the second apostolic journey.)

However, after the two of them decided to go on their second journey, Barnabas, being the man of such a big heart, proposed that they take John Mark with them again. By this one can conclude that Barnabas had forgotten the young man's previous fault completely. He believed there was still much spiritual promise in his cousin. Having seen the partial restoration of John Mark through Peter's ministry, Barnabas was probably anxious to see a full restoration of this young man; and hence, he proposed to Paul that they take John Mark with them once more. Paul, though, vigorously objected, he believing that their former attendant needed to be disciplined further by having him remain with the church in Antioch. Consequently, a sharp disagreement ensued between these two apostles of the Lord. It resulted in Barnabas taking John Mark with him on a journey to Cyprus, whereas Paul, having chosen Silas, went forth, having been "committed by the Antiochan brethren to the grace of God" (see Acts 15:40-41), after which these two traveled together to many places strengthening the churches in Syria, Cilicia, Galatia, and elsewhere in Asia Minor.

Today, we are often asked this question: "Who was right and who was wrong?" These two servants of God had labored together in the work of God and were so blessed; but then, they had clashed to such an extent that they could not be reconciled. They each had to go his own way. In attempting to judge the right and wrong side of this incident, people have usually concluded as follows: "Of course, Barnabas was wrong because after this, neither he nor what he did is any longer mentioned in Scripture. Indeed, the narrative concerning the history of the early church from now on centers upon Paul. Barnabas fades away." True, we do not know what happened to Barnabas after he took John Mark with him to Cyprus. The Scriptures are totally silent, as though, say these same people, the Holy Spirit had declared that Barnabas had "gone off the rails" whereas the church had thenceforth exclusively backed Paul and the Lord had continued to use him everywhere he went. Accordingly, these people have concluded that Paul must have been right and Barnabas wrong.

However, I do not believe that God judges that way. Yes, it would seem as though in this decision of his Barnabas had taken a wrong turn; but if this servant of the Lord had his faults, in this instance it was the fault of possessing an immense generosity due to his having such a big heart. In this respect, Barnabas failed; his heart was too big.

I would have to say that probably both these servants of God were *right*. For we see the sovereign wisdom of God being played out here, in that though Barnabas seemed to have faded away, it was through his continued generous help that John Mark was perfected. For even the apostle Paul would later acknowledge, concerning this younger man, that "he is very helpful to me in my ministry" (II Timothy 4:11b NIV). And God could even put His seal of approval on John Mark in his having been allowed to write the second of the four Gospels which appear in the New Testament: the Gospel according to Mark.

Hence, it would appear that Barnabas died that Mark might live. It was a ministry of love on the part of Barnabas. Therefore, who are we to judge? Barnabas may have been wrong, but if so, it was due to the fault of having a big heart. And in one sense it could possibly be said that God appeared to have overlooked that fault of his, for He still used Barnabas to perfect this young man John Mark.

This is how the body of Christ is to be formed: through the dying of Jesus in one person there emerges the manifestation of the life of Jesus in another person (II Corinthians 4:10). And when that happens, no one can judge anymore. Without the encouragement and help of Barnabas there would probably not have been the great apostle Paul who besides his monumental apostolic work among the Gentile nations of his day, authored 13 of the 27 New Testament books of the Bible. And, again, without Barnabas taking a risk and graciously granting John Mark a second chance, thus restoring him fully to useful ministry (II Timothy 4:11), there would probably have never been the Gospel according to Mark. I think one day when we all appear before the judgment seat of Christ (II Corinthians 5:10a), we will have a different view about Barnabas. I know that not many people have a very high opinion of him, but I wonder whether one day we will alter our opinion about him. He was a true man of God and he had a very special place in the building up of the body of Christ. In fact, Barnabas was a very important bridge. He faded away but the church went on. We therefore need to ask God to raise up not only more Pauls but also more Barnabases. We need them both.

Our heavenly Father, how we praise and thank Thee for the variety of Thy servants whom Thou dost give to Thy church in order that Thy church may be built according to Thy divine design. We thank Thee for Paul; we thank Thee for Barnabas. We pray that there may be many joints of supply and many bands of uniting, so that the body may increase with the increase of God. Oh Father, this is the vessel which Thou art looking for, and we want Thee to have it, so that the Head—even Christ Jesus—may be able to continue to do and to teach. We pray in the name of the Lord Jesus. Amen.

Chapter Eleven

James

Acts 15:1-35—And certain persons, having come down from Judaea, taught the brethren, If ye shall not have been circumcised according to the custom of Moses, ye cannot be saved. A commotion therefore having taken place, and no small discussion on the part of Paul and Barnabas against them, they arranged that Paul and Barnabas, and certain others from amongst them, should go up to Jerusalem to the apostles and elders about this question. They therefore, having been set on their way by the [church], passed through Phoenicia and Samaria, relating the conversion of those of the nations. And they caused great joy to all the brethren. And being arrived at Jerusalem, they were received by the [church], and the apostles, and the elders, and related all that God had wrought with them. And some of those who were of the sect of the Pharisees, who believed, rose up from among them, saying that they ought to circumcise them and enjoin them to keep the law of Moses. And the apostles and the elders were gathered together to see about this matter. And much discussion having taken place, Peter, standing up, said to them, Brethren, ye know that from the earliest days God amongst you chose that the nations by my mouth should hear the word of the glad tidings and believe. And the heart-knowing God bore them witness, giving them the Holy Spirit as to us also, and put no difference between us and them, having purified their hearts by faith. Now therefore why tempt ye God, by putting a yoke upon the neck of the disciples, which neither our fathers nor we have been able to bear? But we believe that we shall be saved by the grace of the Lord Jesus, in the same manner as they also. And all the multitude kept silence and listened to Barnabas and Paul relating all the signs and wonders which God had wrought among the nations by them. And after they had held their peace, James answered, saying, Brethren, listen to me: Simon has related how God first visited to take out of the nations a people for his name. And with this agree the words of the prophets; as it is written: After these things I will return, and will rebuild the tabernacle of David which is fallen, and will rebuild its ruins, and will set it up, so that the residue of men may seek out the Lord, and all the nations on whom my name is invoked, saith the Lord, who does these things known from eternity. Wherefore I judge, not to trouble those who from the nations turn to God; but to write to them to abstain from pollutions of idols, and from fornication, and from what is strangled, and from blood. For Moses, from generations of old, has in every city those who preach him, being read in the synagogues every Sabbath.

Then it seemed good to the apostles and to the elders, with the whole [church], to send chosen men from among them with Paul and Barnabas to Antioch, Judas called Barsabas and Silas, leading men among the brethren, having by their hand written thus: The apostles, and the elders, and the brethren, to the brethren who are from among the nations at Antioch, and in Syria and Cilicia, greeting: Inasmuch as we have heard that some who went out from amongst us have troubled you by words, upsetting your souls, saying that ye must be circumcised and keep the law; to whom we

> gave no commandment; it seemed good to us, having arrived at a common judgment, to send chosen men to you with our beloved Barnabas and Paul, men who have given up their lives for the name of our Lord Jesus Christ. We have therefore sent Judas and Silas, who themselves also will tell you by word of mouth the same things. For it has seemed good to the Holy Spirit and to us to lay upon you no greater burden than these necessary things: to abstain from things sacrificed to idols, and from blood, and from what is strangled, and from fornication; keeping yourselves from which ye will do well. Farewell. They therefore, being let go, came to Antioch, and having gathered the multitude delivered to them the epistle. And having read it, they rejoiced at the consolation. And Judas and Silas, being themselves also prophets, exhorted the brethren with much discourse, and strengthened them. And having passed some time there, they were let go in peace from the brethren to those who sent them. And Paul and Barnabas stayed in Antioch, teaching and announcing the glad tidings, with many others also, of the word of the Lord.

As was pointed out previously chapters 6 through 15 of Acts constitute a record of the formative years of the body of Christ. On the day of Pentecost Christ's mystical corporate body came into being and then it commenced being formed gradually according to the divine design. And in that formative process the body of Christ went through a period of conflict which resulted in the emergence at last of that new vessel fit for the Master's use (cf. II Timothy 2:21b ASV). We may describe that period of conflict as one in which the body of Christ, the church, experienced the pains of growth. Yet through those many pains of growth that new vessel had finally come into its proper form.

Now during this period of painful conflict God raised up a few key men to help direct this formation according to the heavenly pattern. One of them was Stephen, who was indisputably the pioneer of the heavenly way. Through Stephen the church as the body of Christ began to break away from Judaism. During the brief time prior to Stephen's martyrdom people had viewed the church as simply one of several sects in Judaism. But Stephen was one who had vision. He spearheaded, as it were, the break away of this new vessel—the church—from Judaism.

This was further brought forward by Philip, because through his ministry the Samaritans were brought into the church. For centuries past there had been few, if any, relations between the Jews and the Samaritans. On the day of Pentecost when the church was initially formed, she was composed mainly of believing Jews and a few Gentile converts to Judaism who had also believed in Christ. To both the unbelieving Jews and even the believing Jews in the church, the Gentiles had no part in the grace and blessing of God. And hence, the Samaritans, who were of half Jew-half Gentile ethnicity, were despised by the pure Jews. Nevertheless, through the ministry of Philip the Samaritans were brought to a saving knowledge of Christ. However, the Head of the body of Christ purposely withheld the gift of the Holy Spirit from these converts until the two apostles, Peter and John, came over to Samaria where Philip was and laid hands upon these new believers. Then they were filled with the Holy Spirit. Why this delay? It was because in the formation of this body of Christ there would only be one body. And in that one body both the Jews and the Samaritans were to be joined into one. Objectively speaking, the prejudice against each other had been eliminated by the cross; and now the Holy Spirit—in effecting the subjective reality—brought these two opposing groups of people together into one body: a further and significant move away from narrow, exclusive Judaism.

After Philip came Paul, the master builder. Paul was a symbol of the strictest Judaism, but God shattered his Judaism completely. The master Potter made him into a new vessel for the building up of the body of Christ. Indeed, Paul stands as a very special vessel appointed by God.

Then there was Peter, the noteworthy apostle to the Jews; and yet God used him to open the door to the Gentiles. Most likely, Philip was in Caesarea when God sent His angel to Cornelius. But God set aside Philip, as it were, and said through His angel to this Roman centurion: "You must send messengers to Joppa and fetch Peter here to tell you how to be saved." And why this cumbersome action rather than using Philip nearby? Once again, it was for the purpose of preserving the oneness of the body of Christ. Otherwise, there would have emerged a Jewish church and a Gentile church. Because of utilizing Peter instead of Philip, the church remained one in her expression of the oneness of the body of Christ.

After Peter there was Barnabas. Barnabas was a man with a big heart, and he was sent out from the church brethren in Jerusalem to visit the new local churches that had only recently come into being in the cities of Syria and Cilicia. And when he came to Syrian Antioch, he witnessed the grace of God manifested among the brethren in the church there, and so he rejoiced in what he saw. He encouraged the brothers and sisters to go on with the Lord. But seeing that the work there was so extensive, he went forth to find Saul and brought him to Antioch. These two labored together for an entire year, resulting in the church being established there to such a degree that the disciples of Christ were first called Christians at Antioch.

We now come to the last person which I would like for us to focus our attention upon—James. It seems very odd that James should be the one used by God to finalize the formation of the body of Christ according to the heavenly pattern. Who was James? This James was not one of the two sons of Zebedee, both of whom—James and John—were numbered among

Jesus' original twelve disciples. The James who was the brother of John, sons of Zebedee, had been beheaded by King Herod (Acts 12:1-2).

Then who was this James whom we find prominently mentioned in Acts 15? He was none other than the flesh-and-blood brother of the Lord Jesus. In Matthew 13 it is intimated that after Mary had given birth to Christ through the overshadowing of the Holy Spirit, she begat by natural means four sons and a number of daughters. Those sons' names were: James, Joseph, Simon, and Judas (or Jude). Thus the James of Acts 15 was a brother of the Lord Jesus according to the flesh.

We do not know how true it is, but tradition tells us that this James, the son of Joseph and Mary, became a Nazarite. According to Numbers 6, if anyone wants to serve God, he can set himself apart as a Nazarite; that is to say, one who is separated or consecrated to serve the Lord. We are told by tradition that James was a Nazarite from his childhood and set apart to serve God. He was a most righteous person who lived a very godly life. Moreover, James was deeply rooted in Judaism and in the tradition of the Hebrew fathers. It is also believed from tradition that he prayed so much that his two knees began to develop calluses like a camel's knees. And he was deemed to be such a righteous person that even though he was not of the family of Aaron, he was allowed to enter the temple and pray. James was a man greatly admired by the Jews in his time, a most righteous person according to the Law.

But this brother of Jesus was so deeply rooted in Judaism and so brainwashed in the traditions of the fathers that he assumed the same position towards his brother in the flesh, Jesus, as had the Pharisees and the scribes of his time. In fact, he did not believe in the Lord Jesus at all. James grew up with the Lord and must have observed everything about Him; and thus he should have been the first one to notice the uniqueness of this Man who was his brother. Most certainly he should have; yet strange to say, he apparently was totally blind to Jesus' unique character. On the one hand, James might have noticed in the life of his brother something unique and unearthly; on the other hand, because he was so deeply indoctrinated in the religion of Judaism, he could not help adopting the position of looking at his brother as nothing but an impostor.

During the life of the Lord Jesus there was no indication that James believed in Him. On the contrary, one day just prior to the Feast of Tabernacles Jesus' several brothers spoke to Him in the following manner: "If you want to be known by people and become famous, don't hide yourself here in the hilly country of Nazareth but go to Judea where the important people are and show yourself to them." The Lord, however, countered with these words: "The time for you to go up to the Feast is always ready, but My time is not yet come" (see John 7:1-9).

Who were these brothers who mocked Jesus in such a way? For they were actually ridiculing and mocking Him, since they did not believe on Him (John 7:5). Certainly, James was one of them who mocked and ridiculed the Lord here. Indeed, we have absolutely no evidence that during Jesus' lifetime James ever believed.

Oddly enough, however, with the death of Jesus in crucifixion, it would appear as though a change came over James. We do not know if James was at Calvary when the Lord was crucified, but he must have heard what happened there with his brother. At the same time, he who was greatly devoted to the temple must have heard that the veil which had separated the holiest of all from the holy place was rent in two from top to bottom at the death of Jesus (Matthew 27:51a).

We may speculate, but probably the death of his brother in such a cruel manner sealed James's conviction that had most likely been buried down deep within him by the immense weight of tradition all those years. Such a righteous person as James was could not have failed to notice even to the slightest degree something praiseworthy in the life of his brother and to have been touched by it, if even but slightly. There must therefore have been some degree of conviction going on in this man; nevertheless, because James was so deeply grounded in tradition, he could not free himself from that tradition's hold on him. Even so, though he was bound, the conviction was nonetheless there. Hence, upon his hearing of the death of his brother Jesus and what happened with the veil in the temple, it was as though God were saying to him: "This is the Messiah; this is the One you have been waiting for and expecting. It is through Him that the new and living way is opened to God beyond the veil." So most likely Jesus' death sealed that hidden conviction in James and turned him around. In fact, that was perhaps the very reason why, after the Lord was resurrected, that He appeared to James, and did so privately.

We learn of this from I Corinthians 15. We are told there that the risen Lord purposely appeared to James, His brother in the flesh, alone (v.7a). He needed it. Throughout his life James had rejected his brother. After His death, however, James now knew that his brother is the very Son of God, Christ the Messiah, and that he sincerely believed on Him. James probably had wondered whether his brother would ever forgive him, whether Jesus would ever accept him. Consequently, James needed an assurance from the Lord. And, of course, the Lord knew this, and so the risen Lord appeared to him privately. Ever since that time, James would be listed among the believers.

After the Lord's ascension back to heaven those 500 disciples who had witnessed it outside Jerusalem went back to the city. The Lord had told them to wait there until they had received power from on high, then they would be His witnesses from Jerusalem to Judea to Samaria and to the end of the earth (Acts 1:1-8). The brothers and sisters went back to Jerusalem and after ten days only 120 of the 500 were left (v.15b). Among those 120 brethren were the twelve apostles (including now Matthias), the mother of Jesus, some women, and the brothers of the Lord Jesus. Not only did James believe in the Lord but his other brothers had come to the Lord as well, probably through the influence of James (vv. 13-14). Let us not overlook the fact that there would ultimately be two books of the New Testament which were authored by two of the Lord's brothers in the flesh: the Epistle of James and the Epistle of Jude.

From this, then, we see that James was with the 120 believers at the very beginning; and when they were all baptized into one body, James was one of the members of the body of Christ. And though he was not listed among the twelve apostles, nevertheless he would in time become an apostle himself (Galatians 1:19).

When the persecution began after Stephen was stoned to death, the disciples began to be scattered, but the apostles remained in Jerusalem. Now some people have wondered, "Why was it that when the persecution came to the church in Jerusalem, the disciples were scattered but the apostles remained behind?" One reason is that when the persecution broke out, the target had not been the Hebrew Jews but the Hellenistic Jews. The church in Jerusalem was composed of those two classes of Jews, and Stephen himself had been a Hellenistic Jew. The initial perpetrators of the persecution were those members of the synagogue of the Hellenistic Jews (Acts 6:9 ff.), so when the persecution first came upon the church in Jerusalem, their target was mainly the Hellenistic Jews. And when they were persecuted, they were widely scattered and went back to their original homes in Judea, Samaria, Cilicia, Syria and Asia Minor. But the twelve apostles, all of them being Hebrew Jews, were not the main target of persecution, so they remained behind (Acts 8:1b).

After the persecution began to increase, Saul entered the scene and was indiscriminate in his evil conduct towards the disciples. He went into the homes of both Hellenistic and Hebrew Jews equally and brought out both men and women and delivered them up to imprisonment (Acts 8:3). With the scattering of so many Hellenistic Jewish believers elsewhere, this meant that the Hebrew Jewish believers increased their majority even more than before in the Jerusalem church. And quite naturally, during that period of persecution the church was in need of some brethren who would be very firm, steady, strong, deeply rooted and solid, and who could thus stand and lead.

Was Peter such a person? I very much doubt that, since he was one who changed too easily. During this time of persecution, had Peter been the leading brother in the church in Jerusalem, one can hardly imagine the church being able to stand strong, firm and steady against the persecution. During this time of persecution, it would appear that James, the brother of Jesus, began to be manifested as the leading brother in the Jerusalem church. On the day of Pentecost and during the initial period immediately thereafter, Peter seemed to be the leading brother. Of course there were other leaders, but Peter seemed initially to be at the front leading. However, during and after the persecution it was James who led because he was a very solid brother. The church needs people like James who are solid in Christ, and the church also needs brethren who have spiritual stature. We are told that James was not only loved by the believers in Jerusalem but he was admired by the unbelieving Jews in Jerusalem as well. He had a very good testimony and could be used by God to lead the church in Jerusalem in standing against the persecution. Hence, that was probably one of the reasons why James began to assume a frontline position in the church.

There were three brothers who were pillars in the church in Jerusalem—James, John and Peter (Acts 3:1ff.; Galatians 1:18-19, 2:9a). In other words, through their strength the church was supported, but of the three, it seems that James became the leading one in the Jerusalem church. It was not a legal, official appointment; rather, it was a matter of spiritual life. At one time Peter was in advance of the others spiritually; therefore, he did the leading. But it then became evident that James had gone ahead of Peter, and so he began to lead. There was no argument and no strife. It was simply a recognition of the manifestation of the Holy Spirit. And because of that, there was no conflict between this brother and that brother. It was simply the Lord manifesting His spiritual life more in this brother or that brother.

James, being a man with a background such as he possessed, after he believed in the Lord Jesus, he kept the Law of Moses very strictly because it was a transitional period for him as well as for everybody else. On the one hand, he still kept the Law of Moses very strictly, and on the other hand, he was the leading brother in the Jerusalem church. It was therefore quite a mixture, because most of the believers in Jerusalem were Jews and many of them had a Pharisaic background and some were even former priests (Acts 6:7c).

Then some "brothers" in Jerusalem went out on their own to Antioch. Upon arriving there they began to teach and say, "You must be circumcised and keep the Law of Moses. Otherwise, you cannot be saved." Now the believers in Antioch were mostly Gentiles in origin. And yet these Jewish believers (if we may employ this description) who came down from Jerusalem began to teach and say, "No, you Gentiles have to be circumcised; otherwise, you are not saved." Because of that, there arose a very serious commotion in the church in Antioch and there was much discussion. Paul and Barnabas knew this was not the truth of the gospel, but these men from Jerusalem insisted that this was a true teaching; and so, this question could not be solved. Finally, the Antioch church sent Paul and Barnabas with some other brothers to Jerusalem to consult with the apostles and elders for resolving this problem.

It has been mentioned before that in Christ all the natural distinctions among mankind were eliminated. In Christ there is neither Jew nor Gentile, neither circumcision nor uncircumcision, neither barbarian nor Scythian, neither freeman nor bondman, but Christ is all and in all (Colossians 3:11). The Lord will bring both Jews and Gentiles into the body of Christ and make them one. Yet how is this brought about? When the

Lord brings them in through the cross, the Jew is eliminated and the Gentile is likewise eliminated. And having been brought together, they are no longer Jews or Gentiles but they are one in Christ. That is the church, the body of Christ, where there is neither circumcision nor uncircumcision. Whereas the Jews were circumcised and the Gentiles were not, once they are brought into the body of Christ, there is neither circumcision nor uncircumcision because they are now on the other side—on the resurrection side—of the cross.

According to resurrection life there is neither circumcision nor uncircumcision; and why?—because the body of Christ is a new creation. There is also neither barbarian nor Scythian, which is to say that in the church, the body of Christ, there are no civilizational distinctions. Some people in the wider region of gospel outreach back then were considered to be barbarians and others were deemed to be Scythians. Bible commentators have held different opinions about these two groups of people. Some have said that the Scythians were the most barbarous among the barbarians, while others have asserted that the Scythians were the most civilized people imaginable. Whether this or that group is the more civilized is not the point when it comes to the unity of the body of Christ. Whether a person is civilized or uncivilized, that is a worldly consideration. God is intent on bringing the uncivilized in just as He is in bringing the civilized in; for in the body of Christ there is neither civilized nor uncivilized, but all are one in Christ. The same is true with respect to the matter of social or class distinctions. In the world of that day back then there were freemen and bondmen, masters and servants or slaves; but when such people as these are brought into the body of Christ, there is neither of these sets of differences because it is all of Christ. Consequently, in the formation of the body of Christ brethren experienced numerous conflicts with respect to all these distinctions or differences in the world: the cultural, racial, educational, and social or class differences. The Holy Spirit had to break through all these differences by eliminating them all and bringing people with all these backgrounds into the body of Christ and making them one. That is most glorious!

Nevertheless, having no distinctions in the body of Christ does not mean there is uniformity—that everyone is alike because all people therein are now one in Christ. Not so; for let us not ignore the fact that though the body of Christ is one, there are many members. Consider the human body, that its many members are all varied. If all its members were alike there would be nothing but a lump of flesh; and the result would be that there is no body any longer.

Oh, how easy it is for us to go to one extreme or the other. The one extreme is for believers to defy the oneness by allowing all the worldly distinctions to exist in the church as the body of Christ: that those who may be Gentiles insist on bringing in their Gentile background into the church, that those who may be Jewish do the same, or that those who may be Americans or Chinese or South African or European in background do likewise. And thus we begin to divide the church, the body of Christ, along these natural lines. That would be one extreme.

The other extreme is for people to advocate that because all such distinctions were eliminated, therefore, everyone in the church must be uniform in every way: in thought, opinion, outlook, background, or whatever it might be. That is the other extreme. A most revealing example of this kind of understanding and approach concerning the nature of the church, the body of Christ, is what we read about in the opening verses of Acts chapter 15. There Luke reported that supposed Jewish believers in Christ came down from Judea to the brethren in the church at Antioch and commenced teaching them, saying: "If you are not circumcised as we who follow the custom of Moses, you cannot consider yourselves saved. Unless you do exactly as we do and believe as we believe, you cannot be saved. Indeed, unless you conform to our way you cannot be a part of the church, you will need to be excluded."

I do not know if these men from Judea were real believers or not. I say this because in Paul's Letter to the Galatians he had referred to them as "false brethren" (2:4a); but whether Paul meant that they were not true believers or that they were true believers but held to false teaching, I do not know. Regardless of their true identity, what these men were teaching the true brethren in Antioch's local expression of the body of Christ is an example of the other extreme—that of uniformity of everyone in the church: "You must conform, or else you are out."

Do we hear such a voice today? There should be no distinction in the body of Christ, and yet differences should be allowed. We must be open to one another, bear and forbear with one another. Apart from the basic response all people must make towards the gospel of needing to believe in the Person and work of the Lord Jesus or else people are not saved, brethren in the church must allow differences of opinions because there are differences in growth among members. Some may feel they have to observe special days, others feel that every day is the same. Some feel they must abstain from meat; others feel they can eat meat. It is true that those who say they must observe special days are weak in their conscience (I Corinthians 8:7-10), but the strong are not to impose their conviction upon the weak. Rather, the strong should lower themselves and meet their weaker brethren on their level and help to lift them up (Romans 15:1, I Thessalonians 5:14c). Thus, these were differences of opinion and practice relating to secondary matters.

On the other hand, regarding the matter of circumcision, there was a radical difference of opinion. Those Jewish believers insisted in their teaching that all non-Jews must be circumcised, but the Gentiles held to the belief: "We do not need to become Jews following the Mosaic Law in order to be Christians, because the body of Christ is not Judaism but a new creation. We do not need to join Judaism before becoming Christians." To be circumcised or not has nothing to do with salvation; yet those false brethren made circumcision a condition for salvation. However, for the sake of preserving the truth and the liberty concerning the gospel of grace, Paul and Barnabas would not yield an inch on this fundamental truth (Galatians 2:5).

When God brings us together, there is the unity of the Spirit which we all need to diligently keep in the bond of peace because we have one God, one Lord, one Spirit (Ephesians 4:3-6a). Yet, we cannot expect at the outset of our coming together as the body of Christ that we all have the same ideas, opinions, interpretations, or experiences. That is an illegitimate expectation. You have your opinion regarding certain matters coming before the church and I have my opinion regarding those same matters; you have your experience of Christ and I have my experience of Christ; you have your understanding of the Bible and I have my understanding of it. We have all such differences; but let us never forget that in the church as the body of Christ there are no distinctions, there are only differences. Distinctions are eliminated, differences are permitted. Do not try to impose your views upon your brothers and sisters. Do not ever try to make that which is foreign to the truth of the gospel a condition for salvation. Do not ever attempt to make people conform to you. We are to be conformed only to Christ, not to either you or me. We all have to be open to one another; we must all be willing to openly discuss and have fellowship about various matters. Nobody insists; we all allow differences.

If we bear with one another, love each other, and fellowship with each other, you will suddenly discover that your opinion has vanished, that your view has changed. Not only do you change, but your brother changes in the same manner. He knows he has not been changed by you, and you know you have not been changed by him. Who changed both of you? The Lord by His Spirit. We have been commanded to use all diligence to preserve the unity of the Spirit in the uniting bond of peace (Ephesians 4:3). And the wonderful thing is that as we are open to one another, as we love one another and fellowship and share with one another, not being afraid of differences of opinion regarding non-fundamental, secondary matters, we shall discover that, what you have experienced gradually begins to become my experience, that what is my understanding gradually begins to become your understanding. That is precisely what Ephesians 4 calls for among the brethren in the body of Christ: "… until we all attain to the unity of the faith, and of the knowledge of the Son of God, to a mature man, to the measure of the stature which belongs to the fulness of the Christ" (v.13). That is the secret.

Now in contrast to what had been occurring along these praiseworthy lines in the growth of the body of Christ at Antioch, those false brethren came down from Judea and insisted that the brethren in the Antioch church must adopt their Jewish opinions and practices such as circumcision or else they could not be saved. They were attempting to bring the brothers and sisters there into bondage of the Law (Galatians 2:4b-5) because they themselves were under bondage. So finally, the church arranged for Paul and Barnabas to go up to Jerusalem to the apostles and elders concerning this issue. Why were they sent *there*? Did they go to Jerusalem because the church there was the mother church? Or because Jerusalem was the headquarters of Christianity? Not at all! It was mentioned before that in the Bible we find only sister churches and not parent and offspring churches. All the local churches cited therein were sisters to one another. These two apostles from Antioch went to Jerusalem because the trouble had come from there. Had the trouble come from Samaria or elsewhere they would have gone there. The people who were causing the problem had come from Jerusalem, and hence, these two went there to have the problem resolved.

It needs to be underscored that these false brethren had gone to Antioch without having been sent by the church in Jerusalem but they had simply gone there on their own (Acts 15:24). Had James ever preached such a gospel as these men were insisting must be observed by the Gentiles in order to be saved? Not at all! Yes, it is quite true that James kept the Law of Moses very strictly himself, but he never asserted that a Gentile must be circumcised and keep the Law of Moses in order to be saved. Indeed, in his New Testament epistle James never wrote the slightest word which could be interpreted as insisting that Gentiles must keep the Mosaic Law; and it must be noted that he was writing to Jewish believers.

The great Protestant Reformer, Martin Luther, refused to regard the Epistle of James as being on a par with the other canonical New Testament writings, since he believed it contradicted Paul's view of justification by faith and not by works. In fact, Luther viewed James's writing as "a right strawy Epistle." In his opposition to Roman Catholicism Luther had used Paul's Galatians epistle as his sword in his fight for the truth of the gospel.

Though James addressed his epistle to those Jewish believers who had been scattered everywhere abroad (1:1), a careful reading of it reveals that he never commanded those believers to keep the Law of Moses; rather, James wrote for his readers to "keep the royal law"—even "the law of liberty" (2:8, 12). In other words, it is not the letter but the spirit of the law which we are to observe—"the law of the Spirit of life in Christ Jesus" (Romans 8:2). If a person has faith in Christ he or she must prove that faith by his or her works.

That is what James insisted believers should do, and he was a perfect example of that. He had faith in the Lord Jesus and lived a godly life, but never did he write or preach that the Gentile believers must keep the Law. Evidently, however, those false brethren saw that James was a person who strictly kept the Law, and so they began to use him as their champion. In their teaching they might even have used his name: "James said this; James said that. You must be circumcised, otherwise you are not saved." This kind of development has often occurred in church history. For instance, Martin Luther never had a desire or the intention of forming a religious group or party, but he was made the founder of a denomination—the Lutheran Church. John Wesley never had the idea of forming a denomination, but his followers made him the founder of Wesleyan Methodism. That is one of the tragedies in church history. Many great men of God had no desire or intention of being party founders. They had no desire to divide God's people, but circumstances forced them to become leaders of different parties. It has often happened that way.

A Biblical example of this is what happened among the Corinthian believers. The church in Corinth had been brought to birth by Paul when he first went there. Apollos subsequently went there and strengthened them in the word of God. Peter also went there and further reinforced the church. But the creators of the problem which eventually arose in the church were the believers there themselves. Some who were helped by Paul said, "We are of Paul." Others who were helped by Apollos declared, "We are of Apollos." Still others who were helped by Cephas (that is, Peter) made it clear that "We belong to Cephas." There was even a fourth party—a spiritual group, whose adherents proudly proclaimed: "Some of you may belong to Paul, some of you may belong to Peter, and some of you others may belong to Apollos; but *we* belong to Christ," as though saying that none of *them* belonged to Christ—a most spiritual party indeed. And thus there were to be found at Corinth, in the local expression of the church as the body of Christ there, four different parties or groups of believers! (I Corinthians 1:11-12)

Paul, Apollos and Peter had absolutely no ambition to form a party. They went to Corinth to help in building up the church, the body of Christ, that was there. They did not go to Corinth to build the Pauline church, the Apollonian church or the Petrene church. Absolutely not! They all went there to assist in building up the church of God there; nevertheless, with the flesh there is always the desire to divide the body of Christ (3:1-4). But when

Paul learned of what had happened, did he tell Apollos that he should never go to Corinth again? On the contrary, he "begged" Apollos "much" to go there (16:12a). Paul had no territorial concept: "This is my territory, you are not to come." Instead, he greatly encouraged Apollos to go, as if to say to the Corinthians: "If you people are intent on exalting me, then I shall encourage Apollos to visit with you." Let us notice, however, how Apollos reacted. He, too, had no territorial ambition, for his response to Paul's urging was this: that it was not at all his will that he should go at the present time but that he would go whenever the opportunity arises later (16:12b). Thus we discern here that both these servants of God harbored no territorial or party ambition whatsoever.

What a praiseworthy attitude these apostles possessed, which clearly rose above human, selfish motives and ambitions! We can thank God that they were purely for the body of Christ. But how greatly different things are today in this regard! Were a Paul to urge an Apollos in our day to go to a local church some where which Paul had been used by God to establish, Apollos would have most eagerly agreed. And his unspoken hidden attitude would have likely been something like this: "Even if you had not asked me, Paul, I would have been intent on going there anyway, for because I have followers of mine there now, it is my desire to assume sole leadership once I arrive there."

James had no desire at all to be a leader of a party. He had absolutely no such idea. It was those false brethren who were followers of James. They tried to use him as a banner because they themselves were not great enough or influential enough in the Jerusalem church. It often happens that way.

Now when Paul and Barnabas went up to Jerusalem, Paul made it clear later that he went there by revelation (Galatians 2:1-2a). He and Barnabas were definitely sent there by the Antioch church, but at the same time the apostle Paul went there by revelation, not only for the purpose of preserving the truth of the gospel (2:5b), but also for the purpose of maintaining the unity of the body of Christ. Humanly speaking, it was a test of spiritual strength between Paul and James. Had these two men clashed, the church would have been divided into two, and that would have been the beginning of a devastating heresy within Christianity. But let us thank God that James rose above the situation; we have to give him credit for that. Those false brethren were supposedly in support of James, but James would have nothing to do with them.

Now as Paul and Barnabas were passing through Phoenicia and Samaria on their way up to Jerusalem, they reported to all the churches concerning the conversion of the Gentiles, causing the brethren to rejoice greatly in the Lord, these brethren having had no prejudice. And upon arriving in Jerusalem, these two brethren were welcomed by the apostles and the elders. Why the mentioning of the apostles? Because of their ministry of teaching there in Jerusalem. Why, too, were the elders specifically mentioned? Because those false brethren had gone from Jerusalem to Antioch. These two servants of God from the church in Antioch were welcomed by the Jerusalem church elders not because the church in Jerusalem was the mother church or was the headquarters of Christianity but simply because those false brethren had gone out from the believers in the Jerusalem church. In other words, on the one hand, the apostles must be involved in the resolution of this issue because it involved the question of doctrinal teaching concerning fundamental gospel truth; and on the other hand, the church in Jerusalem, as represented by the elders, must also be involved in the resolution of this dispute since it had become a matter of local church discipline of those local false brethren which needed to be addressed by the elders.

When all involved in this entire matter came together, it was thrown open for discussion, and afterwards the apostles and the elders met to decide how to resolve the matter. Some of the sect of Pharisees who were believers in Christ stood up and repeated the very things those false brethren had taught down in Antioch: "The Gentile believers must be charged to keep the Law of Moses and be circumcised." Then Peter rose up (oh, we must thank God for Peter!), and he related how God had used him in the earliest period to open the door of the gospel to the Gentiles. He then went further, saying: "Why should we put upon these Gentile believers the burden of the Law which we ourselves could not bear? We are saved by the grace of Jesus Christ just as they are." He was saying, in other words, this: "It is not because we are Jews and keep the Law of Moses that we are saved but we are saved just as the Gentles are. The Law and circumcision have nothing to do with our being saved but it is by the grace of God through faith in His Son; and hence, why should we put this yoke upon our non-Jewish brethren?" Thank God, Peter had himself been delivered from the bondage of the Law of Moses.

They next listened to Paul and Barnabas relate what the Lord had wrought among the Gentiles through them; and lastly, James gave his judgment. By this time he was the leading brother in Jerusalem and his influence was great; but he did not issue his judgment according to the flesh even though he was a man who kept the Law of Moses and was even a Nazarite. Therefore, those false brethren, as it were, were supporting James, they probably assuming from his strict Jewish lifestyle that he would be in agreement with their teaching, they also probably thinking as follows: "You are our leader and we are standing with you." But James stood up and denied himself. Moreover, he cited God's word in the Old Testament in refuting their position. In fact, he was not afraid to displease these supposed followers of his.

Many church leaders at first begin to lead and then they begin to be pushed. At the beginning they were good leaders; they led the people well, but ultimately they end up no longer leading because they were being pushed by their followers and they could not stop. However, James deeply knew the Lord; and though he himself kept the Law of Moses strictly, he said in so many words to the assembled brethren that day concerning the Gentile believers: "God had originally designed to bring in the Gentiles. Circumcision was for the Jews for a temporary purpose, but the original purpose of God when He rebuilt the tabernacle of David (symbolic of the coming church) was that all the Gentile nations should be joined in. It is therefore my judgment that we must not trouble those Gentiles who turn to God. And hence, the only thing we should ask them to do is to abstain from those things contaminated by idols, from fornication, from what is strangled, and from blood." Please notice that these restraints are not strictly elements within the Law of Moses; they are actually aspects of the universal moral law which one can trace all the way back to the covenant of Noah (Genesis 9:4, 17), and which are still operative for us as believers today: which means we are not above observing such moral strictures. In other words, on behalf of all the apostles and elders James in his judgment did not put the Gentiles under the Law of Moses.

In conclusion, it seemed good to the apostles, elders, and the entire church to send to Antioch from among the Jerusalem brethren Judas and Silas together with Paul and Barnabas, the Jerusalem leadership having written a letter to be carried by all these men and to be read to all the brethren from among the Gentiles located at Antioch, in Syria, and in Cilicia. This letter indicated that a common judgment had been arrived at which had "seemed good to the Holy Spirit and to us." Thus, the Holy Spirit was able to be in charge of the process whereby this decision was arrived at, and this decision was first enunciated by James. He who was a man of the Law, and yet he had the grace and the understanding not to impose the yoke of Law upon others. True, James continued to keep the Law (cf. Acts 21:18ff.) because it was a transitory period in the lives of the Jewish believers in the church, until finally, God in His sovereignty, allowed the destruction of Jerusalem and the temple by the Romans in 70 A.D. Yet, as we have seen here, well before that, James was able to realize that no one should impose anything upon one's brothers and sisters. Even if you as a member of the church as the body of Christ observe certain practices or hold to certain ideas, opinions or understandings, you must not impose the same on others in the church. For by observing this vital principle the unity of the body of Christ shall be preserved.

It can therefore be said that the formation of the body of Christ was finalized through James. This fact, I must confess, is very strange, for humanly speaking, he was the opposite of what one would normally expect to be the kind of vessel to serve God in this critical way; and yet, the divine grace in James enabled him to rise above the distinction between Jew and Gentile, to overcome all human and worldly differences, and to embrace all. We can therefore thank God for James, who himself, according to the Jewish historian Josephus, would suffer martyrdom for Christ by stoning in the early to mid-60s A.D. at the hands of the high priest of that day.

What, then, is the body of Christ? The body of Christ is one, with no distinctions and that which is able to embrace all differences. And thus, through loving fellowship we all may arrive together at the unity of the faith and of the full knowledge of the Son of God.

O Father, do help us to see what the body of Christ truly is, what kind of vessel it is, that it is this new wineskin into which Thou art able to pour the new wine of Thy divine life. Oh, do show us what kind of a body Thou dost desire through which Thy Son can continue to do and to teach on the earth. O Father, deliver us from that which is carnal, from that which is of man. O Father, enable us to rise above all obstacles and fleshly desires and really be fitted together and be able to minister one to another in love, so that we may arrive at the unity of the faith and of the full knowledge of the Son of God, unto the full-grown man, unto the measure of the stature of the fullness of Christ. May all this be so, O Father. We pray in the name of our Lord Jesus. Amen.

Chapter Twelve

The Building Up of the Body of Christ

Acts 13:1-4—Now there were in Antioch, in the [church] which was there, prophets and teachers: Barnabas, and Simeon who was called Niger, and Lucius the Cyrenian, and Manaen, foster-brother of Herod the tetrarch, and Saul. And as they were ministering to the Lord and fasting, the Holy Spirit said, Separate me now Barnabas and Saul for the work to which I have called them. Then, having fasted and prayed, and having laid their hands on them, they let them go. They therefore, having been sent forth by the Holy Spirit, went down to Seleucia, and thence sailed away to Cyprus.

Acts 14:21-23—And having announced the glad tidings to that city, and having made many disciples, they returned to Lystra, and Iconium, and Antioch, establishing the souls of the disciples, exhorting them to abide in the faith, and that through many tribulations we must enter into the kingdom of God. And having chosen them elders in each [church], having prayed with fastings, they committed them to the Lord, on whom they had believed.

Acts 28:30-31—And he [Paul] remained two whole years in his own hired lodging, and received all who came to him, preaching the kingdom of God, and teaching the things concerning the Lord Jesus Christ, with all freedom unhinderedly.

Ephesians 4:11-16—And he has given some apostles, and some prophets, and some evangelists, and some shepherds and teachers, for the perfecting of the

> saints; with a view to the work of the ministry, with a view to the edifying of the body of Christ; until we all arrive at the unity of the faith and of the knowledge of the Son of God, at the full-grown man, at the measure of the stature of the fulness of the Christ; in order that we may be no longer babes, tossed and carried about by every wind of that teaching which is in the sleight of men, in unprincipled cunning with a view to systematized error; but, holding the truth in love, we may grow up to him in all things, who is the head, the Christ: from whom the whole body, fitted together, and connected by every joint of supply, according to the working in its measure of each one part, works for itself the increase of the body to its self-building up in love.

It has been pointed out in earlier messages in this series on the book of Acts that God had sovereignly raised up a number of individuals who were used by Him in bringing about the matured formation of the body of Christ according to the heavenly pattern. Altogether six of these servants whom God used have previously been discussed at some length: Stephen, the pioneer of the heavenly way; Philip, through whom the gospel was preached to the Samaritans; Paul, the master builder; Peter, the one whom God used to open the way of the gospel to the Gentiles; Barnabas, who served as a bridge; and finally, James. And in our having arrived at chapter 15 of Acts during our last discussion together, there could possibly almost be heard among us a deep sigh of relief that all the major problems concerning this new wineskin—the church as the body of Christ—had been solved. The church was not to be a part of Judaism; she was a new vessel, that which was completely new out of heaven, a fit vessel, indeed, for God's use (cf. II Timothy 2:21b ASV).

Yet we are far from having witnessed the full maturation of the body of Christ, since there are thirteen more chapters of this book of Acts; moreover, by the time chapter 28 is reached for reading and understanding, we shall realize that the complete story of the advancement of the church as the body of Christ continues on and on. All who have studied this second treatise of Luke's recognize the fact that the narrative it contains has really no ending because it must continue to be told until one day yet in the future—hopefully in the near future—this body shall have reached its full growth; and only then shall the Lord Jesus, its Head, return to claim the church, the body of Christ, as His bride—even the New Jerusalem of Revelation chapters 21 and 22.

Hence, my intention today, in this final message in this series, is for us to have fellowship together in a very general way concerning the maturing of the body of Christ, since that is what these remaining chapters of Acts are really meant to convey. Or I may phrase this observation another way: our fellowship together today will concern itself with the building up of the body of Christ. In other words, the body of Christ has taken a form on the earth, and now it is to be built up in such a way that this body, like the human body, can arrive at full maturity.

In the building up of the body of Christ there appears to have been one very special chosen vessel—the apostle Paul. Though we have come to see that from chapters 1 through 12 it is a record mainly of the ministry of the apostle Peter, from chapter 13 through chapter 28 it is mainly a record of the ministry of the apostle Paul. With the coming into existence of the new wineskin of God to contain the new wine of the resurrected life of Christ, Paul served as a specially chosen vessel for the building up of the body of Christ. He himself told us in I Corinthians 3 that he is "a wise architect" (v.10b). Some people would rather call him a faithful foreman because actually he was engaged in his building work under the direction of the Chief Architect, Christ himself. Either way, it is a matter of how one understands these terms. Paul was used by God in a very special way for the building up of the body of Christ—the church.

We know that every Jewish boy was trained not only in acquiring knowledge of all kinds but trained also in acquiring skills which would be useful for a future occupation when he grew up. So while Paul was studying as a Pharisee and being trained in the word of God, at the same time, he was trained to be a tentmaker. As a tentmaker he would be required to take materials, dye them, and then make them into tents. That was Paul's earthly occupation, and in a very marvelous way there is a definite similarity or correlation between Paul's earthly occupation and his heavenly one. So to maintain his livelihood he made tents. What were tents made for? They were for people to dwell or live in. And eventually God called him to be the master builder who would build the tabernacle or temple of God for Him to dwell in with His people. God's calling of people is very wonderful. It is most marvelous to see that even in a person's choosing of an earthly occupation God had a hand in it. In the book by brother Watchman Nee—*What Shall This Man Do?*—he shows how even in earthly occupations God had the foreknowledge of everything pertaining to His people.*

Paul was "a wise master builder"—"a wise architect" (I Corinthians 3:10a ASV & Darby versions)—because when he commenced building the church, the body of Christ, he laid a good foundation; and as is well known from this apostle's writing, this good foundation is none other—and cannot be other than—Christ Jesus himself (I Corinthians 3:10a-b, 11). But it is important to assess how any other person builds upon that foundation (v.10c): whether any other person builds with gold, silver, and precious stones or builds with wood, grass, and

---

* Consult Watchman Nee, *What Shall This Man Do?* (Fort Washington PA USA: Christian Literature Crusade, First published 1961, Paperback edi tion 1965), Ch.1, "God's Skilled Craftsmen," pp. 9-19.—*The Publishers*

straw (v.12). For on the day when the work of each person shall be shown or manifested, fire shall test each person's work on the foundation as to what its quality was—whether it shall remain and will thus merit a reward or whether it shall be burned up, resulting in loss for that person, though he or she shall be saved, yet as through fire (vv. 13-15).

This man Paul was apprehended by God in a very special way, the Lord having shattered his Judaism completely. God delivered him completely from the traditions of the Israelite fathers to which he had been bound most firmly. Consequently, he became a free agent in God's hand, making it possible for the Lord to give him the heavenly vision which he received on the road to Damascus. Paul was given to know "the mystery of the Christ" (Ephesians 3:4), and he was faithful to what the Lord had revealed to him. Because of that he became a chosen vessel for the building up of the body of Christ.

It is very interesting to note that though God would be using Paul in such a mighty way, his inward sentiment as a young man before his conversion to Christ on the Damascus road was, as we learned earlier, that of a very strict Pharisee. One could even say that Saul of Tarsus had been *the* Pharisee of all. I believe it would therefore be helpful to review more than previously this man's remarkable background and what he thought of himself both before and after he met the Lord.

Educated as a Pharisee, Saul had subsequently joined the sect of the Pharisees, the strictest of all the sects of Judaism. Not only was he the son of a Pharisee father, Paul himself testified later how most thoroughly he had lived out the Pharisaic lifestyle completely. Moreover, being far more advanced than any and all of his contemporaries, he had already achieved a great deal in his young adult life. In short, Saul of Tarsus had been a great Pharisee—if not the greatest of all! In fact, he had come to think of himself as a somebody—as quite a big man in Judaism. All that was what his biography consisted of prior to meeting Jesus on the way to Damascus. But as was pointed out earlier, in his encounter with the Lord at Damascus this great Pharisee was smitten to the ground and reduced to absolutely nothing. Saul—later to be known as Paul—surrendered his life to Christ and the Lord commenced using him for His purpose (see Galatians 1:13a, 14; Philippians 3:4-6).

Paul began to preach the gospel, and many were saved, and many were helped. While God was using him in such a mighty way, his defense towards his critics had been: "I was in no way less than the greatest of the apostles" (see II Corinthians 11:5). He was not behind any apostles of the first rank or degree. Evidently, among the Lord's apostles there were different magnitudes. Some of them appear to have had greater magnitudes; for instance, Peter and John. Some of the original twelve apostles we have hardly heard about; so they seem to have been of a lesser degree. But Paul, in his defense towards his critics in the church at Corinth, could again say: "If I am nothing in your eyes, I am nonetheless in no way behind those apostles of the first degree or magnitude" (see 12:11). He was a great apostle sent by God and used by Him in a mighty way.

As Paul continued on with the Lord he was moved to write in his Letter to the Ephesians that, having "by revelation" been shown "the mystery of the Christ" (3:3a) (that the Gentiles are to be joint heirs of God's salvation), he was nonetheless "the very least of all saints" (3:8a NASB). This great apostle now saw himself as being less than the least of all the saints. Notice the import of what Paul was saying here: that he was not just the least of the saints but that he was even *less* than the least of all the saints. It was due to the immensity of God's revelation that Paul could do nothing but humble himself before both God and man.

This genuine cycle of self-effacing humility reached its ultimate manifestation in Paul when he declared to Timothy: "I am the foremost of all [sinners]" for whom Jesus had come into the world to save (I Timothy 1:15 NASB). Saul of Tarsus had begun his adult life as the great Pharisee; then he was called to be one of God's greatest apostles; yet, as Paul came to know—in comparison with himself—the Lord more and more, he could only consider himself the less than the least of all believers; and finally, he was moved to confess that he was nothing more than the chief of all sinners. And Paul added that "because of this very fact God was particularly merciful to me … the worst of men" (I Timothy 1:16a Phillips). Whoever is to become a chosen vessel for the building up of the church as the body of Christ must possess this kind of inward sentiment or attitude.

Now in the church in Antioch there were five prophets and teachers (Acts 13:1). These five men served the church in Antioch locally, and as they were ministering to the Lord, they were fasting and praying. We see here that before they ministered to the church, they first ministered to the Lord together in prayer and in fasting. In other words, these servants were seeking the Lord's mind. As they were waiting before Him, the Holy Spirit said, "Separate for me Barnabas and Saul for the work to which I called and am sending them." After the other three fellow workers realized that the Holy Spirit had separated these two among them to be sent out for a special work, they laid hands on them, committed them to the Lord, and then they were sent out by the Holy Spirit. Notice, too, that they were sent out as apostles. From then on, Barnabas and Paul were called apostles because they were sent out for a special work. They were not sent out by men. They were not sent out by the church in Antioch. They were not even sent out by their fellow workers; they were sent out by the Holy Spirit. True, their fellow workers, by means of the laying on of their hands, identified themselves with them, and the church backed them up, but it was the Lord himself who sent them out. And thus they went forth as apostles.

From chapters 13 through 28 of Acts we are told, and it can very clearly be seen there, that Paul traveled forth on four so-called missionary trips. Actually, the word missionary is the modern word for the ancient word apostle, meaning "sent out one." On Paul's first trip he went out with Barnabas. They left Antioch and first went to Cyprus, a Mediterranean island off the Phoenician coast, because it was the native country of Barnabas. After they visited Cyprus they returned to the mainland. They went to Pisidia in what is Turkey today, and there in Pisidian Antioch God began to work; but because of persecution there they proceeded on to Iconium, Lystra and Derbe. Every place they went they preached the gospel and a number of people came to the Lord.

After they had covered this wide area they returned to those same places, encouraging the brothers and sisters who had been saved. From this we clearly see that these two apostles were not simply going forth preaching the gospel and getting people saved, but then leaving them. No, they returned to these same communities for nurturing these new believers and exhorting them to abide in the faith; after which they appointed elders from among them. Thus, they established churches in all these places and then they went back to Syrian Antioch from whence these two servants of God had originally launched forth. That was the substance of Paul's first trip (Acts 13:4-14:26).

With regard to the second trip, Paul and Barnabas were separated for reasons which were discussed in a previous message. Paul therefore went out with Silas (and was early on joined by Timothy). They revisited those same previously visited places—Antioch of Pisidia, Iconium, Lystra, Derbe. Then, after they had passed through the territories of Phrygia and the Galatian country, Paul, with Silas, were now facing west. On the left looking south was the great Roman province of Asia, a very densely populated and important province. Paul had a desire to go there, but the Holy Spirit forbade him to go *there* to preach God's word. Then he and Silas looked to the north with the intention of entering Bithynia, another important Roman province; but once again the Spirit of Jesus forbade them to go *there*. Not having been allowed to go either to the south or to the north, Paul and Silas traveled farther westward through the country of Mysia at the western extremity of modern-day Turkey until they came to the end of land at the port city of Troas (ancient Troy) situated on the coast of the Aegean Sea. Where should they now go? It was at this moment that God gave Paul a night vision: a man was standing and appealing to Paul, saying, "Come and help us here in Macedonia."

The next morning when Paul shared his vision with Silas and Luke, they all concluded that it was the Lord calling them to cross the Aegean Sea into Europe. This was the first time that the gospel would be preached on that continent. People sometimes think that the gospel began in Europe, but as a matter of history it first began in Asia and then was carried by these men into Europe. These servants of the Lord therefore crossed the Aegean Sea and, traveling on land they reached the city of Philippi, and from there they went on to Thessalonica. They next went on to Athens and ended up at Corinth. Corinth, as it were, became the locale where the central work of Paul was carried on during this second apostolic trip. In fact, Paul remained here for 18 months. Now what were these men doing during this entire second apostolic journey of Paul's? Well, wherever they went they preached the gospel; but was that all? By no means! Besides gospel preaching they also established the believers in the faith. And having established churches in all these places, Paul returned once again to Antioch (Acts 15:40-18:22).

Paul then went out on a third apostolic trip. After he had passed through the Galatian country and Phrygia, he was led by God into the province of Asia where he came to Ephesus, and Paul was there for three years. That became the center of his labor until all in this province of Asia had heard the gospel. Again I would inquire, What was Paul doing in all the places he visited during this third journey of his? He not only preached the gospel, he was also used by God to build up the saints and establish the churches more firmly in the Lord (Acts 18:23, 19:1-21:17a).

After that, Paul went to Jerusalem and there he was taken prisoner by the Roman authorities and ended up being taken by ship to Rome. This fourth trip of Paul's was therefore a compulsory journey (Acts 21:17-28:14). But thank God, at the time of the end of the book of Acts, he was given liberty to rent his own house "two whole years," wherein he preached "with all freedom unhinderedly" the kingdom of God to everyone who came to see him (Acts 28:30-31). Figuratively speaking, it may be said that the gospel had come to the end of the world, for Rome at that time was the center of the known world of that day. Such, then, in brief, is the historical account in Scripture of how God used the apostle Paul, in particular, to build up the body of Christ and to bring the church into full maturity in the Lord.

Why does the Holy Spirit relate these historical facts to us? In reading about the apostolic ministry of Paul in all these various places, do you discern a divine principle behind his multifarious work? In other words, how does one build up the body of Christ?—by means of what working principle? I think people today are very much interested in this question. During these past five years God's people everywhere have been talking especially about the body of Christ. Prior to these years we would rarely hear even the term the body of Christ being mentioned. Some people might have written about it, but that was very rare. During the last few years, however, not only those who greatly love the Lord and are searching and seeking His best are occupied quite much with this subject but also even those who hold to a very liberal apprehension of Christ—and of Christianity as a whole—are likewise talking much about the body of Christ. Everybody, it seems, is keenly interested in this topic.

How is the body of Christ built? How does this body of Christ grow into full maturity? I think this is what Acts chapters

13 through 28 are meant to convey to us. This building process is not accomplished by God's servants by simply traveling here and there preaching the gospel wherever they may go. On the contrary, gospel preaching is undertaken for a purpose. Let us notice that after Paul had preached the glad tidings of salvation, invariably something was established, which was, that a church was established in every place he visited. In every locality where this apostle preached the gospel he left behind a gathering, a testimony, a church in that place as a lampstand. And that is clearly what we see was occurring throughout the record of these concluding chapters of the book of Acts.

Here I would like to tell you the story of one of God's modern-day choice servants. I do not know if you are acquainted with brother Bakht Singh of India personally or simply by name or not at all. We have some of his writings here on the literature table. I know Bakht Singh personally, and we are good friends. I wish to use his story because it illustrates that which we are presently discussing today. He comes from a fairly wealthy family, since his father was a prominent contractor.

Born in 1903 of devout Hindu parents, Bakht (Chabra) Singh was the Chabra family's firstborn son; and for family reasons the parents dedicated him to the Sikh religion. Such dedication thus made him a Sikh, and, like all Sikhs, he thereafter bore the surname of Singh. His father did become a baptized born-again believer, but his mother remained a most devout Hindu.

Now when our brother was studying in India, he did so in a Christian mission school, but he would have nothing to do with Christ and would even make fun of the name Jesus. After he finished studying in India he wanted to go to England for further education. His mother helped him to gain his father's permission to send him to England to study, but on the one condition that he would not change his religion. He therefore promised his mother that he would never change his religion.

So, off he went to England, and after he arrived there he met some of his friends from India, who began to influence him in adopting the ways of English culture. He tried to be as English as possible. Indeed, that soon became a matter of pride for Bakht Singh. Everything an Englishman would do he would himself emulate to prove that he was not in any way inferior.

Once there was a group of students who were intent on going on a trip to Canada, and Bakht Singh joined that trip. While he was on the boat, there was a Sunday Christian service and it was held in the first-class salon. Due to his pride he wanted to experience the first-class salon, so he attended that service. Someone was preaching there, but Bakht Singh later reported that he could not remember a single thing from the sermon; but after the sermon was finished, the preacher asked everybody to kneel down and pray. And everybody around him knelt down. He was the only one who remained seated there.

Of course, Bakht Singh was very, very embarrassed by this situation, and so he tried to extricate himself and exit the service; but he could not do so because he was completely surrounded by those who had knelt down and were praying. At that moment Bakht Singh recalled that when he was a child his mother used to take him on visits to all kinds of temples, even temples belonging to other religions which were not of the Sikh faith. And his mother had continually reminded him: "When you go to any temple you must show respect even if you are not a follower." So at this moment in the boat's Sunday Christian service his mother's word came back to him that he must show respect, even though he did not know this Christian God. Consequently, to show respect Bakht Singh knelt down. And while he was kneeling there something remarkable happened, as he himself would later describe it: the presence of God was quite living and real to him, even though he did not understand what was happening. Nothing more than an initial spiritual awakening, however, occurred on this occasion.

After Bakht Singh arrived in Canada, one day his friend asked him, "What gift do you want me to give you?" He replied, "A Bible." And upon receiving it he started to read it. When he came to John chapter 3 he was soundly saved, this having occurred while he was still in Canada. After his conversion our brother continued his studies as a mechanical engineer. In his days both before and after his conversion Bakht Singh had been very critical of the missionaries in India because he felt they lived such a high-class lifestyle. So he was determined that he would contribute whatever money he would earn to the preaching of the gospel but not to those missionaries. One day, however, the Lord spoke to him and asked, "How about you?" His response was: "Lord, I will return to India and earn money, and then I will financially support Your work." But the Lord persisted: "No, I do not want your money, I want you."

Hence, upon his return to India, Bakht Singh talked to whoever would listen to him about the Lord Jesus. Often his only meal was when people invited him to have tea. That was how he first began in evangelism. The Lord began to use him, and as he traveled all around India many, many people got saved. However, upon his revisiting these converts to see how they were faring spiritually, Bakht Singh was confronted with a major disappointment: all of them had disappeared. This outcome greatly troubled our brother. He mused on the matter as follows: Children in the Lord are born, but who is available and willing and able to take care of them? The so-called churches in the relevant areas were so weak that they were unable to take care of these new-born babes, and so he did not know what to do.

Then one day Bakht Singh received a letter from a dear sister, a widowed Englishwoman, whom I knew very well. This elderly Englishwoman had come to India from Honor Oak, brother T. Austin-Sparks's place in London where she had been an attendee at the Christian meetings which were held there; and so she had written to Bakht Singh, saying, "If you need rest, you can come to my home." And the Lord spoke positively about this to our brother. He had become so busy that he realized he needed some quiet time and rest. In response to the Lord's urging, Bakht Singh went to this elderly sister's home. And I was told that for about two months four people—including Bakht Singh—would come together every morning doing nothing but praying and asking the Lord to show our brother the pattern concerning what God wanted him to do and revealing how this major problem which had confronted Bakht Singh so long could be solved. After these four brethren had prayed during this two-month period, God revealed to brother Bakht Singh what he should do. So he went down to Madras and commenced his life work of service under the guidance of the Holy Spirit. And today there are hundreds and hundreds of local church gatherings all over India and Pakistan.*

I have recounted this story in order to point out what I believe is the principle by which this problem which Bakht Singh encountered can and should be solved. Indeed, this is the same problem which many of God's best servants are facing. They faithfully serve the Lord, going here and there, having many souls saved; but how do you take care of them? In other words, what is the way to build the body of Christ?

Most likely many view the body of Christ solely in terms of the universal understanding of it. We do thank God that the body of Christ is universal in scope, with Christ as the Head. Yes, indeed, the body of Christ as the church is everywhere on the earth. Yet, how is the universal church to be built up?

---

* For more on this servant of God, consult Bakht Singh, *The Skill of His Loving Hands* (Beamsville, Ontario: Worldwide Evangelization Crusade Bookroom, 1959, formerly published in two parts, 1936 and 1952—his personal testimony; Dan Smith, *Bakht Singh of India* (Washington DC: International Students, Inc., 1959); and T. E. Koshy, "Bakht Singh's Movement Still Full of Grassroots Vitality," *Christianity Today* (22 Feb. 1980): 51.—*The Publishers*

The book of Acts shows us the working principle. Paul was not disobedient to the heavenly vision which God gave him on the Damascus road. There he saw the body of Christ, and he thereafter was continually engaged in building the body of Christ, but in what way? The body of Christ is to be built up in each place, locally. In other words, the body of Christ universal is to be built through the body of Christ local.

After Paul preached the gospel and converts were brought in, he did not leave them to fend for themselves initially. He encouraged them, established them, a church was established and a testimony raised up in that locality. Then the apostle went to another place and another church was established. It was not just evangelism; it was evangelism with a definite purpose in view. There was the church in Antioch, the church in Lystra, the church in Derbe, the church in Philippi, the church in Thessalonica, the church in Corinth, the church in Ephesus, and the church in Rome. Here and there and everywhere there were many local churches established and brethren nourished and encouraged in the faith. The local expression of the body of Christ universal appeared here and there. Were all these churches different from the church of God universal? No. They were simply the local expression of the church universal. In building the local church, you at the same time are building the church universal. Let us understand that in building the body of Christ in the local sense, the building of the body of Christ in the universal sense is being accomplished. That is the only practical way of building the body of Christ.

Permit me to use another illustration. When I first take up a book to read, I usually absorb the contents of the first two or three pages and then I go to the last two or three pages and do the same. Why do I do this? It is because I am so anxious to know what the end is, since the end is the goal. In reading the book of Revelation, for example, if we read the first three chapters and immediately thereafter go to the last two chapters, what do we see as having been played out? Well, in the first three chapters we are given to see the seven local churches which had been established in the relevant seven cities situated throughout Asia Minor; and in the last two chapters we behold New Jerusalem. In other words, we have revealed to us how New Jerusalem has been built: the New Jerusalem that appears at the consummative end of God's working is actually the result of what has been built in those local churches cited and discussed in Revelation chapters 2 and 3.

Now it is because the Lord was building the church local in these seven churches which would make it possible for the coming into view of the finally accomplished church universal as represented by New Jerusalem. That is the way and that is the principle to be followed if ever the goal of the building up of the church universal is to be achieved. We are all very much interested in seeing New Jerusalem because it is perfect and so full of God's glory. In contrast to that, though, our reading of Revelation chapters 2 and 3 leaves us all somewhat dejected and depressed; for of the seven churches cited, only the church in Philadelphia received all praise and no rebuke; and yet, even with respect to *that* local church, there came forth from the risen Lord Jesus: "Hold fast what thou hast, that no one take thy crown" (3:11).

The Lord was dealing with the church local in those churches cited in order to bring into perfection the church universal. The same effort by the Lord is taking place today: it is in the church local where the Lord is working today in order that tomorrow He shall have the perfect, matured church universal. That is exactly what Christians need to see and understand as having been God's working principle throughout all these centuries since the initial formation of the body of Christ. Otherwise, if we adopt the notion that what we Christians are building is the church of God universal, such an understanding is quite vague and most impractical in accomplishing the goal. How, actually, are we to build the church as the body of Christ? It can only be accomplished by our focusing entirely upon the local place where we live, for it is in the local churches on earth where the building up process of the body of Christ can take place and nowhere else. True, it is difficult work and not necessarily all pleasant and may be marked by many problems. And furthermore, it may require, as was the case with most of the seven churches cited in Revelation, a great amount of repentance now and then. Nevertheless, it is in the church local where the work of building up the body of Christ must occur if the achieving of a mature and perfect church universal is to become a reality for the Lord Jesus to be satisfied.

Jesus declared to His disciples: "I will build my church upon this rock and the gates of Hades shall not prevail against it" (see Matthew 16:18b). Where is He building? If the building work is not taking place in the churches local—with a testimonial lampstand being established here and a similar lampstand there, then there is nothing being built. The building work is very real and most practical in bringing about God's desired outcome. That, I believe, is what the last part of the book of Acts is meant to show us—how this body of Christ is to be built.

We are told in Ephesians 4 that the risen, ascended Lord gives to the church some apostles, some prophets, some evangelists, and some pastors and teachers (v.11). Why does He do this? The next verse tells us: "for the perfecting of the saints" and "with a view to the work of ministry, with a view to the edifying of the body of Christ." These four classes of people mentioned here are the Lord's gifts to the church. Let us take note that this listing of gifts is different from what is found in I Corinthians 12 and Romans 12, in that what are described as gifts in these latter two letters of Paul's are spiritual gifts as the manifestations of the Spirit given according to grace (cf. Romans 12:6 with I Corinthians 12:1, 7), whereas in Ephesians 4 the four classes of *people* are gifts given to the churches local.

What is the work of these people given by the Lord as gifts? Their work is for the perfecting or equipping or preparing of the saints. These men are given to the church to perfect or equip and prepare the saints; that is to say, they are given, first of all, to help the saints grow in Christ, to help them to know the Lord more, and to help them to have more of the life of Christ; and, second, to help them to develop their gifts and to fulfill their functioning.

So what is the purpose in perfecting the saints? The verse goes on to say, "with a view" towards. These words indicate that there is a purpose to be mentioned thereafter: "to the work of the ministry" or the work of service. Too many Christians too often think of ministry or service as being exclusively confined to these four kinds of people doing all the work. Too many Christians believe that apostles, prophets, evangelists, and pastors and teachers are the only ones involved in ministry of the church. Not so; for their ministry is a very special kind as was intimated earlier; but the ministry here cited in this Ephesian passage is the ministry or works of service that is to be done by all the members of the body of Christ. *That* is the ministry which is in view here.

We often hear people talk about body ministry, and what they have in mind is the special ministry which these four classes of servants mentioned in Ephesians chapter 4 perform towards the body of Christ. No, body ministry is that which the body members minister to and among themselves whereas those special classes of servants of God are given by the Lord to activate, reinforce and help build up the spiritual life of the saints. And as the saints are growing stronger in the Lord and made spiritually healthier, then the saints in the body begin to do the works of service. Thus, the ministry here is that of the body, not the ministry of these four kinds of people given as gifts to the body.

I was made very happen in reading Anglican Bishop Lightfoot's notes on these verses in Ephesians 4. He was a fine scholar and a true man of God. When he commented on this verse 12, he said that the ministry in view here is the ministry of the body. However, when certain kinds of people are ministering to the body, the body cannot be seen in action, for all body members are simply present as an audience receiving ministry from those special people, whose ministry should nonetheless not be discounted in the least, since the effect of those special ministries upon the saints is meant to produce true body ministry.

Let us understand, though, that their special ministries are not at all meant to be a substitute or a replacement of body ministry nor meant to monopolize all spiritual ministry. Rather, their purpose is to encourage, stimulate and bring forth true body ministry. At the same time the Spirit of God and the life of Christ are working in every member of the body; yet such working is not the same from member to member but is different in each believer. And hence, as members' spiritual life is being built up, all the saints begin to contribute that portion of the Lord's working in him or her, and thus all are contributing to the body, with the result being that the body of Christ is being built up in love (4:16c).

The body of Christ is not built by those special people's ministries. The body of Christ is built directly by the members of the body themselves functioning. If the members of the body are not being perfected, equipped or properly prepared, they do not grow; and thus they are not able to fulfill body ministry. And if they are not able to fulfill the ministry of the body, the body can never be built up. People may preach, preach and preach for a hundred years, but if that is all which is taking place, the church shall only be a congregation, not a body that is being built up. You may build up a congregation of two or three thousand people, but it is only a congregation. Where, then, is the body? If the body local is not being built up, where is the body universal?

God is very practical. We have to see that the way, as just now outlined, is the way by which He has sought to work from the very moment when the body of Christ was first formed. Every member of the body, as it grows and matures, begins to function together distinctly but coordinately under the body's Head by means of the Holy Spirit. When this happens, the body builds itself up in love.

The body of Christ begins to build itself up in love and this is what Paul and the others were doing as described in the book of Acts. They preached the gospel, souls were saved, they encouraged these new body members, and so various ones among them were being equipped for the works of service. Having begun to manifest more mature life, these equipped ones were put in responsibility, while other members of the body began to function in fulfilling body ministry. And hence, here, there, and everywhere the churches as local expressions of the body of Christ began to grow and mature. That is how the building up of the body of Christ is to occur, and this shall eventually bring about the realization of Revelation 21 and 22—New Jerusalem.

May the Lord therefore show us through the book of Acts the working principle of God. If we are able to see this and implement this working principle among us, then we shall be working *with* God and not simply *for* God. Many are working for God, but few are working with Him. When the Lord Jesus was on earth, He did the work of the Father. He was not doing His own work or only doing some work for the Father. Far more than that, He was working the work of the Father. May this be true with all of us—that our laboring on earth may not be merely working for God, but truly working with Him.

O Lord, do reveal to us continually Thy mind as to the way Thou wilt build Thy church, the body of Christ. We ask Thee that Thou wilt not only lead us to the third heaven to behold the great revelation but also lead us right here on earth in dealing with all practical matters relating to Thy church. We do desire to see Thy church built and Thy people grow spiritually so that each one may fulfill his or her function in the building up of the body of Christ in love. Oh, that this may be real and true everywhere locally in every gathering of Thy saints. We commit ourselves to Thee, O Lord; for if this is what Thou art wanting to do, we desire to work with Thee. We pray in Thy precious name. Amen.